GLOBALIZATION

Globalization
Educational Research, Change and Reform

Edited by

Nicholas Sun-keung Pang

The Chinese University Press

Hong Kong Institute of
Educational Research

 香 港 教 育 研 究 學 會
THE HONG KONG EDUCATIONAL RESEARCH ASSOCIATION

Globalization: Educational Research, Change and Reform
  Edited by Nicholas Sun-keung Pang

© **The Chinese University of Hong Kong**, 2006

ISBN 962–996–268–3

THE CHINESE UNIVERSITY PRESS
The Chinese University of Hong Kong
SHA TIN, N.T., HONG KONG
Fax: +852 2603 6692
      +852 2603 7355
E-mail: cup@cuhk.edu.hk
Web-site: www.chineseupress.com

**HONG KONG INSTITUTE OF
EDUCATIONAL RESEARCH**
The Chinese University of Hong Kong
SHA TIN, N.T., HONG KONG
Fax: +852 2603 6850
E-mail: hkier@cuhk.edu.hk
Web-site: www.fed.cuhk.edu.hk/~hkier

Printed in Hong Kong

Hong Kong Institute of Educational Research

The Hong Kong Institute of Educational Research (HKIER) was in-augurated in September 1993. Its founding was made possible by the fervent support of the Tin Ka Ping Foundation with a generous donation designated as the setting-up costs and operating capital. The Institute helps to strengthen the roles of The Chinese University of Hong Kong as a leading centre of educational research, as a responsible institution that addresses the needs of the teaching profession, and as an active consulting agent for international organizations, public agencies, and local education bodies. It also helps to strengthen the University's ties with local schools and overseas institutions. Projects initiated by the Institute are to facilitate educational planning, produce policy alternatives, and enlighten policy makers and members of the educational profession.

The objectives of the Institute are to conduct strategic research with strong policy implications for educational developments in China and Hong Kong; to effectively deploy resources for educational research; to disseminate research ideas and findings in publications of journals and books; to promote the role of the Institute as a consultant and a development agent; and to win international recognition of its work.

Director   Professor Leslie Lo Nai-kwai, Faculty of Education
                     The Chinese University of Hong Kong

Associate Directors Professor Hau Kit-tai, Faculty of Education
                     The Chinese University of Hong Kong

                     Professor Tsang Wing-kwong, Faculty of Education
                     The Chinese University of Hong Kong

                     Professor Wong Hin-wah, Faculty of Education
                     The Chinese University of Hong Kong

Hong Kong Educational Research Association

The Hong Kong Educational Research Association (HKERA) was registered with the Government in accordance with the Society Ordinance in May, 1984 and its inauguration was officiated by the then Chairman of the Education Commission, Dr. the Honourable Q. W. Lee, at the opening ceremony of the first annual conference held at The Chinese University of Hong Kong in November, 1984. Since then, the Association has built a strong foundation with supports from various educational institutions and it has been able to assemble educational researchers to participate on a cooperative basis in research activities and scholarly communication. In the past years, members from different institutions worked together towards the improvement of education and they made the annual conferences momentous events every year in Hong Kong.

In May 2001, the Hong Kong Educational Research Association Limited was successfully incorporated. The Executive Committee, based on members' views solicited from a survey, has resorted to holding the HKERA conference biennially instead of annually. Such change has allowed the Executive Committee more time and room to form conference organizing committees and to make better planning and preparation for quality conferences. Through continuous efforts and contributions from its members and the executive committees, the Association to date has established its strengths in the areas that it is still the largest organization engaged in educational research in Hong Kong and that it has the widest representation and participation across educational institutions.

Contents

—⁓ꟿ⁓—

Acknowledgements xi

Notes on Contributors xiii

Introduction

Chapter 1. Globalization and Educational Change 1
    Nicholas Sun-keung PANG

Part I: Globalization, Comparative Education and Educational Research

Chapter 2. National Educational Systems and 25
    Comparative Education: From State Formation
    to Globalization
    Andy GREEN

Chapter 3. Comparative Education in the Era of 51
    Globalization: Evolution, Missions and Roles
    Mark BRAY

Part II: Globalization and Change in Higher Education

Chapter 4. Globalization and Higher Education Reform 73
    in China
    Kinglun NGOK

Chapter 5. Quality Assurance in the Context of 101
    Globalization and Its Impact on Higher Education
    David GAMAGE & Jaratdao SUWARNABROMA

Chapter 6. Developing Higher Degrees in Context 133
    and Culture for Globalization
    Alan T. LARKIN

Chapter 7.   Community Colleges in a Global Society: 179
             Is There One Best Governance Model?
             Cheryl D. LOVELL & Catherine TROUTH

Part III: Globalization and Educational Reform

Chapter 8.   The Formation and Transformation of 195
             the Teaching Profession in the Global Era
             Brian CALDWELL

Chapter 9.   Internationalizing Teacher Subjectivities: 213
             English Language Teachers, Post-colonial
             Contexts and Global Educational Markets
             Dianne BLOOMFIELD & Cathryn McCONAGHY

Chapter 10. The Curriculum and Cultural Identity 249
             Transformation
             Candace SCHLEIN

Chapter 11. Contrasting the Profiles of Schools 271
             in Extreme Stages of Organizational Learning:
             Localization in Globalization
             Jack Yee-lay LAM

Chapter 12. Managing School Change Through Self- 291
             evaluation in the Era of Globalization
             Nicholas Sun-keung PANG

Acknowledgements

—〜〜—

This book is a collection of selected articles from the Hong Kong Educational Research Association 2002 International Conference on "Globalization: New Horizons for Educational Change." The HKERA 2002 International Conference was co-organized by The Hong Kong Educational Research Association, the Faculty of Education and the Hong Kong Institute of Educational Research of The Chinese University of Hong Kong, and the Hong Kong Teachers' Centre. It took place on the campus of The Chinese University of Hong Kong during the period of December 20 and 21, 2002. The Conference brought together over 600 educational researchers, policy-makers, teacher educators, curriculum developers, practitioners and other concerned participants from different parts of the world to: (1) search for the very meaning of globalization and its implications for schools and students, (2) explore the connections that globalization is bringing about in education trends, policies and practices, and (3) explore new areas for educational research and development in the 21st century. The Conference drew upon the wisdom and experience of experts who have intimately involved in important educational reforms in Hong Kong, mainland China, Taiwan, Japan, Australia, Canada, the United Kingdom, and the United States and invited them to share their insights and experience with the conference participants in various presentation formats. The gathering afforded an opportunity for a synthesis of ideas and synergy of efforts.

The Conference was made possible with the assistance and support of many organizations. On behalf of the Conference Organizing Committee, we would like to express our deep gratitude to the Faculty of Education and the Hong Kong Institute of Educational Research (HKIER) of The Chinese University of Hong Kong as well as the Hong Kong Teachers' Centre. They served as the co-organizers and hosts of that conference. Thanks are extended to Professor Stephen Yue-ping Chung (the then Dean of the Faculty of Education) and Professor Leslie N. K. Lo (the Director of HKIER), who served as Honorary Advisors for the Conference. I would like to extend sincere thanks to the members of the Conference Organizing Committee, whose encouragement and innovative ideas had contributed much to the success of that Conference. They were Professors Hung Fan-sing, Cheung Sin-pui Derek, Ming-ming Chiu, Dr. Joshua Ka-ho Mok, Dr. Siu-wai Wu, Mr. Kwok-wai Ko, Mr. Kee-huen Wu, Ms. Sylvia Wing-tin Tsoi and Sr. Cecilia Yeuk-han Wong. I would also like to thank those sponsors who generously supported the conference financially and with other means, in particular, the Hong Kong Institute of Education, the Hong Kong Baptist University, the Comparative Education Policy Research Unit at the City University of Hong Kong, Sik Sik Yuen, Causeway Bay Victoria Kindergarten, Hong Kong (Ascot) Preschool, and Braemar Hill Nursary School. Special thanks are also extended to the enthusiastic and dedicated members of the Secretariat, Ms. Erica Kwai-hing Ho, Ms. Virginia Chun-ying Wan, and Ms. Grace Ka-yee Wong, who took care of every detail of the conference. Furthermore, the Editor would like to thank The Chinese University Press and the Hong Kong Institute of Educational Research for making the publication of this book possible, the reviewers for their constructive comments for improving the manuscript, and Ms. Audrey Lok-yee Ma of the HKIER for her editing support for this book.

Nicholas Sun-keung Pang

Notes on Contributors

—⁓⁓—

Dianne BLOOMFIELD is Director of Professional Experience at the University of New England, Australia. She has responsibility for all professional experience and practicum programs within teacher education. Her research interests focus on student teacher subjectivity and professional experience relationships.

Mark BRAY is Director of UNESCO's International Institute for Educational Planning (IIEP) in Paris, France. Prior to taking that post, he worked for two decades at the University of Hong Kong where, among other roles, he was Director of the Comparative Education Research Centre and Dean of the Faculty of Education. He is also President of the World Council of Comparative Education Societies (WCCES) and former President of the Comparative Education Society of Hong Kong (CESHK).

Brian CALDWELL is Managing Director of Educational Transformations Pty Ltd in Melbourne, Australia and Associate Director of iNet (Global) (International Networking for Educational Transformation) of the Specialist Schools and Academies Trust in England.

David GAMAGE is Associate Professor and Director of the Master of Leadership and Management in Education (MLMEd) Program of the School of Education, University of Newcastle, Australia. He has published 5 books, 19 book-chapters, a large number of articles in 42 different journals and over 100 presentations at learned forums. His research interests include: leadership and management in education; school-based management; higher education; and international and comparative education.

Andy GREEN is Professor of Comparative Education at the Institute of Education, London University and Co-director of the Department for International Development project on *Globalization, Education and Development*. He is co-author of a few books which have been translated into Chinese, Japanese and Spanish. These include: *High Skills: Globalization, Competitiveness and Skills Formation* (2002); *Convergences and Divergences in European Education and Training Systems* (1999); and *Education, Globalization and the Nation State* (1997).

Jack Yee-lay LAM is Professor Emeritus at Brandon University, Manitoba, Canada and former Chairman of the Department of Educational Administration and Policy, The Chinese University of Hong Kong.

Alan T. LARKIN is Director of the Flinders Institute of International Education and Adjunct Senior Lecturer in School of Education at the Flinders University in Adelaide, Australia.

Cheryl D. LOVELL, is Associate Dean of the College of Education at the University of Denver where she is also Associate Professor of Higher Education. She specializes in postsecondary public policy. Specifically she is interested in the relationships between and among state and federal governments and institutions of higher education. She has written extensively about issues of institution and statewide governance.

Cathryn McCONAGHY is Associate Professor in Educational Contexts at the University of New England, Australia. Her research interests include postcolonial and psychoanalytic studies in education and the sociology of education in difficult contexts.

Kinglun NGOK is currently Associate Professor at School of Government, Sun Yat-sen University, China. Before he joined Sun Yat-sen University, he taught at the Department of Public and Social Administration, City University of Hong Kong. His research interests include contemporary Chinese politics and public administration, public policy and social policy in China. He has published articles and chapters on China's public policies, especially education and labor policy.

Nicholas Sun-keung PANG is Associate Professor in the Department of Educational Leadership and Policy, The Chinese University of Hong Kong. He was Chairman of the Hong Kong Educational Research Association for the years 1999–2001. He has published widely in international and local journals and is co-author of an academic book entitled *Leadership and Management in Education: Developing Essential Skills and Competencies* (2003).

Candace SCHLEIN is currently a Ph.D. candidate in Teacher Development at OISE/ University of Toronto. She is an English as a Second Language teacher who taught at public high schools in Japan. Her research interests involve a qualitative investigation into the experiences of Canadian teachers who have worked respectively in Hong Kong and Japan and returned to Canada.

Jaratdao SUWARNABROMA is Lecturer at the School of Nursing, Siam University in Thailand. She completed her Ph.D. at the School of Education, The University of Newcastle in Australia. Her research interests are educational administration and quality assurance in higher education.

Catherine TROUTH is Research and Assessment Analyst at the University of Denver, where she is also a Ph.D. candidate in Higher Education. She recently completed a Policy Research Internship at the Education Commission of the States and was a Ford Foundation Fellow at the Western Interstate Commission of higher education. She has worked with international students at the University of Colorado at Denver and Teikyo Loretto Heights University.

1

Globalization and Educational Change

Nicholas Sun-keung PANG

—ᨦ—

Introduction

This volume is dedicated to a topic which has been attracting increasing interest in recent years: the impact of globalization on education. One conference after another has been examining the potential impact of globalization on education. It is being hotly debated in leading education journals and specialized publications (Burbules & Torres, 2000; Daun, 2002; Stromquist & Monkman; 2000; Mok & Chan, 2002; Uvalié-Trumbié, 2002; Mok & Welch, 2003a). This volume is spawned by the Hong Kong Educational Research Association's International Conference on "Globalization: New Horizons for Educational Change" in the year 2002 and is a collection of some of the proceedings of that conference which investigate how globalization has been affecting education and how education has been responding to the challenges thus posed.

As a result of globalization, not only is educational change occuring in the development of secondary and higher education, but also in the ways educational research is conducted. The authors in this volume will examine the effects of globalization on educational policies and practices, in their own areas of investigations and expertise based on their own research findings and observations. This volume will also review the trends of educational research which can be identified as having specifically come about to deal with these changes.

Before looking at the details of the various issues in this volume, this introductory chapter will first outline what is meant by globalization, how it has impacted on education and what changes in principle have come about. Then, more specifically, it will explore how school, and higher education have been responding to globalization, and what the implications have been for educational research in this unprecedented era of global change.

The Advent of Globalization

Globalization is not a new process. Bates (2002) comments that migration of ideas, artifacts and people has been a constant part of human history but that what appears to be new is the rapidity with which such migrations are now accomplished and the relative weakness of the barriers to them, constructed by nation states in order to maintain their social, political and cultural integrity. Although current concepts of globalization are still blurred and hard to define, it is generally accepted as relating to the global reach of processes of the exchange of goods, the formation of gigantic multinational enterprises, and the virtual abolition of time because of the instantaneous quality of communication all over the world (Capella, 2000). Carnoy (1999) argues that globalization means more competition, which means that a nation's investment, production, and innovation are not limited by national borders. Globalization has become possible only because of the technological infrastructure provided by telecommunications, information systems, microelectronic equipment, and computer-controlled transportation systems.

There is no universally accepted conceptualization of globalization. Globalization has many faces, thus different theorists view globalization differently. Held (1991) defines globalization as "the intensification of worldwide social relations which link distant localities in such a way that local happenings are shaped by events occurring many miles away and vice versa" (p. 9). Pieterse (1995) speaks of globalization in terms of "the ideas that the world is becoming more uniform and standardized, through technological, commercial and cultural synchronization emanating from the West, and that globalization is tied up with modernity" (p. 45). Parker (1997) views globalization as "a growing sense that events occurring throughout the world are converging rapidly to shape a single, integrated world where economic, social, cultural, technological, business, and other influences cross traditional borders and boundaries such as nations, national cultures, time, space, and industries with increasing ease" (p. 484). Capling, Considine, and Crozier (1998) argue that, "globalization refers to the emergence of a global economy which is characterized by uncontrollable market forces and new economic actors such as transnational corporations, international banks, and other financial institutions" (p. 5). Blackmore (2000) described it as "increased economic, cultural, environmental, and social interdependencies and new transnational financial and political formations, with both homogenizing and differentiating tendencies" (p. 133).

Globalization is a product of the emergence of a global economy. The process of globalization is seen as blurring national boundaries, shifting solidarities within and between nation-states, and deeply affecting the constitution of national and interest group identities (Morrow & Torres, 2000). The term "globalization" is generally used to refer to a complicated set of economic, political, and cultural factors. As a result of expanding world trade, nations and individuals experience greater economic and political interdependence (Wells, Carnochan, Slayton, Allen, & Vasudeva, 1998). New communication technologies that facilitate expanded world trade as well as cultural interaction are considered the determinants that lead to the emergence of globalization. It is widely believed that globalization is transforming the political, economic and cultural lives of people all around the world, whether in the developed countries or developing ones, and that globalization is driving a revolution in the organization of work, the production of goods and services, relations among nations, and even local culture.

The Impact of Globalization on Education

The potential effects of globalization on education are many and far-reaching, due to its scale and nature. Because the main bases of globalization are knowledge intensive information and innovation, globalization should have a profound impact on education (Carnoy, 2002). Almost everywhere in the world, educational systems are now under pressure to produce individuals for global competition, individuals who can themselves compete for their own positions in the global context, and who can legitimate the state and strengthen its global competitiveness (Daun, 2002).

Economic and technological globalization is challenging the nation-state in different ways. Countries differ in their response to the processes of globalization according to their size, economic and technological level, economic position in world markets, cultural composition, relationships between the state and economy (Daun, 2002; Green, 1997). Carnoy (2002) argues that analyzing how nation-states respond to globalization is crucial to the understanding of the effects of globalization on education. He posits that the approach a nation-state takes in education reform, their educational response to globalization, depends on three key factors: their real financial situation, their interpretation of that situation, and their ideological position regarding the role of the public sector in education. These three factors are expressed through the methods that a nation-state has adopted for the structural adjustment of its economy to the new globalized environment (Mok & Welch, 2003b).

Globalization is having a profound effect on education at many different levels. That education has been a national priority in many countries is largely understood in terms of national economic survival in a fiercely competitive world. It is commonly recognized that the production economy is being rapidly overtaken by the knowledge economy. Many countries have taken action to enhance their competitive edge through the development of the knowledge-producing institutions and industries. The development of the knowledge economy through the enhancement of skills and abilities, that is, improved human capital, has become an important agenda in many countries' educational policy (Bates, 2002). Globalization will have even greater effects on education in the future. Because global financial flows are so great, governments rely increasingly on foreign capital to finance economic growth. One way to attract finance capital is to provide a ready supply of skilled labor by increasing the overall level of education in the labor force.

Global competition results in an overall demand for higher skills. Daun (2002) argues that global competition leads to an increasing demand for higher skills in the population as a whole, and lifelong learning for all. Global competition also leads to a techno-economic shift. Such a shift results in unemployment in the short term but to a higher standard of living and higher employment in the long term. As the arrival of a global society will also herald that of a knowledge society, the role of education is to enhance a nation's productivity and competitiveness in the global environment. Bate (2002) foresees that the challenges ahead for most education systems and their success in global competition will depend on: (1) whether they can determine the skills and attitudes required by the young and by lifelong learners; (2) the construction of an appropriate global curriculum; (3) the development of an appropriate technologically mediated pedagogy; (4) the specification of the universal standards by which performance can be evaluated; (5) the management of the system through which these achievements can be realized (p. 139).

Globalization and Educational Change

Globalization has brought a paradigm shift in educational policies and administration in many countries. Under the impacts of globalization, Mulford (2002) observes that the old-fashioned values of wisdom, trust, empathy, compassion, grace, and honesty in managing education have changed into those so-called values of contracts, markets, choice, and competition in educational administration. At present, school administrators are probing more into the instrumental skills of efficiency, accountability and planning than the skills of collaboration and reciprocity. School education nowadays puts more stress on the short term, the symbolic and expediency, having the answers and sameness, than those of the past, which focused on the long term, the real and substantive goals and objectives, discretion and reserving judgment, and character.

In the competitive global economy and environment, nation-states have no choice but to adjust themselves in order to be more efficient, productive, and flexible. To enhance a nation's productivity and competitiveness in the global situation, decentralization and the creation of a "market" in education have been the two major strategies employed to restructure education (Lingard, 2000; Mok & Welch, 2003b). Decentralization and corporate managerialism have been used by most governments to increase labour flexibility and create more autonomous educational institutions while catering for the demand for more choice and diversity in education (Blackmore, 2000). The emergence of education markets has also been central to education reform for globalization in many states. Carnoy (2002) argues that if education is restructured on market principles and based upon competitive market relations where individual choice is facilitated, education will become more efficient.

While it is true that many educational developments are due to globalization, the dynamics, complexity, and mechanism of such impacts are still not fully grasped. Martin Carnoy (1999) analyzes how globalization has been affecting education systems, directly and indirectly, and summarizes that globalization has recently brought the following major educational changes (pp. 15–17):

1. Globalization has had an impact on the organization of work and on the work people do. Usually this work demands a high level of skill.
2. Such demands push governments to expand their higher education, and to increase the number of secondary-school graduates prepared to attend post-secondary education.
3. Most governments are under greater pressure to increase spending on education to produce a more educated labour force.
4. The quality of education is increasingly being compared internationally. The TIMSS and PISA studies are cases in point.
5. There have been greater emphases on mathematics and science curricula, English as a foreign language and communication skills, in school education.
6. Use of information technology, such as, the use of the Internet and computer assisted instruction are becoming more common in the classroom.

In the following sections, the impact of globalization on higher education and school education will be discussed more specifically and in greater details.

Restructuring Higher Education in the Era of Globalization

There have been a variety of important social, cultural, economic, and political forces that link to the global development of higher education. Schugurensky (2003) identified (1) the globalization of economy, (2) the commodification of knowledge, and (3) the retrenchment of the welfare state as three important forces, among others, for the changes in higher education. Globalization leads to the emergence of a knowledge economy, in which the importance of information technology and knowledge management is coming to outweigh that of capital and labour. Globalization also leads to the intensification of the transnational flows of information, commodities, and capital around the globe. That, in turn, renders both production and dissemination of knowledge increasingly commoditized. In parallel with the onset of globalization, more and more welfare states have adopted a neoliberal ideology geared to promoting economic international competitiveness through cutbacks in social expenditure, economic deregulation, decreased capital taxes, privatization and labour flexibilization. All these forces are implicit in a restructuring of higher education systems worldwide (Peters, Marshall & Fitzsimons, 2000; Welch, 2003).

The impacts of these forces on the change to higher education are manifest in the drastic restructuring of higher education systems, in which values, such as accountability, competitiveness, devolution, value for money, cost effectiveness, corporate management, quality assurance, performance indicators, and privatization are emphasized (Mok & Lee, 2002; Ngok & Kwong, 2003). Though nations vary widely in their social, political, cultural and economic characteristics, what is striking is the great similarity in the unprecedented scope and depth of restructuring taking place. In general, most of these changes are expressions of a greater influence of the market and the government over the university system. At the core of these changes is a redefinition of the relationships among the university, the state, and the market (Schugurensky, 2003).

Currie (1998) has been able to identify certain trends in the restructuring of higher education, in the globalizing practices in Anglo-Pacific and North American universities. These trends have important implications for the development of higher education systems in other countries in this era of globalization. These trends include (1) a shift from elite to mass higher education, (2) the privatization of higher education, (3) the practice of corporate managerialism, and (4) the spread of transnational education.

There has been a shift from elite to mass higher education

globally, driven by the fact that in a knowledge-based economy, the payroll cost to higher levels of education is rising worldwide. This is a result of the shift from economic production to knowledge-intensive services and manufacturing. Rising relative incomes for higher educated labour increases the demand for university education, pushing governments to expand their higher education (Carnoy, 2002).

In the face of limited resources and the rapid expansion of higher education, governments have been forced towards the privatization of higher education and corporatization of public universities. Privatization is another global trend in higher education, which means a reduction in the level of state provision, and correspondingly, the encouragement of the expansion of private provision (Lee, 2000). The underlying ideology of privatization is based on the belief that the public sector is ineffective, inefficient, and inflexible, while the private sector is deemed more effective, efficient, and responsive to the rapid changes that are needed in the globalizing world.

By corporatization, public universities are run like business corporations. The adoption of business-like approaches will result in financial cost savings; increased administrative efficiencies; and retain academic staff through the offering of competitive market remunerations (Lee, 2000). Such a global change reflects the fact that higher education institutions are increasingly required to secure additional funds from external sources and to reduce dependence on the government (Ngok & Kwong, 2003).

A unique feature of the rapid expansion of private higher education is the emergence of offshore programmes that are offered by foreign universities. The emergence of foreign-linked programmes reflects a growing trend of transnational education, which means that there is a growing volume of higher education being delivered across national boundaries. Education has become increasingly affected by commoditization. In the global context, the boundaries of how, where, and under whose authority education is carried out and certified are becoming less clear as universities internationalize their campuses, curricula, and teaching staff (Lee, 2000)

There are some backwash effects created from these global currents of restructuring of higher education due to globalization. First, a rapid expansion in higher education may inevitably lead to a fall in the average academic standard of performance of graduates. It is likely that the definition and establishment of quality will become the prerogative of management rather than academic professionals. When universities become more corporatized, they will be linked more to the market and less to the pursuit of truth. Intellectuals will become less the guardians of the search for truth, and administrators will assume a dominant role (Stromquist & Monkman, 2000). In this regard, norms that have traditionally been part of university life may be questioned. Stromquist and Monkman (2000) warned that when guided by a climate of knowledge as production, the university may become indifferent to subjects dealing with ethics, social justice, and critical studies.

Globalization and School Educational Reforms

While higher education systems worldwide have been undergoing restructuring as a response to the challenges posed by globalization, school education systems inevitably have to reform also. Based on the strategies the nation-states adopted in school educational reforms implemented in the context of globalization, The International Labor Organization (1996, pp. 6–12) and Carnoy (1999) have been able to identify three different models of educational reforms and make a distinction between: (1) competitiveness-driven reforms, (2) finance-driven reforms, and (3) equity-driven reforms. The competitiveness-driven reforms are implemented in order to improve a country's competitiveness in the world market and the major strategies include decentralization, centralization, improved management of educational resources and improved teacher recruitment and training. Finance-driven reforms consist of privatization, shifting public funding from higher to lower levels of education, and the reduction of costs per student as the major strategies, while equity-driven reforms are often targeted towards groups that are neglected or are more affected by the consequence of structural adjustment programmes. Different countries will adopt these models of educational reform to a greater or lesser extent according to their financial situation, culture and interpretation of globalization.

Though different nation-states may have varying perceptions of globalization and adopt different strategies in school educational reforms, similarly to the strategies in restructuring higher education described in previous sections, decentralization, marketization and choice are the major approaches seen.

The main argument for decentralization stems from the assumption that increased flexibility and control allow for a better fit between educational methods and the students served, as well as greater accountability for educational results. Decentralization is cast in the role of a reform that increases productivity in education and thus contributes significantly to improving the quality of a nation's human resources. Many schemes have been tried to achieve decentralization of school education, such as voucher plans, magnet schools, zero-based budgeting, school consultative committees and school-based management (Brown, 1990).

Decentralization in education systems is typically the legacy of the New Right's neoliberal ideology of school reform in Western countries in the early 1980s (Cooper, 1988). Both Ronald Reagan of the United States and Margaret Thatcher of Great Britain were committed to breaking the monopoly of schools and the introduction of more choice, competition and measurable results. They both believed that strong state control of schools rendered them ineffective, inefficient and not responsive enough to rapid global societal changes. Their basic beliefs were that the market is the most efficient instrument to allocate resources, that competition will motivate people to raise their standards of performance and that school improvement will not occur if they are not held accountable and given the necessary resources to do their job.

These two Governments came into office on a platform of motivating schools' internal initiatives and reducing the governments' roles in and control over education by creating competitive markets in the school system and devolving authority to schools. The New Right's language articulated in school reform is, "choice," "competition," "market mechanism" and such like. In order to promote a market mechanism in the school system and to allow schools to compete with each other, state (government) schools should be dissolved, deregulated and even "privatized" (Pang, 2002), be given the chance of self-management (Caldwell & Spinks, 1988) and be accountable for their own performance. "Market" and "school-based management" are the two prime ideological foci of the New Right's school reforms.

When the concept of a market is applied to the school system, the notion of choice is crucial. Choice may be bi-directional in the sense that schools compete for students and students also compete for schools. The two-way competition is the driving force for both schools and students to improve and to raise their standards of performance. In the face of competition, students would strive for excellence in order to get into a "good" school, and schools would ensure they provided quality education in order to compete for the best students. When market forces are introduced into the school system, competition is created, and the quality of education will be assured effectively, efficiently and automatically.

When there is a market mechanism in the education system, schools are responsive and accountable. The right choice is to devolve the system to schools (Chapman & Boyd, 1986). School-based management (site-based management, self-budgeting and self-management are other terms coined) is the most popular form of school management reform to revitalize schools in terms of responsiveness, flexibility, accountability and productivity. When the functions of market and school-based management in schools are at full strength, the quality of education will be assured.

Implications and Further Research

Though there is still no universally accepted conceptualization of globalization, what we call "globalization" has brought numerous and profound changes to the economic, social, cultural and political life of nations as well as changes in education. Globalization seems to be leading to some homogenizing tendencies, but it is also opening a space for new identities and contesting established values and norms (Stromquist & Monkman, 2000). The global flow of information and culture as well as the rapid spread of new technologies has enormous consequence for education. Globalization might entail the imposition of the concepts of competition, market, choice, decentralization and privatization on education, that is, the further infiltration by business forces into education. It might also lead to increased commoditization of education and making quality education only accessible to elite elements of society who can afford it (Kellner, 2000).

The globalization of education might involve the privileging of

Western, most particularly English-language, culture in the whole world. It is evident that in many places, globalization has led to greater economic and social inequality; and that educational access, whilst expanded, has also become more unequal in quality. Greater decentralization and privatization of education has generally not increased equality in educational services, rather leading to more inequality (Carnoy, 2002).

There exist dichotomous accounts of globalization in the literature, for example, (1) the relations between the global and the local; (2) between globalization viewed as a trend toward homongenization around Western norms and culture and globalization viewed as an era of increased contact between diverse cultures, leading to an increase in hybridization and novelty; and (3) between the material and rhetorical effects of globalization (Burbules & Torres, 2000, pp. 13–14). There is also a question of whether globalization is a "good thing." Is globalization beneficial to economic growth, equality, and justice, or is it harmful? Has globalization led to development or division in education, and to what extent? (Welch & Mok, 2003) The question whether globalization in its various manifestations, is bad or good for education, remains largely unanswered. Further research into these controversial issues should be carried out, as long as globalization continues to affect education. The challenge ahead for research on globalization is not only whether progress is being made, but whether it is being made quickly enough.

About the Book

This book is about the educational research, change and reforms that are taking place around the world in the name of globalization. It brings together an outstanding group of international authors and is divided into three parts on the following themes and focuses on how globalization has been impacting on educational policy and practice around the world. The themes are: (1) to discuss the roles of educational research in the era of globalization and how comparative education can contribute to such investigation (Arnove, 2003; Torres, 2003), (2) to explore the relationships between the development of higher education and globalization in different countries, and (3) to examine the impacts of globalization on school education and how schools can respond to the challenges ahead.

Part I comprises two chapters, which focus on the relationship of globalization, comparative education and education research. Andy Green and Mark Bray have provided new insights into the roles of comparative education in educational research in the era of globalization. They both review the development of comparative education historically, but from different perspectives. They both posit that, complex as the concept of globalization is, the very nature of comparative education as an interdisciplinary field, does provide a meeting point between globalization and comparative education. Both chapters review research methodology in comparative education and explore the new horizons for educational research. Though the authors have addressed similar issues in the two chapters, readers will find that their approaches to and delineation in the issues are quite different.

In Chapter 2, Green explores how globalization is changing education and the implication of this for comparative education. He examines why we should study education systems in general and national education systems in particular. He suggests what else comparativists should study, and attempts to define the field of comparative education under the impacts of globalization. In the critical analyses, he approaches the above issues historically and methodologically.

In Chapter 3, Bray introduces the argument that the field of comparative education is more closely related to globalisation than most other fields of academic enquiry, because comparative education, by its very nature, encourages scholars to be outward looking. Reviewing the history of comparative education, Bray suggests that the field of comparative education is being shaped by globalization and posits that comparative scholars have become much more global in their approaches than used to be the case. Such cross-national forces of change are reflected in dominant paradigms, methodological approaches, and the foci of comparative studies.

Part II is a collection of four chapters, which focus on the relationship between globalization, and changes and restructuring in higher education. These four chapters indicate that the recent development and reforms of higher education around the world have mostly been a response to the requests and challenges of globalization. Most states, under the impact of globalization, have been restructuring their higher education, in order to (1) establish a diversified, multi-channel, flexible and interlinked system of higher education; (2) to increase post-secondary learning opportunities, and (3) to nurture quality people who possess knowledge and virtues, broad-mindedness, commitment, global vision, creativity and adaptability (Education Commission, 2000). Though most higher education institutions (HEIs) have been impacted by similar global demands, the response in different countries has been quite diverse. The various issues discussed in these chapters include: the evolution and transformation of higher education in China Mainland under the impacts of globalization; the issue of quality assurance in higher education in Australia; the issues surrounding the development of higher degrees in the context of and culture of globalization in Australia; and the governance model of community colleges in the United States.

China's accession to the WTO in 2001 has accelerated its integration into the global community. In Chapter 4, Kinglun Ngok analyses Chinese higher education reform in the context of globalization. He focuses his discussions on the changes in educational governance, educational financing and provision, curriculum, and educational competition in higher education in China, in the last two decades. After about two decades of restructuring and transforming under the impacts of globalization, the unified, centralized, closed, and static higher education system of China is becoming more diversified, decentralized, open, and dynamic. All these changes have exposed higher education in China to increasing international exchange and co-operation, as well as wider use of modern educational technology. Ngok speculates that along with the further opening of the Chinese higher education sector following China's accession to the WTO, international competition and pressure will be intensified and he predicts that further restructuring and transformation will be introduced.

In Chapter 5, David Gamage and Jaratdao Suwarnabroma argue that Total Quality Management (TQM) may be a useful model to assure the quality of higher education as well as to ensure its competitiveness. In this chapter they first explicate what TQM is, how the concept evolved, and what it means in the context of higher education. They have offered a range of definitions of TQM by different researchers, which help explore its applicability in assuring the quality of higher education. In addition to the discussion of the impacts of TQM on higher education, the authors also explore what difficulties need to be confronted when the concept of TQM is applied to assuring the quality of higher education. They ask what approaches are possible and what the advantages are in adopting TQM in quality assurance measures. They finally argue that TQM is a quality culture, which allows higher education institutions to move beyond notions of quality control and to provide a philosophy and methodology which helps them manage change and set their own agendas for dealing with the external competitive world.

In Chapter 6, Alan Larkin, drawing on comments, gathered in various informal discussions, in class seminars and discussion activities, through written assignments and student research projects, from many international students, offers a thorough reflection and a fresh perspective on how to develop higher degree courses in the context and culture of globalization. He has keenly followed the study programme, social programme, cultural experiences and family welfare of some hundreds of post-graduate international students in past years. He is of the view that globalization offers extensive opportunities for truly worldwide development, but it is not progressing evenly. Higher education providers who are delivering education, training and research expertise to students from developing countries may assist these countries by helping them integrate more quickly into the global economy. However, Larkin warns that the successful provision of higher degree courses in a truly global context requires far greater depth of understanding of all of the issues and a shared and coherent "vision" and agreed "mission" across the various areas of a university, than presently exists. He stresses that academic teaching and research staff, general and administrative staff, staff prospecting in markets overseas for new students in many locations and those who develop and coordinate academic programmes all need to come together to share their perspectives on globalized courses.

From just one institution in Illinois in 1901, the community college system in the United States has evolved during the last century, to over a thousand institutions. However, little is known about how statewide governance systems shape or influence community colleges in the United States and the extent to which they are effective (Raby, 2000). Cheryl Lovell and Catherine Trouth, in Chapter 7, review the different types of community college governance models in the United States, and make observations about them to determine if there is one best model. Their analysis is based on two different criteria: the decision-making authority for an organization and statewide (as opposed to nationwide) coordination. In their analysis, they have identified five taxonomies of the governance models, two of which describe statewide governance for all public higher education institutions, the other three describing governance specifically for community colleges. The specific question they ask is, "Is there one best model that most adequately describes the U.S. governance systems for community colleges in the U.S.?" This is simple question to ask but a very complex one to answer, and they both directly admit that there is no one best model, since each of the taxonomies identified has unique features that are useful to an understanding of community college governance. Nevertheless, they have suggested a few matters for other countries to consider, when they have to adopt or are considering adopting the U.S. community college model.

Part III is a collection of five chapters, which look at the relationship between globalization, school reforms and the transformation of teaching. The first, is an article focusing on the transformation of schools and the teaching profession under the impacts of globalization. The next two articles share a similar theme, namely that English language teaching has become a globalized educational market. While the first of these aims to explore the complex interplay of subjectivity, context, culture, desire, economy and discourse that merge within the dynamics of globalizing teacher subjectivities, the second examines how the author as a native English-Speaking teacher experienced the cultural identity shocks and transformation when teaching in different countries and what roles native English-Speaking teachers play in implementing curricular changes that aim for globalization. The last two chapters in Part III, focus on the importance of a schools' capacity for organizational learning and self-evaluation. The theses in the last two chapters are that under the highly external competitive environment, the continued survival of the school as a public institution is no longer guaranteed and that if schools are to survive the turbulent uncertain external environment, they should resort to transforming into "learning organizations" to enhance their on-going self-evaluation and self-renewal capacity.

Based on the seminal work by the OECD on the future of education, Brian Caldwell in Chapter 8 foresees that there will be a transformation of schools on a dramatic scale in the early years of the 21st century. In his analysis, transformation means change that is significant, systematic and sustained, and the transformation of schools means the transformation of work for those engaged in the core business of learning and teaching. In his words, the transformation of schools and the transformation of the teaching profession are opposite sides of the same coin. He argues that if the profession is transformed then the way in which the professional is formed will also be transformed. Caldwell contends that a central theme in the transformation of the teaching profession is that of knowledge management. A successful transformation of schools calls for a "new professionalism" in which teachers' work will be increasingly research-based, outcomes-oriented, data-driven, and team-focused at the same time as it is globalized, localized and individualized, with lifelong professional learning as the norm for teachers. It is readily apparent that though Caldwell in this chapter put forwards his observations, insights and arguments on the formation and transformation of the teaching professions to the International Baccalaureate Organization (IBO) and IB schools, the contexts and rationales of such transformations and their implications are also applicable to schools in general and to the future development of teacher education in particular.

In Chapter 9, Dianne Bloomfield and Cathryn McConaghy assert that the major outcome of economic globalisation is a reduction in the defining power of nation states. With expanding international employment opportunities, the issue of what shapes an 'internationalized teacher identity' and what are the appropriate responses in terms of teacher education curriculum and pedagogy in shaping teacher subjectivities are securing more attention and investigation.

As traditionally defined identity and culture break down, spaces are emerging for new cultural forms and identities. The globalization of education has called for a new identity construct of the "internationalized teacher."

The place of English language teaching in this globalizing educational market is complex. Bloomfield and McConaghy report on their investigation into a collaborative venture between the Faculty of Education, Chinese University of Hong Kong (CUHK) and the University of New England, Armidale (UNE) in Australia. The project entitled, "Enhancing English Proficiency through School-Based Learning," was supported by the Hong Kong Government's Quality Education Fund, and involved the native English-speaking student teachers from Australia who were placed in English language programmes in a number of Hong Kong schools under the Native English Teachers (NET) scheme. There was evidence that the NET scheme in its present form was somewhat problematic and required reforms. The focus of the reforms was related to the selection of suitable teachers, induction and support for NETs. The authors in this chapter attempted to explore the success of, and resistance in the process of internationalizing teachers and the quality of the student teachers' learning journeys when they participated in the project.

While Bloomfield and McConghy have identified the importance of English as the language of the global market and consider that native English language teachers have become a global commodity, Candace Schlein, in Chapter 10, a Canadian native English-speaking language teacher reflects on her personal and professional experience of being just such a commodity in Japan. Her experience affirms that curriculum reform efforts around the world have focused on globalization as a prime goal and many of the reforms often include the addition or strengthening of programmes in English as a Second Language (ESL). ESL educators play a crucial role in implementing curricular changes that aim for globalization. Many countries, such as Japan and China have recruited numbers of teachers from Western countries to teach English in their respective "NET" programmes, the Japan Exchange and Teaching (JET) Programme in Japan (Parmenter, 2000) and the Native English Teachers (NET) Scheme in Hong Kong are two cases in point.

Schlein shows how narrative inquiry into experience, that is qualitative research, can be a prime methodology for investigating teachers and teaching. Reflecting on her own experience as a Canadian ESL teacher who participated in the JET programme for a period of two years, she shares stories of her intercultural experience of acculturation and reacculturation. Her stories indicate how foreign teachers and the curriculum are impacted under the movement towards globalized education in Japan and how they allow themselves to develop professionally in foreign educational situations. In particular, Schlein explores, in her analysis, the theories regarding cultural adaptation and reentry in the context of teachers and teaching as well as the relationship between teachers' experiences and the actualized curriculum (Gough, 2000). The findings of the author's inquiry show that the interweaving of educational landscapes leads to the transformation of teachers' cultural identities, which influences the enacted curriculum in both the foreign and native educational contexts as well as that the decisions and actions that are made in curricular situations are based on teachers' past personal and professional experiences.

In Chapter 11, Jack Lam has synthesized a model of a school's developmental stages of organizational learning. Based on his empirical research into the organizational learning processes and outcomes of schools in both Taiwan and Hong Kong (Lam & Pang, 2003), he was able to identify the positions of the schools falling on each of the quadrants and their stages of school development. Schools falling into Quadrant 1 are those stagnating schools, which result where there are factors that exert stronger pressure for inertia than change and where no collective learning is taking place. Schools in Quadrant 4 are those, which have successfully evolved into "learning organizations." Schools which fall into either Quadrants 2 or 3 are those undergoing certain transitional phases in their search for new directions for development and are in a state of flux. In his study, what accounted for the variations among these groups of schools is the focal point of his investigation. By comparing and contrasting the forces of change at work, Lam was able to identify both the global and local factors that schools in each setting seem to respond to. He warns that the numerous attempts at conceptually segregating globalization and localization become futile academic exercises when we actually apply these concepts separately to dissect the impacts of the contemporary school reforms. It seems quite impossible to sort out the effects of localized factors in order to assess global influence, neither is it beneficial to parcel out globalized effects to ascertain the role of local factors. Following on from this, Lam subscribes that intermingling globalized and local effects constitute a very rewarding and enlightening aspect of comparative education research.

Global trends in the development of school systems, are to adopt a two-pronged approach to the assurance of quality of school education. This two-pronged approach, that is, employing whole-school inspections as the external force and school self-evaluation as the internal force, will be more likely to produce better results in managing organizational change when schools are confronted with the challenges arising from globalization. In Chapter 12, Nicholas Pang asserts that the school principal acts as an important agent for change in response to the ever-increasing expectations of school education and should make use of these two forces in managing organizational change. Pang recommends three basic strategies to school administrators for planning the management of school organizational change, that is, (1) rational-empirical strategy, (2) power-coercive strategy, and (3) normative-re-educative strategy. Of course, it is acknowledged that these three strategies are descriptive tools, and will rarely be used in a "pure form" and most likely will be seen being used conjointly.

Taken as a whole, the book illustrates the quite different views of globalization held by various academics. While there are research papers exploring the impacts of globalization on education in general, there are also papers specifically examining the experience of restructuring education in China, Hong Kong, Taiwan, Japan, Singapore, Australia, Canada, and the United States. This work produces an overview of principal changes in different national societies and their educational systems, definitions and arrangements of educational restructuring and educational research. These changes imply decentralization/centralization, freedom of educational choice, application of market forces in education or systemic reforms. We trust that this volume can make a significant contribution to extending this field of knowledge by identifying, characterizing, and clarifying some of the debates surrounding the phenomenon of globalization and improve our understanding of some of the multiple and complex effects of globalization on educational policy and practice.

References

Arnove, R. F. (2003). Reframing comparative education: The dialectic of the global and the local. In R. F. Arnove & C. A. Torres (Eds.), *Comparative education: The dialectic of the global and the local* (2nd ed., pp. 1–23). Lanham, MD: Rowman & Littlefield Publishers.

Bates, R. (2002). Administering the global trap: The roles of educational leaders. *Educational Management & Administration, 30*(2), 139–156.

Blackmore, J. (2000). Globalization: A useful concept for feminists rethinking theory and strategies in education. In N. C. Burbules & C. A. Torres (Eds.), *Globalization and education: Critical perspectives* (pp. 133–155). London: Routledge.

Brown, D. J. (1990). *Decentralization and school-based management*. London: The Falmer Press.

Burbules, N. C., & Torres C. A. (2000) Globalization and education: An introduction. In N. C. Burbules & C. A. Torres (Eds.), *Globalization and education: Critical perspectives* (pp. 1–26). London: Routledge.

Caldwell, B. J., & Spinks, J. M. (1988). *The self-managing school*. London: The Falmer Press.

Capella, J. R. (2000). Globalization, a fading citizenship. In N. C. Burbules & C. A. Torres (Eds.), *Globalization and education: Critical perspectives* (pp. 227–251). London: Routledge.

Capling, A., Considine, M., & Crozier, M. (1998). *Australian politics in the global era*. Melbourne: Addison-Wesley.

Carnoy, M. (1999). *Globalization and educational reform: What planners need to know*. Paris: UNESCO & International Institute for Educational Planning.

Carnoy, M. (2002). Foreword. In H. Daun (Ed.), *Educational Restructuring in the Context of Globalization and National Policy*. New York: Routledge Falmer.

Chapman, J., & Boyd, W. L. (1986). Decentralization, devolution, and the school principal: Australian lessons on statewide education reform. *Educational Administration Quarterly, 22*(4), 28–58.

Cooper, B. S. (1988). School reform in the 1980s: The New Right's legacy. *Educational Administration Quarterly, 24*(3), 282–298.

Currie, J. (1998). Globalization practices and the professoraite in Anglo-Pacific and North American Universities. *Comparative Education Review, 42*(1), 15–29.

Daun, H. (Ed.). (2002). *Educational Restructuring in the Context of Globalization and National Policy*. New York: Routledge Falmer.

Education Commission. (2000). *Review of the education system: Reform proposals*. Hong Kong: The Printing Department.

Gough, N. (2000). Globalization and curriculum inquiry: Locating, representing, and performing a transnational imaginary. In N. P. Stromquist & K. Monkman (Eds.), *Globalization and education: Integration and contestation across cultures* (pp. 77–98). Lanham, MD: Rowman & Littlefield.

Green, A. (1997). *Education, globalization and the nation state*. London: Macmillan Press Ltd.

Held, D. (Ed.). (1991). *Political theory today.* Standford, CA: Standford University Press.

The International Labor Organization. (1996). *Impact of structural adjustment on the employment and training of teachers.* Geneva: ILO, Sectoral Activities Programme.

Kellner, D. (2000). Globalization and new social movements: Lessons for critical theory and pedagogy. In N. C. Burbules & C. A. Torres (Eds.), *Globalization and education: Critical perspectives* (pp. 299–321). London: Routledge.

Lam, Y. L. J., & Pang, S. K. N. (2003). The relative effects of environmental, internal and contextual factors on organizational learning: The case of Hong Kong schools under reform. *The Learning Organization: An International Journal, 10*(2), 83–97.

Lee, M. N. N. (2000). The impacts of globalization on education in Malaysia. In N. P. Stromquist & K. Monkman (Eds.), *Globalization and education: Integration and contestation across cultures* (pp. 315–332). Lanham, MD: Rowman & Littlefield.

Lingard, B. (2000). It is and it isn't: Vernacular globalization, educational policy, and restructuring. In N. C. Burbules & C. A. Torres (Eds.), *Globalization and education: Critical perspectives* (pp. 79–108). London: Routledge.

Mok, J. K. H., & Lee, H. H. (2002). A reflection on quality assurance in Hong Kong's higher education. In J. K. H. Mok & D. K. K. Chan (Eds.), *Globalization and education: The quest for quality education in Hong Kong* (pp. 213–240). Hong Kong: Hong Kong University Press.

Mok, J. K. H., & Chan, D. K. K. (Eds.). (2002). *Globalization and education: The quest for quality education in Hong Kong.* Hong Kong: Hong Kong University Press.

Mok, J. K. H., & Welch, A. (Eds.). (2003a). *Globalization and educational restructuring in the Asia Pacific region.* New York: Palgrave Macmillan.

Mok, J. K. H., & Welch, A. (2003b). Globalization, structural adjustment and educational reform. In J. K. H. Mok & A. Welch (Eds.), *Globalization and educational restructuring in the Asia Pacific region* (pp. 1–31). New York: Palgrave Macmillan.

Morrow, R. A., & Torres, C. A. (2000). The state, globalization and education policy. In N. C. Burbules & C. A. Torres (Eds.), *Globalization and education: Critical perspectives* (pp. 27–56). London: Routledge.

Mulford, B. (2002). The global challenge: A matter of balance. *Educational Management & Administration, 30*(2), 123–138.

Ngok, K. L., & Kwong, J. (2003). Globalization and educational restructuring in China. In J. K. H. Mok & A. Welch (Eds.), *Globalization and educational restructuring in the Asia Pacific region* (pp. 160–188). New York: Palgrave Macmillan.

Pang, N. S. K. (2002). Towards 'school management reform': Organizational values of government schools in Hong Kong. In J. K. H. Mok & D. K. K. Chan (Eds.), *Globalization and education: The quest for quality education in Hong Kong* (pp. 171–193). Hong Kong: Hong Kong University Press.

Parker, B. (1997). Evolution and revolution: From international business to globalization. In S. R. Clegg, C. Hardy, & W. R. Nord (Eds.), *Handbook of organization studies* (pp. 484–506). London: Sage Publications.

Parmenter, L. (2000). Internationalization in Japanese education: Current issues and future prospects. In N. P. Stromquist & K. Monkman (Eds.), *Globalization and education: Integration and contestation across cultures* (pp. 237–254). Lanham, MD: Rowman & Littlefield.

Peters, M., Marshall, J., & Fitzsimons, P. (2000). Managerialism and educational policy in a global context: Foucault, neoliberalism, and the doctrine of self-management. In N. C. Burbules & C. A. Torres (Eds.), *Globalization and education: Critical perspectives* (pp. 109–132). London: Routledge.

Pieterse, J. N. (1995). Globalization as hybridization. In M. Featherstone, S. Lash, & R. Robertson (Eds.), *Global modernities* (pp. 45–68). London: Sage.

Raby, R. L. (2000). Globalization of the community college model: Paradox of the local and the global. In N. P. Stromquist & K. Monkman (Eds.), *Globalization and education: Integration and contestation across cultures* (pp. 149–172). Lanham, MD: Rowman & Littlefield.

Schugurensky, D. (2003). Higher education restructuring in the era of globalization: Toward a heteronomous model? In R. F. Arnove & C. A. Torres (Eds.), *Comparative education: The dialectic of the global and the local* (2nd ed., pp. 292–312). Lanham, MD: Rowman & Littlefield.

Stromquist, N. P., & Monkman, K. (2000). Defining globalization and assessing its implications on knowledge and education. In N. P. Stromquist & K. Monkman (Eds.), *Globalization and education: Integration and contestation across cultures* (pp. 3–26). Lanham, MD: Rowman & Littlefield.

Torres, C. A. (2003). Comparative education: The dialectics of globalization and its discontents. In R. F. Arnove & C. A. Torres (Eds.), *Comparative education: The dialectic of the global and the local* (2nd ed., pp. 446–461). Lanham, MD: Rowman & Littlefield.

Uvalié-Trumbié, S. (Ed.). (2002). *Globalization and the market in higher education: Quality, accreditation and qualifications.* Paris: UNESCO & the International Association of Universities.

Welch, A., & Mok, J. K. H. (2003). Conclusion: Deep development or deep division? In J. K. H. Mok & A. Welch (Eds.), *Globalization and educational restructuring in the Asia Pacific Region* (pp. 333–356). New York: Palgrave Macmillan.

Welch, A. (2003). Globalization, structural adjustment and contemporary educational reforms in Australia. In J. K. H. Mok & A. Welch (Eds.),

Globalization and educational restructuring in the Asia Pacific Region (pp. 262–301). New York: Palgrave Macmillan.

Wells, A. S., Carnochan, S., Slayton, J., Allen, R. L., & Vasudeva, A. (1998). Globalization and educational change. In A. Hargreaves, A. Lieberman, M. Fullan, & D. Hopkins (Eds.), *International handbook of educational change* (pp. 322–348). Dordrecht, The Netherlands: Kluwer Academic Publishers.

2

National Educational Systems and Comparative Education: From State Formation to Globalization

Andy GREEN

—⟆⟆—

Abstract

Comparative education has traditionally meant the study of national education systems. The field first developed in the early nineteenth century in parallel with the rise of national education, and it took the national system as its main object of enquiry (Noah & Eckstein, 1969). The twentieth century comparativists who consolidated it as an academic subject, including Michael Sadler, Isaac Kandel and Nicholas Hans, continued to focus on the classification and explanation of characteristics of different national systems. But how far is this approach valid today? Doesn't the "decline" of the nation state make national systems obsolete? And isn't the very idea of a "system" anachronistic in a world of market triumphalism and global disorganization? As Peter Jarvis asks in a recent edition of Comparative Education: "Why should we undertake comparative analysis at all in this Global Village?" (Jarvis, 2000).

These are tough questions for comparative educationalists because the concept of the national education system forms the keystone of the whole mental architecture of comparative education. It may be hard to think comparative without it. Nevertheless, the question has been rightly posed and needs answering. The purpose of my lecture is to explore how globalization is changing education and the implication of this for comparative study. Why study education systems and why study national education systems in particular? What else should comparativists study, and how? What defines the field of comparative education? I approach these questions first historically and secondly methodologically.

Introduction

National education systems and comparative education have a parallel history. Since the first cross-national studies, the idea of the national system has been a central paradigm of comparative work. But how apt is this notion in the face of rapid globalization? Will the decline of the nation state make national systems obsolete; and is the very idea of a "system" anachronistic in a world of market triumphalism and global disorganization? These are tough and trenchant questions. Trenchant because globalization does question historical ideas of national education systems, and it behoves us to understand how. Tough because the concept forms the keystone of the whole mental architecture of comparative education and it would be hard to think comparative without it—although that, in part at least, is what we must learn to do.

I want to do two things in this article. The first is to trace in outline the origins and development of the national education system in Europe and North America, and to ask if, and if so how, "globality" fundamentally challenges the model. The second is to ask what implications this process has for the comparative study of education. What does comparative study of education and learning mean in a global era?

National Education Systems—Definition and Origins

What are—or were—national education systems? Margaret Archer, in her landmark book, *The Social Origins of Educational Systems* (1979), defines them as systems of formal schooling at least partly funded and supervised by the state, which sought to provide universal education to school age children in a given nation. A set of institutions constituted a national system when it supplied the majority of the nation's needs in formal education and did so with at least a degree of coordination and integration. This was what started to occur in much of Europe during the early nineteenth century.

National networks of elementary schools were developed with state assistance and gradually free tuition and compulsory attendance laws ensured near universal participation; secondary and technical schooling expanded from their tiny elite bases, so that they could allow a small trickle of upward mobility and give credibility to the Napoleonic maxim of "the career open to talents." Except in the American North and West, the secondary schools represented a parallel system separate from the mass elementary school system for a good further century, but gradually institutions did became more articulated with one another, and systems emerged which were increasingly regulated by the state. Some of these systems, like that in France, with origins in what Archer calls state "restriction," tended to be more centralized and "unified" with higher levels of bureaucratic integration and more systematized linkages between the parts. Others, which developed through middle class ìsubstitutionî of new schools for traditional schools, as in England, tended to be more decentralized, with lower levels of integration, more differentiation and more specialization (Archer, 1979). In either case, although at different rates, as public schools came to predominate over private and voluntary institutions, governments increased their control over systems, providing the majority of funds, licensing and inspecting schools and teachers, organizing teacher training through growing networks of dedicated Normal schools and, in most cases, overseeing national certification and standard school curricula.

The creation of a set of dedicated educational institutions with a putative monopoly of formal learning and training for diverse occupations, signalled a revolution in the concept and forms of education, and a transformation in the relations between schooling, society and the state. Education not only became a mass phenomenon; it also became a central function of society and feature of social organization. Compared with the old clerical forms of learning, this form of national system was radically new and *sui generis*.

The Origins of National Systems

How and why did such systems develop? In brief, they were created as part of the long state forming process which established the modern nation state (Green, 1990). The origins of national education go back to the central European absolutisms, for instance in Prussia and Austria, which first created compulsory and state-funded schools. Absolutism marked the beginning of the modern state-forming process with its development of the principles of sovereignty, bounded territoriality and administrative integration. Absolutist states already had the air of modernity, developing standing armies and bureaucracies, and the taxation systems to support them, and, in some cases, giving support to fledgling capitalist manufacturing industries (Anderson, 1974). Schooling played an important if still limited role in this, providing state bureaucracies, enterprises and armies with administrators, engineers and loyal military recruits.

However, it was in the post-revolutionary period that the project of national schooling came into its own, for it was then that the people—the nation—were brought decisively into the equation of the sovereign, territorial state. In the absolutist, Hobbesian meaning of the term, sovereignty had resided in the person of the absolute ruler, as supreme authority over the territory and the subjects within it. The impact of the Enlightenment and the French Revolution was to transform the notion of sovereignty so that the nation itself became constitutive of that authority. The nation became the body of citizens whose collective sovereignty constituted them as a state which was their political expression (Hobsbawm, 1990). Or such anyway was the principal.

The post-revolutionary nation state completed what the absolutist state had started (de Tocqueville, 1856/1955). It consolidated national boundaries, creating defined borders around preferably unbroken territory; it continued to centralize authority, breaking down the old feudal particularisms and creating a more unified and integrated administrative apparatus; and it entrenched state powers in new civil codes and administrative procedures, with bureaus and statistics to make them effective and to extend the reach of official surveillance and monitoring (Giddens, 1985). However, what was most novel about the nation state was not so much the state but the nation. States had to create nations and the citizens who composed them since these did not come ready made and since states now had to prove their legitimacy with reference to the people.

States created nations of citizens in a multitude of ways. They conscripted and disciplined them in the national defence; they registered their births, marriages and deaths; they monitored and regulated their movements across borders and their political activities; they punished and incarcerated them; they enlisted them into new state rituals, convened them under national flags, and rallied them to the mobilizing sounds of anthems and national declarations; and they recorded their collective characters in a mountain of officials statistics. But most of all they educated them. As Baron Dubin wrote in 1826: "Practically all modern nations are now awake to the fact that education is the most potent means of development of the essentials of nationality" (Fuller & Robinson, 1992, p. 52).

Through national education systems states fashioned disciplined workers and loyal recruits; created and celebrated national languages and literatures; popularized national histories and myths of origin, disseminated national laws, customs and social mores, and generally explained the ways of the state to the people and the duties of the people to the state. At times they even reflected on the rights of citizens and the responsibilities of the state to the people. National education was a massive engine of integration, assimilating the local to the national and the particular to the general. In short, it created, or tried to create, the civic identity and national consciousness which would bind each to the state and reconcile each to the other, making actual citizens out of those who were deemed such in law by virtue of their birth or voluntary adoption.

It did not, of course, do this equally or disinterestedly. Civic rights were in theory universal, but citizenship in practice involved a hierarchy where each class and each gender had differential rights and opportunities both socially and politically (Marshall & Bottomore, 1992). Schools generally reflected this differentiation, educating all according their station, except where the need for a meritocratic safety valve allowed a talented trickle through to careers and upward mobility. However, there was a still a common notion of nationhood and national culture even where each class was apportioned a differentiated slice. Education was the preeminent author and guardian of this national identity and culture.

In practice, not all nations developed nationhood in the same way, and nor did they develop their national education at the same time or in the same forms. Generally speaking, the states in Protestant-dominated northern Europe created national education in advance of the Catholic nations of the Mediterranean, just as did the Puritan states of the northern United States relative to the slave-owning Anglican states of the South (Cipolla, 1969). Protestantism, with its culture of the book, its individualistic work ethic and its proselytizing mission, saw more use for education than the Catholicism of Saints, martyrs and images (Stone, 1969), until, that is, the Counter-Reformation spurred the Jesuits into action as the "schoolmen of Europe."

Significant also to the timing and character of national education was the nature of state formation in the different countries. Where the process of state formation was particularly compacted and intensive, so too was the development of national education. Typically, where countries were forced into accelerated state formation, either by revolution, as in France or America, or by territorial conflict and defensive nationalism, as in Prussia, or simply by the desire to reverse a history of economic underdevelopment relative to some dominant power, education was pressed into service by the state as a vehicle of national development. In these cases national systems were developed early. On the other hand, where nation state formation was peculiarly protracted and retarded, as in Italy, or simply lethargic due to precocious state formation in earlier times, as in Britain, then the development of national education was fitful or delayed (Green, 1990).

In either event, it would seem to have been the nature and timing of the process of state formation that largely determined the course of development of national education systems. This process, more than theories of industrialization or urban development, would seem best to explain the uneven growth of national education across Europe and North America. It explains both why national education developed so early in predominantly preindustrial and rural societies like eighteenth century Prussia and Austria (and even post-revolutionary France which was still a land of small peasants and artisans) and why it developed so late in Britain despite its early industrialization and early concentration of proletarian urbanites. It also explains why Italy, heir of the Roman civilization and the Renaissance, and home of the great city-states and the Papacy, did not develop a national education system until after unification in the 1870s.

National education systems were not a functionally necessity of early industrialization, although they played their part later in industrial development. Nor were they exclusively a response to the conflicts emerging in anomic and class-divided urban environments. Above all they were a state instrument for the forming of the nations of citizens that would give them legitimacy and ensure their survival, both at home and within the European interstate system.

Education, Nationalism and Empire

The ideological work performed by national education in the early phase reflected the imperatives of nation state formation in the post-revolutionary era. The liberal ideal of the nation state, up at least until the second half of the nineteenth century, was generally aggregative and emancipatory, involving the integration of smaller units into larger states which might be both viable and progressive and which were inevitably heterogeneous, both culturally and linguistically (as, in fact, they had usually been).

Nationality for the liberal nationalists, as for the Jacobins of the French Revolution meant, essentially, statehood. It was not dependent on ethnicity or language, so much as conferred by virtue of citizenship gained by birth or by voluntary adoption. The nation consisted of those who wished (and were eligible) to make a commitment to citizenship. Whereas in all states there might be a dominant ethnic, to use Smith's term (Smith, 1995), in countries where this citizen notion of the nation was dominant, as in France or the new nations of America and Australia, nationalism tended to take a "civic" rather than a cultural or ethnic form. Education systems tried to promote such inclusive civic ideologies. They embraced principles of secularism or *laicité* to avoid divisive confessional conflicts, and they emphasized the modern republican heritage and its future goals, as in France and America, rather than the traditional histories and characters of peoples and their cultures and religions.

The later nineteenth century, however, saw the emergence in Europe of a new kind of nationalism which stressed language, traditional culture and, at its extreme, race. This had its ideological roots in the romantic nationalism of Fichte and Herder, both products of a Germanic culture perennially prone to stress the defining principles of language and ethnicity in reaction to the historic dispersal of German-speaking peoples across a territorially unstable Diaspora. However, it was during the period from 1870 to 1918, the Age of Empire, when various factors coalesced to produce a reactionary and aggressive nationalism of race and cultural exclusivism: the rise of Gobineau's pseudo "race science," the effects of large-scale migrations; the insecurity of petit-bourgeois populations caught in the cross-fire between capital and labour; and the growing alienation of some social groups from the standardization of the modernizing process were amongst these (Hobsbawm, 1990). Above all it was Imperial expansionism and rivalry that paved the way. In the face of rising democracy and popular agitation towards the end of the century, governments increasingly sought to secure their legitimacy by appeals to a nationalism which was both ethnic and exclusivist in its rhetoric and symbolism.

Towards the end of the century this more strident nationalism was reflected in different ways in schools across Europe and elsewhere. In Japan a reactionary backlash followed the initially liberal reforms of the 1868 Meiji Restoration and led to the Imperial Rescript on Education of 1890. This became, until 1945, "the basic sacred text of the new religion of patriotism" (Dore quoted in Burke, 1985, p. 349). In Germany, after unification in 1871, education was increasingly influenced by "Volkisch" ideas of national character and destiny and textbooks, as in Jules Ferry's Republican France, became increasingly nationalistic (Albisetti, 1983; Gildea, 1988). Imperialism in Britain, fuelled by German trade competition and later by the Boer war, led to a national efficiency movement which endorsed, amongst other things, para-military training in schools, The Boys Scouts Movement, the narcissistic cult of leadership in the public schools, and a national drive on technical education. As Fabian socialist Sidney Webb once said: "it is in the classroom ... that the battles of the Empire for commercial prosperity are being lost." (Simon, 1965, p. 174)

The empire nationalism of the *fin-de-siécle* was of course only a prelude to the worse things to come. Imperial rivalries brought on the First World War, whose settlement at Versailles only intensified the rebarbative nationalisms that would lead to a further world war within two decades. The period from 1918–1945 has rightly been regarded as the apogee of nationalism in its most reactionary racial and ethnocentric forms (Hobsbawm, 1990). Racism and ethnic nationalism found their way into the heart of education in a number of states during this period. Hitler used German schools to promote his Aryan supremacist doctrine and to fuel anti-Semitism. Japanese schools also became breeding grounds for an aggressive and militaristic nationalism (Schoppa, 1991). Not all countries succumbed to such practices, but the period of the World Wars certainly built an understandable liberal antipathy to nationalistic appropriations of education. The role of education in state formation would be very different thereafter.

Education and Post-war Nationalism

The post-war world brought a new international order. Whilst the Cold War was soon to divide the world into conflicting power blocs, internationalism, initially at least, was the official or ideal currency of interstate relations. Education continued to be associated with nation-building and state formation even though its typical official modality stressed civic integration and cultural pluralism; in fact this association had if anything been strengthened by its prevalent adoption in newly independent states. However, arguably, there were important changes underway in the relations between education and state formation in the western world, as well as growing divergences between the older and newer states in the meaning they assigned to national education.

Amongst the older post-war states were some clear examples of education used as an agent of state formation. Most obviously, in those countries faced with the task of political and economic reconstruction, like Japan, Germany, and France, education was often at the forefront of policies for national development. A major change, however, can be seen in western states in the relation between education and state formation. Increasingly, where education was identified with the national interest, as it often was, this was in terms of the national economy and economic competitiveness rather than citizenship and national cohesion. Skills formation was replacing citizen formation as the main object of national policy (Green, 1997). Where citizenship was a concern, there was increasing confusion about what this should mean in a modern pluralistic society and how education could contribute to it. There are signs now of renewed state interest in promoting social cohesion through schools, as the socially fragmenting effects of globalization become more evident, but Governments are no more clear about what to do about it.

In the developing world, of course, there has been an even more explicit link between education and state formation, with education unequivocally linked with both citizen-formation and national economic development. New states have not always been successful in using education as an instrument of nation-building. What is striking, however, is the frequent coincidence of successful nation-building and planned educational development. As in nineteenth-century Europe, rapid educational growth today is often associated with countries undergoing peculiarly intensive periods of state formation, as in East Asia. In many cases this has been induced by crises of national identity born of war, national division, and social transformation. It has also been linked with concerted national drives for economic development, usually aimed at catching up with some more advanced regional power, which acts as a role model.

The East Asian "tiger" states have provided the most dramatic example of this in the recent period. Each has experienced crises of national identity, born of regional conflicts or internal strife (Castells, 1992): South Korea forced to reconstruct after civil war and in the face of continuing hostility from its communist northern neighbour; Taiwan, like Korea, at the heart of regional and cold-war tensions with its sovereignty still disputed by mainland China; and Singapore, cast adrift by the British and Malaysia, and thereafter struggling to create a state which no-one had thought viable. Each has sought rapid economic expansion, both for its own sake and to catch up with the regional champion and former occupying power, Japan. In all of these countries nation-building has been seen as a question of national survival, with education at its heart.

Education in a Global Age

National education systems, though changing, clearly remained fully intact well into the post-World War II era. The 1960s represented an exceptional period of growth for public education in most advanced states: school and university provision expanded to make upper secondary enrolment near universal and higher education a mass phenomena; governments, on advice from human capital economists, invested increasing proportions of GDP in public education to raise skills levels and accelerate economic growth; and national electorates generally believed education systems to be matters of national interest—so much so in fact that when the Treaty of Rome was drawn up and ratified in 1957, it contained no references to education at all since national sovereignty was still thought to remain supreme in such matters. So what happened in the remaining decades of the last century to cause us to consider whether education systems may now be in decline, the brief answer is globalization.

What is Globalization?

Globalization can be defined as the rapid intensification of cross-border movements of capital, goods, labour, services, and ideas. This process, though not new, was massively accelerated from the 1970s as a result of three factors: cheap energy and transportation (particularly after containerization); the exponential growth of new information and communications technologies allowing faster, cheaper, and more efficient global communication; and by the financial de-regulation which began with the post-Bretton Woods floating of exchange rates and gathered pace with the rise of neo-liberal politics under Thatcher and Reagan. The latter encouraged rapid increases in Foreign Direct Investment and the proliferation of multinational enterprise. What is decisively new about the process is not only the sheer scale of financial movements and the market domination of MNCs (responsible for some 53% of world value-creation, much of which channelled through untaxable off-shore accounts, see Beck, 2000); but also the extension of the process beyond capital, goods, and labour, to services, knowledge, and culture. In fact globalization is not, of course, purely a matter of economics. Equally important, though more complex, is the globalization of politics and culture.

Internationalization, as Hirst and Thompson (1996) remind us, is by no means a new phenomenon. International trade has a long history and movements of capital and people reached high levels even before the First World War (in terms of capital movements not reached again until the 1970s). However, the recent surge of globalization, starting in the 1970s and still ongoing, is both quantitatively and qualitatively distinct. So much is agreed in most current debates about globalization. What is not agreed amongst current theorists is how far these economic trends will change the political and cultural landscape. Does globalization mean the end of the nation state as the main unit of political and social organization? Does it mean the end of cultural differences and the creation of a MacWorld of homogeneous cultural space? So far social and political science has found little agreement.

Some useful distinctions can be made, however. As Ulrich Beck (2000) notes, globalization—an objective, empirically verifiable process—is different from globalism, a political ideology which holds the transformation of the world along neo-liberal market lines to be inevitable, linear and wholly desirable. The latter approach is not only deeply ahistorical; it is also blind to the dangers of globalization which are readily apparent to the poorer countries.

Globalization has certainly compressed our notions of time and space (Harvey, 1990; Waters 1995). However, the so-called "borderless world" of Kenichi Ohmae (Ohmae, 1990) and company—a world without frontiers, and beyond national politics and national culture—is no doubt a figment of neo-liberal fantasy. It issues from a kind of economic determinism, most redolent of nineteenth-century political economy, which holds that political and cultural changes can be read off more or less mechanically from economic shifts. In fact, there is no certainty that economic globalization, even if it continues in its current direction, will lead to the eclipse of the nation state as a political force and to the waning of national cultural differences. History tends to be more dialectical and reality is more complex than that. So much is pretty clear from current politics. Despite the proliferation of supranational political organizations and the emergence of what Beck calls "transnational civil society" (Beck, 2000), there are still as yet no transnational political entities of sufficient democratic legitimacy or effectiveness to reduce the need and desire for national states as the primary units of political organization and loyalty.

Nor is the world becoming culturally homogenized except at a superficial level. It is true that the reach of global media is extending, and that people's aspirations are increasingly shaped by images deriving from distant cultures, so much so that Eric Hobsbawm can convincingly argue that this was a major factor in the final collapse of the Soviet State (Hobsbawm, 1994). It is also true the transnational companies like Coca-Cola and Nike do, as Naomi Klein (2001) argues, seek to create global brand images. But global media and advertising images are not swallowed whole. Global marketing to Disney and Coca Cola is still essentially global localization—Disney's Mickey Mouse is still Topolino to children in Italy (Beck, 2000) and Donald Duck Anders And in Denmark; antiglobalization protesters are increasingly using "culture-jamming" to subvert the images of the brand advertizers and to reclaim local cultural space. Despite—and perhaps because of—the pervasiveness of American commercial culture, different nations and cultures are far from throwing in the cultural towel.

The last decade has seen the creation of more new nation states, and more ethnic secession movements, than any other equivalent period in history, not least because of the break up of the former Soviet Union and Yugoslavia. Even amongst the old states, American global culture is not taken neat and still jostles up against other cultural forms. In fact a much more accurate metaphor for cultural change than homogenization is the notion of "glocalization" developed by cultural analyst Roland Robertson (1995). Time/space compression actually means hybridization and pluralization of cultures—dominant cultural forms mutated by receiving cultures, mixing with local cultures which globalization make ever more globally visible. A global mélange: Thai boxing by Moroccan girls in Amsterdam; Asian rap in London, Irish Bagels and Chinese Tacos.

I do not hold with the doomsday vision of Samual Huntington's *Clash of Civilizations* (1997). But September the 11th does tragically illustrate the contradictions of a globalization process which harbours the seeds of its own destruction. The belief, however simplified, that globalization leads to cultural domination and global inequality (the latter said to be 30 times higher than 150 years ago[1]) can certainly incubate extreme reactions, particularly against its perceived U.S. standard-bearers; the ensuing struggles are largely fought out by nation states—although against an "terror" which is amorphously global. Globalization is certainly not a one way historical street.

Globalization and Education

So how has globalization impacted on education? The answer must be fundamentally, but not in the ways that are often argued.

Globalization itself has not yet buried the national education system. Governments still seek to control their national systems— indeed, in some ways, more actively than before with ever proliferating targets and audits. They know that education remains one area where they still have some control. As Robert Reich (1991) has pointed out, despite the waning of the "national economy" and despite the internationalization of most of the factors of production, human skills remain relatively immobile and national.

Education systems are not all converging on a single model—

despite the influence of transnational agencies and the proliferation of policy borrowing. New global policy rhetorics—like lifelong learning—are certainly emerging, but in practice educational structures and processes do still vary considerably by region.

Nor is it necessarily the case that education systems have lost their original Durkheimian function of transmitting national cultures and promoting social cohesion. The means to do this in modern pluralistic societies certainly require some radical rethinking, but why should we assume it impossible? When national systems were first developed, nations were not only more divided than now by class, region, and religion; they also contained populations that rarely spoke the same language and which were divided between rural and urban lifestyles which belonged virtually to different historical times. It is salutary to remember that at the time of the French Revolution less half of France spoke French and there was no national system of weights and measures (Hobsbawm, 1990). Rural people could barely communicate and do business with others outside their own regions. As Eugene Weber has graphically demonstrated, it took an education—lead nation-building effort of epic proportions to create a viable modern French identity (Weber, 1979). Modern societies are certainly more individualized; they have lost many of the ties of solidarity that formerly bound communities together; but they are also more likely to have a common language and cultural idiom. Were we able to envision new forms of solidarity and civic culture appropriate to our pluralistic world, it should be possible still for education to play its part in promoting it.

However, in certain key respects, the prospects for traditional education systems are changing. I will briefly mention four:

Firstly, higher education, in the English-speaking states at least, is becoming genuinely internationalized because there is a growing market for it and because governments see international higher education as a major commercial opportunity. Consequently, and with the substantial support of international bodies such as the European Commission, universities, particularly those in the metropolitan heartlands of the developed world, take increasing numbers of foreign students, either on home-based courses, or on international courses delivered by mixtures of in-person home-based and foreign-based tuition and through virtual learning. Research is also increasingly internationalized. Universities have lost their quasi-monopoly on knowledge generation and transmission. They are increasingly competing with corporate and other private, non-university, global knowledge and learning networks, many of them on a scale which dwarfs the traditional universities. Hence the current trend for global university partnerships. The trend is unmistakable and likely to continue, as major universities seek to profit from developing their global brand recognition.

Secondly, whilst compulsory schooling remains predominantly a national affair, new transnational spaces are beginning to open up within and across school structures—I am thinking here of the proliferation of international schools, the creation of new "faith" schools, the cultural spaces in traditional schools created by immigrant or internationally mobile students and teachers, and—although it has yet to develop far—the possibility of corporation-backed schools crossing frontiers and taking on what governments find themselves unable to do (see Klein, 2001). There is already substantial evidence of curricular penetration by the global brands which not only invade educational space with their brand logos but which also produce widely used educational materials to achieve this.

Thirdly, there is the increasing trend towards the marketization of the school sector, either through the creation of more private schools, or through commercial sponsorship of state schools, or through new forms of public/private partnership in school administration as with the Education Action Zones in the United Kingdom. The trend is most apparent in Anglo-Saxon countries but not restricted to them, and this has the potential, more than other aspects of globalization, to undermine the whole notion of the public educational system. Marketization is not, of course, a necessary corollary of globalization per se, although it is an article of faith for globalism. How far it will go nobody yet can really say, but while unregulated globalization increases "social dumping" and pressures on governments to reduce public spending, it is hard, though not impossible, for governments to resist, even if they may prefer it otherwise.

Lastly, and perhaps most important, is the impact of globalization on the demand for skills and qualifications. Globalization has undoubtedly increased the attraction to advanced nations of the so-called "knowledge economy." With increased global economic competition, advanced economies can no longer compete with low wage economies in cost-competitive manufacturing and retain their living standards—hence the rush towards the high value-added sectors which constitute the so-called knowledge economy (Brown, Green, & Lauder, 2001).

There has been much hype about the miraculous new virtual or "weightless" economy. The new economy sectors did not provide that many jobs—the software industry in the United States, for instance, still employs less than a quarter of the number employed by General Motors—and there was never a prospect of it shifting everyone into high-skilled high-paid work. Now, with the bursting of the IT bubble, Charles Leadbeater's prescription (1999) for "Living on thin Air" seems rather foolish. However, it is still the case that, on balance, work is becoming more skills-intensive, and there is increasingly pressure on individuals to gain higher qualifications or risk marginalization in the job market. Hence the pressure on governments to provide more and more diverse learning opportunities intensifies.

Lifelong learning—that most globalized of educational discourses—is the ubiquitous response to this. As technological change drives up the employer demand for skills, and as individuals increasingly compete for career-enhancing certificates, so governments have to find new ways to meet the demand. Lifelong learning is an ingenious solution, made possible in part by the new learning technologies. By declaring learning a lifelong and "life wide" process—occurring everywhere from the school to the home, the workplace and the community—governments are able both to respond to individual demands for more diverse learning opportunities which mesh with their modern lifestyles, and to shift the costs, which they can no longer bear, onto employers, individuals and their families and communities.

This, more than any other development, challenges the notion of the "education system." We have been used to thinking about education in terms of schools and colleges and other institutions. In years to come these may well cease to be the main locus of learning activity. To this extent the idea of the educational system does become marginalized. We will have to start to think more about informal learning, workplace learning, and learning in the community and home (see Broadfoot, 2000).

Implications for Comparative Education

So what are the implications of globalization for Comparative Education? One conclusion we could draw is that cross-national comparison is now redundant. Ulrich Beck has taken this view (Beck, 2000). Social science, he says, has for too long been the creature of the nation state; since the founding fathers first treated society and state as coextensive the state has operated as a kind "container" of all concepts and data. Now in an age of globalization, says Beck, a "nationally based sociology is becoming obsolete." The message is clear: social science should abandon the "methodological nationalism" of its intellectual past rather as Marx claimed to caste off his "erstwhile philosophical conscience" in abandoning Hegel. The new mission should be to analyse world society and transnational space—"reading the world" as Bob Cowen (2000) puts it.

This is a tall order for comparative education. Like social science in general, and indeed probably more so, comparative education as a field has its origins in national thinking. From Jullien, Levasseur, and Sadler, through to Kandel, Hans, and Mallinson, comparative education has taken the national system as its main object of enquiry and "national character" as its main explanandum. This exclusively national way of thinking is now surely outdated. Explaining educational structures and outcomes in terms of national character and culture was always a somewhat essentialist exercise, in danger of reifying national culture as some irreducible and homogenous property. Now, with the glocalization of culture, and the creation of transnational cultural spaces, this approach will surely not do. Comparativists should cease taking national states as the only—or even main—units for comparison.

There is certainly a need for more studies of education and learning across sub-national regions and communities—like the so-called "home international" studies conducted by David Raffe and colleagues in Scotland, or Karen Evans' multilayered comparisons of youth learning and transitions in cities in different countries. Recent doctoral theses are using new approaches: for instance Jack Keating's two-dimensional comparisons of regional differences within Australia and the United Kingdom (Keating, 1999). Much more comparative work could be done in this area. In Belgium for instance, the language group forms the main basis for educational administration, and so a natural unit for comparing the combined effects of different structures and cultures on outcomes. Likewise, as Joseph Kay observed a century and a half ago, Switzerland, with its French-speaking and German-speaking regions with different educational structures and cultures, similarly provides an ideal laboratory for comparative work.

There is also room for studies across supranational regions. Bob Cowen's work on "rims" opens up a new perspective in regional comparison (Cowen, 2000). My own work on convergences and divergences with Alison Wolf and Tom Leney (Green, Wolf, & Leney, 1999) found strong evidence of regional clustering in system characteristics and trends within Europe which we sought to explain with reference to historically defined cultural and institutional affinities between states in particular regions. Likewise, the "High Skills Project," which I conducted with Phil Brown and Hugh Lauder, was an explicitly cross-regional Euro-Asian study which, whilst setting out to analyse "national routes to the high skills economy," ended up finding more potential for comparison of regional and sectoral differences (Brown, Green, & Lauder, 2001). Our late realization of the importance of comparing economic sectors suggests another important point regarding units of comparison. So long as the units being compared have "societal" characteristics(that is, in terms of characteristic institutional structures and rules)—there is no reason for limiting comparison to territorially defined units. Diasporic language groups, distributed communities and "virtual communities," are all—in theory at least—amenable to comparative educational research.

This need not mean, however, that Beck is correct to argue that cross-national study is obsolete. School systems, unlike some higher education systems, are still very national institutions. Their structures and processes are shaped primarily by national legislation and the national institutional and cultural contexts in which they operate. To understand the structural (that is, institutional and cultural) factors that determine their forms and outcomes may often require that we compare across countries—especially where there is too little system variation within countries to allow within-country comparison (Noah & Eckstein, 1969).

Nations are still the preferred units for comparative social science for good reasons. Many of the data are still collected at national level. Many of the operative societal variables are measured at the national level because they concern structures and institutions—labour markets, industry structures, political systems, cultural traits—which are still essentially national. Countries do still vary regularly and substantially on a whole range of demographic, economic, and cultural indicators. As Ronald Inglehart tersely concludes from his exhaustive study of data for 25 countries in the World Values Survey (1990), "The peoples of different societies are characterized by enduring differences in básic attitudes, values and skills: In other words they have different cultures" (p. 3). These cultures are not monolithic and nor are they immutable. However, in given times and places they act as important determinants of social and political behaviour which cannot be left out of account.

The country level, therefore, remains important for comparative analysis—but it is only one of a number of levels at which comparison can be effectively used. The question of units of comparison should not in any case be decided *a priori*, but rather according to research criteria. As Neil Smelser has argued, the main criteria for choosing the unit of comparison should be that it is: (1) appropriate to the theoretical problem, (2) causally related to the phenomenon being studied, and (3) that there are data available at this level (Smelser, 1976). This allows for comparison at various different levels, including multilevels.

The main methodological challenge for comparative educationalists is not, in any case, about levels of analysis; it is about the nature of comparative analysis per se and whether to do it all. Like Roger Dale before him, Peter Jarvis poses the question in a recent edition of Comparative Education: "Why should we undertake comparative analysis at all in this Global Village?" (Jarvis, 2000). I would answer, as do they, that Globalization doesn't undermine the utility of comparative analysis, providing, that is, that we understand by this analysis across societal units. Globalization may alter the spatial dimensions of what we take to be a meaningful societal unit, but even Beck would not argue that society has ceased to exist.

It can be argued that all social science is essentially comparative. Durkheim famously wrote that "comparative sociology is not a particular branch of sociology, it is sociology itself, in so far as it ceases to be purely descriptive and aspires to account for the facts" (Smelser, 1976, p. 2). But for Durkheim accounting for the facts meant understanding the pattern of relationships between collectivities—or what he terms "social facts"—since this is what distinguishes sociology from other disciplines such as psychology. The study, statistical or otherwise, of variations in individual traits and behaviours is therefore, rightly in my view, not generally considered to be comparative study. Collectivities, or societies, are, as Durkheim conceded, made up of individuals and their actions; but they represent more than the sum of those. The patterns of variation between collective or societal properties and behaviours, and the determining relationships between them, cannot be explained by the mere aggregation of individual characteristics and actions. This requires analysis of the effects of structures and characteristics which are integral to the collectivity or society itself, and which have meaning only at that level. Distributional properties, for instance, such as income or skills spread—have no meaning at the level of the individual. Comparative research is thus about analysing the pattern of relationship between characteristics of societal or collective entities, whether they be at national or other levels (Shriewer & Holmes, 1988). Such analyses can be qualitative or quantitative, depending on the nature of the problem and the data available.

One problem with contemporary comparative education research is that much—or even most—of it is not actually comparative. This is well illustrated by Angela Littles recent survey of articles published in the journal *Comparative Education* between 1977 and 1988 which shows that over 50% have been single country studies (Little, 2000). Some of these may be what Leach and Preston call "comparisons in a single nation" but Little concludes that "only a small percentage [of articles] have adopted an explicitly comparative approach" (Little, 2000, p. 285). Probably the vast majority of published studies in comparative education generally are either noncomparative analyses of single countries or parallel descriptions of education practices and policies across a group of countries. Whatever the merits of these types of study, neither necessarily uses comparative methods to analyse or test hypotheses about cause and effect relationships.

We may believe, as I do, that it is not helpful to police disciplinary frontiers or to draw sharp lines around field of study. But any field or discipline needs some core and distinguishing methodological criteria. In comparative education, and indeed any field of comparative research, these must include the use of comparison to test hypotheses and explain causal relationships. In the absence of natural experiments in social science, the comparative method is the next best thing to scientific "proof."

There are, of course, many ways of using comparative methods to understand cause and effect. John Stuart Mill famously wrote about the Method of Agreement, the Method of Difference, and the Indirect Method, which is a combination of the two (Mill, 1888/1970). All methods of comparison in social science, whether quantitative or qualitative, are essentially variations on this theme, although it is rarely possible to meet Mill's ideal requirements that all possibleoperative variables are considered, because we cannot know in advance what they all are. Comparison works by the manipulation of variables, holding certain variables constant, so as to test the independent effects of other observed variables on outcomes. Quantitative comparison does this statistically, establishing probabilistic relationships between independent and dependent variables, and has the advantage that it can simultaneously test correlations amongst a large number of variables. Qualitative comparison can rarely analyse the effects of all possible causes of a phenomenon (therefore generally failing Mill's ideal criterion), but it should, where possible, include a wide range of instances of the phenomenon in question, so long as these are sufficiently comparable not to increase indefinitely the number of possible variables. Where it does this it has the advantage that it can identify a range of causal chains, whereas statistical methods are likely only to bring out the most dominant (Ragin, 1981). Qualitative comparison also looks at "real" cases, seeking to show the mechanisms of cause and effects in their actual context: something that statistical analysis alone cannot do.

The methods of qualitative comparison are mostly variations of the Indirect Method that Mill thought peculiarly suitable for phenomena which had multiple causation. Basically, the investigator examines multiple instances where a particular phenomenon occurs, noting whatever conditions they have in common, and compares these with a range of instances where the phenomena does not occur. If certain conditions are common to the first set and are absent in the second set, and if the cases are otherwise similar, you can assume that these conditions represent causes of the phenomenon in question. The method is always liable to the accusation that there are "third causes" which it has failed to observe, but this can be the case also, although it is less likely, in quantitative analysis, where a correlation may be due to an unobserved variable which affects both of the correlated variables simultaneously. Neither of the methods can determine for sure what is cause and what is effect, although quantitative methods have more chances of doing this where there is a longitudinal element and qualitative methods where there is some examination of the causal process. Only natural experiments and randomized controlled trials, with controlled samples and time frames, can escape these flaws but, even there, social scientists may fail to understand what attribute of the intervention is having a given effect.

Comparative education needs to compare and to do this systematically, if it is to avoid the accusation that it too often degenerates into a catalogue of traveller's tales, policy advocacy and opportunistic rationalizations of unscientific policy-borrowing. One way that it can do this is to draw more on the mainstream of comparative social science research for its concepts, methodology and evidence. But it is striking, when you revisit the central texts of the Comparative Education canon, how insulated comparative education has been from some of the main currents in comparative social science, not only from my original field of comparative historical sociology, but also from other fields such as comparative political science and comparative political economy.

The pioneers of comparative education certainly drew wide and deep on humanistic thought, especially on philosophy and history, but made relatively little use of comparative historical sociology. You may find echoes of the ideas of Durkheim, Tönnies, and Weber in the works of Michael Sadler, Isaac Kandel, and Nicholas Hans but no sustained engagement. When the historical humanist legacy of the pioneers was superceded in the 1960s with a more social scientific approach this was, on the one hand, through the new scientism of Noah and Eckstein and, on the other, through the pragmatic problem-solving approach of Brian Holmes. These indeed pulled comparative education closer to social science, somewhat at the expense of historical depth, as Andreas Kazemias has noted (2001). However, much of the new comparative education remained narrowly empirical—either positivist or policy-reform-oriented—and still adrift from much of the more theoretically fruitful work in other comparative social science disciplines.

Margaret Archer drew heavily on Max Weber, but many key works in comparative historical sociology—say, Norbert Elias on the civilizing process, Barrington Moore and Reinhard Bendix on modernization, Theda Skocpal on states and revolutions, though highly germane to educational development, have left little trace on historical studies in comparative education. Comparative students of contemporary education have also shunned important comparative work in cognate fields. Students of education and citizenship, for instance, engage little with Rogers Brubaker's seminal comparative work on national identity (Brubaker, 1992), or with the works on civic culture by comparative political scientists like Almond and Verba. Likewise comparative students of skills and training have made rather less use than they might of work in comparative political economy by the likes of Dore, Streeck, Thurow, Albert, and Esping Anderson. Equally, textbooks on comparative education methods rarely mention the major contributions of Stein Rokkan, Neil Smelser, and Charles Ragin, all leading figures in comparative social science methodology.

It is hard not to conclude that comparative education has been at times somewhat insular; sometimes perhaps too preoccupied with self-referential internal debates, including those perennials about the limits of policy borrowing and the boundaries of comparative and international approaches. We would do well to take more account of relevant comparative work in cognate fields, as well as to remember the important work in comparative education carried out by "unbaptized" comparativists who do not go to comparative conferences and who do not see themselves as professional comparative educationalists (Alexander, 2001). Opening up comparative education in the 21st century should mean embracing all those who use comparative methods and whose work can help in understanding educational problems.

Comparative analysis remains the most powerful tool for causal explanation of societal aspects of the educational process. Globalization does not reduce its usefulness, although its creation of educational spaces which belong exclusively to neither nations nor systems, should make us look to broadening our units of analysis. The major challenges posed for comparative education today, as ever

48 *Globalization: Educational Research, Change and Reform*

before, are essentially twofold: firstly, to make the field genuinely comparative; and secondly, to bring it back from its relative isolation into the mainstream of comparative social science where it rightly belongs. The enormous richness of the current social science debate around globalization should at least help to make the second challenge attractive.

References

Albisetti, J. (1983). *Secondary school reform in imperial Germany.* Princeton, NJ: Princeton University Press.

Alexander, R. (2001). Border crossing: Towards a comparative pedagogy. *Comparative Education, 37*(4), 507–524.

Anderson, P. (1974). *Lineages of the absolutist state.* London: Verso.

Archer, M. (1979). *The social origins of educational systems.* London: Sage.

Beck, U. (2000). *What is globalization?* Cambridge, United Kingdom: Polity Press.

Broadfoot, P. (2000). Comparative education for the 21st century: Retrospect and prospect. *Comparative Education, 36*(3), 357–372.

Brown, P., Green, A., & Lauder, H. (2001). *High skills: Globalization, competitiveness and skill formation.* Oxford, United Kingdom: Oxford University Press.

Brubaker, R. (1992). *Citizenship and nationhood in France and Germany.* Cambridge, MA: Harvard University Press.

Burke, A. W. (Ed.). (1985). *The modernizers: Overseas students, foreign employees and Meiji Japan.* Boulder, CO: Westview Press.

Castells, M. (1992). Four Asian Tigers with a dragon's head: A comparative analysis of the state, economy and society in the Asian Pacific rim. In R. Appelbaum & J. Henderson (Eds.), *States and development in the Asia Pacific rim* (pp. 33–70). London: Sage.

Cipolla, C. M. (1969). *Literacy and development in the West.* Harmondsworth, United Kingdom: Penguin.

Cowen, B. (2000). Comparing futures or comparing pasts? *Comparative Education, 36*(3), 333–342.

de Tocqueville, A. (1955). *The old regime and the French Revolution* (S. Gilbert, Trans.). New York: Anchor Books. (Original work published 1856)

Fuller, B., & Robinson, R. (Eds.). (1992). *The political construction of education.* New York: Praeger.

Giddens, A. (1985). *The nation-state and violence.* Cambridge, United Kingdom: Polity Press.

Gildea, T. (1988). *The third republic from 1870–1914.* New York: Longman.

Green, A. (1990). *Education and state formation.* London: Macmillan.

Green, A. (1997). *Education, globalization and the nation state.* Basingstoke, United Kingdom: Macmillan.

Green, A., Wolf, A., & Leney, T. (1999). *Convergences and divergences in education and training systems.* London: Institute of Education.

Harvey, D. (1990). *The condition of postmodernity.* Oxford, United Kingdom: Blackwell.

Hirst, P., & Thompson, G. (1996). *Globalization in question: The international economy and the possibilities of governance.* Cambridge, United Kingdom: Polity.

Hobsbawm, E. J. (1990). *Nations and nationalism since 1780: Programme, myth and reality.* Cambridge, United Kingdom: Cambridge University Press.

Hobsbawm, E. J. (1994). *The age of extremes.* London: Michael Joseph.

Huntington, S. (1997). *The clash of civilizations: Remaking the world order.* New York: Simon and Shuster.

Inglehart, R. (1990). *Culture shift in advanced industrial society.* Princeton, NJ: Princeton University Press.

Jarvis, P. (2000). Globalization, the learning society and comparative education. *Comparative Education, 36*(3), 343–356.

Kazemias, A. (2001). Re-inventing the historical in comparative education: Reflections on a protean episteme by a contemporary player. *Comparative Education, 37*(4), 438–450.

Keating, J. (1999). *Upper secondary education and the state in Australia: A comparative study of regional variations within two nation states.* Unpublished doctoral dissertation, Institute of Education, University of London.

Klein, N. (2001). *No Logo.* London: Flaming.

Leadbeater, C. (1999). *Living on thin air: The new economy.* Harmondsworth: Penguin Books.

Little, A. (2000). Development studies and comparative education: Context, content, comparison and contributors. *Comparative Education, 36*(3), 279–296.

Marshall, T. H., & Bottomore, T. (1992). *Citizenship and social class.* London: Pluto Press.

Martin, H. P., & Schumman, H. (1996). *The global trap.* London: Zed Books.

Mill, J. S. (1970). Two methods of comparison. In A. Etzioni & F. DuBow (Eds.), *Comparative perspectives: Theories and methods* (pp. 205–213). Boston: Little Brown. (Original work published 1888)

Noah, H., & Eckstein, M. (1969). *Towards a science of comparative education.* London: MacMillan.

Ohmae, K. (1990). *The borderless world.* London: Collins.

Reich, R. (1991). *The work of nations: A blueprint for the future.* New York: Vintage.

Robertson, R. (1995). Globalization: Time-space homogeneity-heterogeneity. In M. Featherstone, S. Lash, & R. Robertson (Eds.), *Global modernities* (pp. 25–44). London: Sage.

Schoppa, J. (1991). *Educational reform in Japan: A case of immobilist politics.* London: Routledge.

Shriewer, J., & Holmes, B. (Eds.). (1988). *Theories and methods in comparative education.* Frankfurt: Peter Lang.

Simon, B. (1965). *Education and the labour movement, 1870–1920.* London: Lawrence and Wishart.

Smelser, N. (1976). *Comparative methods in the social sciences.* Englewood Cliffs, NJ: Prentice Hall.

Smelser, N. (1993). The methodology of comparative analysis. In D. Warwick & S. Osherson (Eds.), *Comparative research methods.* Englewood Cliffs, NJ: Prentice Hall.

Smith, A. D. (1995). *Nations and nationalism in the global era.* Cambridge, United Kingdom: Polity Press.

Stone, H. (1969). Literacy and education in England, 1640–1900. *Past and Present, 42,* 69–139.

Waters, M. (1995). *Globalization.* London: Routledge.

Weber, E. (1979). *Peasants into Frenchmen: The modernization of rural France, 1870–1914.* London: Chatto.

Note

1. The wealthiest 20% of world population were three times richer than the poorest 20% in the mid-nineteenth century. The ratio is now about 86 to 1 (Martin & Schumman, 1996).

3

Comparative Education in the Era of Globalization: Evolution, Missions and Roles

Mark BRAY

—ɯ—

Abstract

This chapter examines the evolving field of comparative education. Perhaps even more than other fields, comparative education seems to promote globalization. The field is naturally concerned with cross-national analyses, and encourages its participants to be outward-looking. At the same time, the field responds to globalization. Cross-national forces of change are reflected in dominant paradigms, methodological approaches, and topics studied. The Internet is one instrument through which this globalization is achieved and manifested.

The chapter includes particular focus on the history, role and functioning of the World Council of Comparative Education Societies (WCCES). This body was created in 1970, and has 30 member societies. As its name suggests, the WCCES is a global body—with all the positive features and tensions that it implies. The chapter notes the extent to which there is a global field of comparative education, while also commenting on distinctive features of the field in different countries and regions.

Earlier versions of this paper were published in the *Revista Española de Educación Comparada* and in *Policy Futures in Education*. The work is republished here with permission from the author.

Introduction

Globalization is a dynamic process which has major implications for many domains of activity. The field of comparative education is one of these domains. Yet this is not just a passive, one-way influence; comparative educationists can themselves promote and shape elements of globalization. The field of comparative education is arguably more closely related to globalization than most other fields of academic enquiry. Comparative education is naturally concerned with cross-national analyses, and the field encourages its participants to be outward-looking. At the same time, the field responds to globalization. Cross-national forces of change are reflected in dominant paradigms, methodological approaches, and foci of study.

In order to provide a context for subsequent discussion, this paper begins by considering some of the meanings of globalization. The paper then turns to the nature of the field of comparative education, noting dimensions of evolution over the decades and centuries. Moving to relatively recent times, the paper focuses on the World Council of Comparative Education Societies (WCCES), which was created in 1970 and currently has 30 constituent societies. As its name suggests, the WCCES is a global body—with all the positive features and tensions that that implies. The paper notes the some characteristics of the global field of comparative education, while also commenting on distinctive features in some countries and regions. The paper highlights some specific domains in which globalization has changed the agenda in which comparativists can and should work.

Globalization: Concepts and Debate

Held, McGrew, Goldblatt, and Perraton (1999), presenting one of the most thorough analyses of the nature and impact of globalization, began their book with the observation that:

> Globalization is an idea whose time has come. From obscure origins in French and American writings in the 1960s, the concept of globalization finds expression today in all the world's major languages. (p. 1)

However, they added, the term lacks precise definition. It is used widely and vaguely, and can mean different things to different people (p. 1).

At a general level, Held et al. suggest (1999), globalization may be thought of as "the widening, deepening and speeding up of worldwide interconnectedness in all aspects of contemporary social life" (p. 2). The range of dimensions, Held et al. observed, stretch "from the cultural to the criminal, the financial to the spiritual" (p. 2). Elsewhere, Held and McGrew (2000) have noted that globalization:

[H]as been variously conceived as action at a distance (whereby the actions of social agents in one locale can come to have significant consequences for 'distant others'); time-space compression (referring to the way in which instantaneous electronic communication erodes the constraints of distance and time on social organization and interaction); accelerating interdependence (understood as the intensification of enmeshment among national economies and societies such that events in one country impact directly on others); a shrinking world (the erosion of borders and geographical barriers to socio-economic activity); and, among other concepts, global integration, the reordering of interregional power relations, consciousness of the global condition and the intensification of inter-regional interconnectiveness. (p. 3)

All these dimensions have impact on the field of comparative education as well as on other fields of endeavour.

Nevertheless, interpretations of the precise nature of dynamics depend strongly on the perspectives of the observers. Held et al. (1999) distinguished between three broad schools of thought on globalization:

1. The hyperglobalists define contemporary globalization as a new era in which peoples everywhere are subjected to the disciplines of the global marketplace. Emphasizing economic forces, this view argues that globalization is bringing about "denationalization" of economies through the establishment of transnational networks of production, trade and finance. In this "borderless" economy, national governments are "relegated to little more than transmission belts for global capital or, ultimately, simple intermediate institutions sandwiched between increasingly powerful local, regional and global mechanisms of governance" (p. 3).

2. The sceptics, by contrast, maintain that contemporary levels of economic interdependence are not historically

unprecedented. The 19th century era of the classical Gold Standard, they note, was also a period of economic integration. The sceptics consider the hyperglobalist thesis to be fundamentally flawed and politically naïve since it underestimates the enduring power of national governments to regulate international economic activity. The sceptics recognize the economic power of regionalization in the world economy, but assert that by comparison with the age of world empires the international economy has become considerably less global in its geographical embrace.

3. The transformationalists, like the hyperglobalists, consider globalization to be a central driving force behind the rapid social, political and economic changes that are reshaping societies. However, they are less certain of the direction in which trends are leading and about the kind of world order which it might prefigure. For transformationalists, the existence of a single global system is not taken as evidence of global convergence or of the arrival of a single world society. Rather, they argue, "globalization is associated with new patterns of global stratification in which some states, societies and communities are becoming increasingly enmeshed in the global order while others are becoming increasingly marginalized" (Held et al., 1999, pp. 7–8). The new patterns require reformulation of vocabulary from North/South and First/Third World, recognizing that new hierarchies cut across and penetrate all societies and regions of the world.

These remarks show that the concept of globalization is complex. The term is viewed differently even within particular academic disciplines, and across disciplines the variation increases further. Comparative education is by nature an interdisciplinary field. This provides a valuable meeting point for disciplinary perspectives, but also increases the potential for confusion.

Comparative Education: Historical Development and Evolution

To place in context subsequent remarks about the contemporary nature of the field and the extent to which it has become globalized, it is useful to sketch some dimensions of its history and evolution. It is commonly asserted (see, e.g., Epstein, 1994; Van Daele, 1993) that the origins of comparative education as a clearly-defined scholarly activity lie in 19th century France. Specifically, Marc-Antoine Jullien, who in 1817 wrote a work entitled *Esquisse et Vues Préliminaires d'un Ouvrage sur l'Éducation Comparée*, has been widely described as the "Father of Comparative Education" (see, e.g., Berrio, 1997; Leclerq, 1999). The field is then commonly considered to have spread to other parts of Europe and to the United States, before reaching other regions of the world. An alternative view might be that the field had multiple origins (Bray & Gui, 2001; Halls, 1990; Zhang & Wang, 1997); but it is undeniable that significant work was developed in Europe and the United States. Further notable landmarks include the first university-level course in 1899, taught at Teachers College, Columbia, the United States (Bereday, 1964a), and a famous 1900 speech by Sir Michael Sadler in the United Kingdom (Sadler 1900/1964). During the 20th century, the field gathered momentum and spread. Nakajima (1916) published a book in Japanese entitled "Comparative Study of National Education in Germany, France, Britain and the United States," which was translated into Chinese with some adaptation by Yu (1917). Further early works include Sandiford (1918) and Kandel (1935).

The extent to which these early works may be considered global deserves some examination. Jullien's (1817) work was explicitly confined to the states of Europe—though that may perhaps already be considered quite a broad canvas for that point in history. Sadler (1964) used examples from both Western Europe and North America, and Nakajima (1916) focused on Germany, France, Britain and the United States. Interestingly, although Nakajima's book was written in Japan, it did not include focus on Japan; but Yu's (1917) translation and adaptation did add some material on China. Like Nakajima, Sandiford (1918) and Kandel (1935) focused on Germany, France, Britain and the United States, but Sandiford also included Canada and Denmark, while Kandel included Italy and Russia.

During the second half of the 20th century, the field blossomed in a spectacular way with the publication of many journals, including:

1. *Comparative Education Review*, an English-language journal launched in the United States in 1957;
2. *Comparative Education*, another English-language journal launched in the United Kingdom in 1964;
3. *Foreign Education Conditions*, a Chinese-language publication which was launched as an internal publication in Beijing in 1965, became a full journal in 1980, and was retitled *Comparative Education Review* in 1992;
4. *Compare: A Journal of Comparative Education*, an English-language publication which began in the United Kingdom as a newsletter in 1968, and which became a fully-established journal in 1977;
5. *Canadian and International Education/Éducation Canadienne et Internationale*, which was launched in Canada in 1973 to publish both English-language and French-language articles;
6. *Comparative Education Research*, a Japanese-language journal which was launched in 1975;
7. the *Journal of Comparative Education*, a Chinese-language publication which began as a newsletter published in Taiwan in 1982 and which in 1997 evolved into a full journal;
8. *Educazione Comparata*, an Italian journal which commenced publication in 1990;
9. the *Revista Española de Educación Comparada*, which was launched in Spain in 1995;
10. *Current Issues in Comparative Education*, an electronic journal which commenced publication in the United States in 1998; and
11. *Comparative and International Education Review*, which was launched in Greece in 2003.

Other journals used the word "international" in their titles without "comparative," but nevertheless published many comparative articles. In 1931 a journal under the trilingual title of *Internationale Zeitschrift für Erziehungswissenschaft, International Education Review* and *Revue International de Pédagogie* was launched in Germany and published articles in German, English and French. After a hiatus in World War II, it was re-launched in 1947 and proceeded with publication for another 4 years. Another hiatus occurred in 1951, but in 1955 the journal was again re-launched with the almost the same original title except that the English name was *International Review of Education* rather than *International Education Review* (McIntosh, 2002). In 1971, UNESCO in Paris launched *Prospects: Quarterly Review of Education*, initially in parallel English and French versions, then from 1973 also in Spanish, and by the 1990s also in Arabic, Chinese and Russian. In 1995, the subtitle of the journal was changed to *Quarterly Review of Comparative Education*. The English-language *International Journal of Educational Development* was launched in the United Kingdom in 1981, and is also considered a major journal in the field.

To these journals were added many seminal textbooks. Towards the end of the century they became too numerous to list, but significant English-language works in the decades immediately following World War II included Hans (1948), King (1958), Bereday (1964b) and Havighurst (1968). Hans' book to a large extent followed existing geographic traditions, with four case-study chapters focusing on England, the United States, France and the Soviet Union, but it did also refer to other countries in all continents. King's work was also dominated by the traditional focus. Like Sandiford's book (1918) four decades previously, King had individual chapters on France, Great Britain, the United States and Denmark; but whereas Sandiford's fifth and sixth countries of focus were Germany and Canada, King's were the Soviet Union and India. The inclusion of India reflected the emergence to sovereignty of a group of colonies—a trend that gathered speed in the 1960s and which brought much broader focus to the field of comparative education. Bereday's book focused on the traditional United States, United Kingdom, France and Germany, but also on the Soviet Union, Turkey, Poland and Colombia. Havighurst focused on France, the Soviet Union, Japan, Brazil, China, Ghana, South Africa, New Zealand, the Sudan and the Netherlands, and, with an unusual slant, also included chapters on the Hopi Indians (U.S.A.) and Tudor (15th and 16th century) England. During the next three decades the field further broadened its geographic scope, placing much more emphasis on less developed countries as well as on industrialized ones, and this in a sense becoming more globalized.

The WCCES: A Global Body in Comparative Education

The WCCES was formed in 1970, having evolved from an International Committee of Comparative Education Societies which had been convened by Joseph Katz, of the University of British Columbia in Canada, in 1968 (Epstein, 1981, p. 261). Five societies came together to form the council, namely:

1. the Comparative & International Education Society (CIES) of the United States, which had been founded in 1956;
2. the Comparative Education Society in Europe (CESE), which had been founded in 1961;
3. the Japanese Comparative Education Society (JCES), which had been founded in 1964;
4. the Comparative & International Education Society of Canada (CIESC), which had been founded in 1967; and
5. the Korean Comparative Education Society (KCES), which had been founded in 1968.

Over the decades, the number of constituent societies in the council has fluctuated, but in 2003 the WCCES had 30 societies. Of these, 23 were national or sub-national societies (Brazil, Bulgaria, Canada, China, Czech Republic, Cuba, Hong Kong, Germany, Greece, Hungary, India, Israel, Italy, Japan, Korea, Philippines, Poland, Russia, Spain, Taiwan, United Kingdom, Ukraine, and United States), 5 were regional societies (Australia and New Zealand, Europe, Nordic countries, Southern Africa, and Asia), and 2 were language-based societies (French and Dutch).

While the total list of constituent societies was impressive, in some countries and regions the societies have been fragile. The organizations have depended on the enthusiasm of a few individuals, and have commonly operated on a voluntary basis with low budgets. The fragility can be illustrated by comparing the 2003 WCCES list of constituent societies with that for 1993. In 1993, the WCCES had 31 constituent societies, but only 25 were still on the list a decade later because 6 had ceased to exist. These were:

1. the Asociación Argentina de Educación Comparada (AAEC),
2. the Asociación Colombiana de Educación Comparada (ACEC),
3. the Egyptian Group for Comparative Education (EGCE),

4. the London Association of Comparative Education (LACE),
5. the Nigerian Comparative Education Society (NCES), and
6. the Portuguese Comparative Education Society (PCES).

However, five new societies had joined the list, namely:

1. the Asociación de Pedagogos de Cuba (Sección de Educación Comparada) (APC-SEC),
2. the Comparative Education Society of Asia (CESA),
3. the Comparative Education Society of Hong Kong (CESHK),
4. the Comparative Education Society of the Philippines (CESP), and
5. the Ukraine Council for Comparative Education (UCCE).

Also, a new Argentinean group had formed and had expressed intention to apply for admission to the council; a parallel group had been formed in Venezuela; and in France a body had been created under the title Association Française pour le Développement des Échanges Internationales et de la Comparaison en Éducation (AFDECE).

The most obvious activities of the WCCES have been the organization of periodic World Congresses of Comparative Education. The first congress was held in Canada in 1970, and was followed by ones in Switzerland (1974), United Kingdom (1977), Japan (1980), France (1984), Brazil (1997), Canada (1989), Czechoslovakia (1992), Australia (1996), South Africa (1998), South Korea (2001) and Cuba (2004).

Other WCCES activities include advocacy for the field. The WCCES is affiliated to UNESCO as a non-governmental organization (NGO), and makes official representations to the international community through that body. The WCCES also operates a website (www.hku.hk/cerc/wcces), which contains links to organizations and educational institutions related to the field. One part of that website connects readers to Ministries of Education in over 120 different countries.

Like all such global bodies, however, the WCCES has constraints in its operation. As noted by King (1997):

> In all academic circles there are prima donnas and factions, and in a world society of members from so many traditions and contexts it is often difficult to reconcile the diversity of interests and priorities. There are

also diplomatic difficulties in finding acceptable venues which are also convenient for the gathering-in of colleagues from all over the world. (p. 81)

The WCCES statutes do not declare any official language, but most WCCES affairs are conducted in the English language. English has gained dominance as an international language, but this is not a neutral form of globalization. By convention, arising from the fact that the original secretariats were located in Ottawa (Canada) and then Geneva (Switzerland), French has also been a permitted language for communication for the WCCES. During the last decade, however, French has been little more than a token vehicle for official deliberation of WCCES affairs. The WCCES officers are very aware of the imbalances that can be associated with language, and welcome suggestions on ways to promote the field of comparative education in multiple languages.

Another bias arises from the geographic spread of WCCES member societies. Although the WCCES has constituent societies in every continent, and has also held congresses in every continent, several parts of the world do not have direct representation in the council. Thus in 2003, following the demise of the Nigerian and Egyptian societies, the only African society was that serving Southern Africa. South America was represented only by Brazil; and the Arab States were not represented at all. By contrast, Europe and Asia were well represented.

Nevertheless, the WCCES may certainly be considered a global body; and in many respects it is also globalizing. It brings together scholars from different parts of the world for exchange of ideas, and promotes joint projects. Certainly a great deal more can be done to facilitate the development of comparative education in different regions of the world and to promote the global dimensions of the field; but the WCCES does at least provide one vehicle to do this.

Paradigms, Methods and Foci in Comparative Education

The field of comparative education, at least in some parts of the world, has drawn strongly on the theoretical bases of the social sciences. To some extent, therefore, shifts in dominant paradigms within the social sciences have been reflected in shifts in the field of comparative education. This includes the rise of positivism in the 1960s and 1970s, and the popularity of post-modernism in the 1980s and 1990s (Crossley, 2000; Epstein, 1994; Paulston, 2000; Psacharopoulos, 1990). However, comparative education scholars have tended to use a fairly limited set of tools from the social sciences. Books and journal articles display many commentaries based on literature reviews, but relatively few studies based on survey research, and almost no studies based on experimental methods.

In order to gain deeper understanding of this phenomenon, Rust, Soumaré, Pescador, and Shibuya (1999) analysed articles in three major English-language journals in the field, namely *Comparative Education Review* published in the United States, *Comparative Education* and *International Journal of Educational Development*, both published in the United Kingdom. Reviewing articles in the 1960s, they found that 48.5% were mainly based on literature review and 15.2% were historical studies. For the 1980s and 1990s, they found a marked drop in the two categories—to 25.7% mainly based on literature review, and 5% historical studies (p. 100). Reviews of projects had increased, as had participant observation and research based on interviews and questionnaires. In this respect, the field had increased its use of some standard social science instruments.

Rust et al. (1999) also scrutinized the qualitative/quantitative biases of the articles. Their survey of 427 articles published in 1985, 1987, 1989, 1991, 1993 and 1995 showed that 71.2% were based on qualitative methods, 17.3% on quantitative methods, 10.8% on a combination of qualitative and quantitative, and 0.3% on other strategies. Commenting on this, Rust et al. suggested that scholars in the field of comparative education:

> [T]end to rely on similar philosophical assumptions. Concerning the nature of reality, comparative educators would tend to see reality as somewhat subjective and multiple, rather than objective and singular. Epistemologically, comparative educators would tend to interact with that being researched rather than acting independently and in a detached manner from the content. Axiologically, comparative educators would tend not to see research as value free and unbiased; rather, they would accept the notion that their research is value laden and includes the biases of the researcher. (p. 106)

A third aspect of the study by Rust et al. (1999) concerned the geographic foci of the articles. During the 1960s, the dominant focus was on high-human-development countries (using the classification of the United Nations Development Programme). By the 1980s and 1990s, however, the balance had shifted significantly. It still showed bias towards these countries, but included a much greater focus on low-human-development countries. Thus, whereas in the 1960s, 73.1% of the articles in *Comparative Education Review* and *Comparative Education* focused on high-human-development countries, and 15% focused on the low-human-development countries, in the 1980s and 1990s these proportions were 43.1% and 23.3% respectively.

However, the nature of the themes, and the methodological approaches, have been very different in various parts of the world at particular periods in history. Thus, although Rust et al. (1999) referred throughout their article to "the field" of comparative education, their analysis focused only on English-language journals, and only on ones published in the United States and the United Kingdom. Cowen (2000, p. 333) has highlighted the co-existence of multiple comparative educations. His observation, on the one hand, applies to different groups within particular countries who have different methodological approaches and domains of enquiry, and who may or may not communicate with each other. On the other hand, it also applies to groups in different countries who operate in different languages with different scholarly traditions, and who also may or may not communicate with counterparts in other countries and language groups.

Concerning the differences in scholarly traditions in different countries, it is instructive to compare the work of Harold Noah and Max Eckstein during the three decades from the mid 1970s with that of Gu Mingyuan. Sets of collected works by these authors have been published by the Comparative Education Research Centre at the University of Hong Kong, and thus may easily be placed side by side (Gu, 2001; Noah & Eckstein, 1998). Among the major concerns of Noah and Eckstein, who were based in the United States and who operated mainly in the English-speaking arena, were methodological issues in the positivist framework and oriented to First World concerns. Gu, by contrast, operated mainly in the Russian- and Chinese-speaking arenas. His writings, particularly during the early part of his career, were couched within a Marxist-Leninist framework, and he was especially concerned with the lessons that China could learn from industrialized countries. Especially during the 1970s and 1980s, the comparative education world in which Gu lived was a very different environment from that in which Noah and Eckstein lived.

During the 1990s, however, these two worlds showed some signs of convergence. As China opened up, and as English became more widespread, scholars in China paid more attention to the literatures and to methodological approaches in Western countries. Academic interchange between the two cultures increased, facilitated by translations of English-language books into Chinese and by cross-national visits by both sides. It is arguable that the flow of ideas from the opening up was unbalanced: Chinese scholars were influenced by Western traditions much more than Western scholars were influenced by Chinese traditions, and the number of books translated from Chinese to English was considerably smaller than the number translated from English to Chinese. However, some Western scholars have certainly explored Chinese academic traditions in depth, and have gained from doing so. In this context, the work of Ruth Hayhoe (e.g., 1999, 2001) immediately comes to mind.

The 1990s and initial years of the present century have also brought some broadening of geographic interest among the different scholarly communities. Throughout their histories, albeit growing over time, the major English-language journals listed at the beginning of this paper have contained a significant number of papers on the less developed countries of Africa, Asia and Latin America in addition to work on Western Europe, Northern America and Australasia. In China, the volume of scholarly analysis of education in less developed countries has been much more modest. This has partly reflected priorities, insofar as policy makers have felt that less can be learned from poor countries than from prosperous ones. It has also reflected the fact that although overseas-Chinese communities exist in many parts of the world, China has had fewer political and cultural links with Africa, Western Asia and Latin America. Nevertheless, some broadening of geographic interest has been evident in Chinese-language publications, both in the mainland and in Taiwan (e.g., Lee, 1999; Yung, 1998).

Despite these observations about convergence, however, it remains the case that the topics chosen for comparative analysis, and the methodological approaches, have continued to vary considerably in different parts of the world. Gender, for example, has been a much stronger topic for focus in Western countries than in Asian societies; and analyses of the World Bank and other international agencies have been much more common in the English-language journals than in the Chinese, Japanese or Korean journals. Similarly, not all societies have been equally interested in themes of post-colonialism, multi-culturalism and civil strife. Thus, while it is increasingly possible to talk of about a global field of comparative education, it is necessary to recognize continued variations.

Missions and Roles in the Era of Globalization

Crossley (1999, 2000) and Watson (2001) have presented insightful analyses of the field of comparative education at the turn of the century, and have stressed the need for reconceptualization. The forces of globalization, they suggest, provide both an imperative and an opportunity. The imperative arises from the changed environment brought by globalization, and the opportunity arises from the increased interest in international affairs among academics, policy-makers and practitioners. The field of comparative education, they argue, can be revitalized and can secure fresh relevance within the new environment.

Various other scholars have also noted ways in which the field of comparative education can grapple with issues of globalization. They include Sanz (1998), Burbules and Torres (2000), Tickly (2001), Welch (2001), and Carnoy and Rhoten (2002). Particularly useful to the present paper is the work of Marginson and Mollis (2001, pp. 611–614), who presented five implications of globalization for a reforged comparative education. These implications may be summarized as follows:

1. Analytical frameworks: Scholars should locate nation-to-nation comparisons in wider frameworks. At the same time, they should note that global effects are contested and uneven, and vary among nations, regions and institutions. Important work by comparativists has already been conducted along these lines, but more is needed.

2. Units of analysis: The traditional comparative map of the

world, in which all nations are formally similar and ranked according to their level of development on a single scale, is more inadequate than ever. It fails to explain power relations between nations, and it hides qualitative national differences. Globalization requires "a new geopolitical cartography that traces the flows of global effects and the patterns of imitation, difference, domination, and subordination in education policy and practice" (Marginson & Mollis, 2001, p. 612).

3. Focus on cross-border international education: Cross-border trade in international education has become an important object of research in itself. Such trade raises questions about the identities of mobile students, and about the attributes required for educators, institutions and systems. Sub-themes include tensions between pedagogical practices and national cultures, and the mushrooming of on-line education communities.

4. Forms of identity: Globalization opens up a new potential for forms of identity other than national identity. The traditional focus on the nation state downplayed supranational cultural and religious identities, and obscured intra-national regional variety in educational participation, resourcing and outcomes.

5. The Impact of Globalization at the National Level: Modern education systems are still organized locally and nationally, and are still subject to national regulation. The trends of increased mobility and cosmopolitanism, Marginson and Mollis suggest, have major implications for policies on the preparation of citizens in education (p. 613). Further research is also needed on the extent to which international agencies and others shape national education policies.

No doubt this list could be extended. It is, however, a useful starting point to show that comparative education can and should play a very different role in the era of globalization. It should address new questions, and it should be reinvigorated as a vehicle to assist academics and practitioners to understand the changes around them. This is not to say that the nation-state should be discarded as a unit of analysis, but that an expanding agenda could focus on wider issues which impact on education within individual countries.

Conclusions

This paper commenced by noting that the field of comparative education is arguably more closely related to globalization than most other fields of academic enquiry. One major factor is that comparative education is naturally concerned with cross-national analyses, and by its very nature encourages its participants to be outward-looking. At the same time, the paper has pointed out that the field of comparative education is shaped by globalization. Cross-national forces of change are reflected in dominant paradigms, methodological approaches, and foci of study. Reviewing the history of the field, the paper has noted that comparative scholars have become much more global in their approaches than used to be the case.

The first part of this paper quoted the observation by Held et al. (1999) that globalization may be thought of as "the widening, deepening and speeding up of worldwide interconnectedness in all aspects of contemporary social life" (p. 2). Along similar lines, Delanty (2000) refers to "the diminishing importance of geographical constraints," and has described globalization as "the deterritorialization of space" (p. 81). These phenomena have certainly been seen in the field of comparative education. As noted by Wilson (2003), whereas early scholars had to rely on the printed word and on slow communications through the postal system and other mechanisms, their contemporary counterparts can access the Internet and liaise inexpensively by e-mail. Further, reductions in the cost of air travel have facilitated face-to-face contact with colleagues and cultures in a way that was unimaginable in former decades. Time-space compression and improved access to people, places and societies have assisted the field to develop in important ways.

Among the institutions which promote globalization are the various national, regional and language-based comparative education societies and the global body which brings them together, the WCCES. Most of the national, regional and language-based societies hold annual and biennial conferences which attract participants from outside the countries, regions and language groups which the societies mainly serve; and every few years the WCCES organizes a World Congress of Comparative Education. These events increase the interflow and promote internationalization. However, imbalances in access remain, and comparative education is certainly not yet (and may never become) a homogeneous field to which scholars from all countries and language groups have equal access.

Within the field, globalization has itself become an important topic for study and has affected the nature of discourse. For many scholars the nation-state remains a favoured unit for analysis, but an increasing number of studies draw instructively on multi-level analysis (Alexander, 2000; Bray & Thomas, 1995; Crossley, 2000). Multi-level studies can show how global forces do or do not shape patterns within particular countries, provinces, districts, institutions and even classrooms. The field of comparative education contains some hyperglobalists who, like their counterparts in other fields, argue that the world is becoming borderless and that national governments, using the words quoted above from Held et al. (1999), are "relegated to little more than transmission belts for global capital" (p. 3). However, scholars with this perception are a minority in the field. The majority recognize that cross-national forces exist and that in some ways they have become stronger than in the part, but who point out that cross-national forces have long been an important influence on education systems and that national governments still retain major roles in the education sector.

It would be unrealistic to assert that the field of comparative education will ever reach unanimity in perspectives on globalization. One obstacle is that, as noted above, the term itself is viewed differently even within particular disciplines; and across disciplines the variation increases further. Since by nature comparative education is an interdisciplinary field, the potential for common conceptions seems very limited.

Nevertheless, the field of comparative education can contribute to one important agenda identified by Held et al. (1999), namely analysis of the extent to which globalization is associated with new patterns of stratification in which some states, societies and communities are increasingly enmeshed in the global order while others are increasingly marginalized (pp. 7–8). This theme again underlines the value of multilevel analysis which identifies the impact of supra-national, national and sub-national forces on education systems. Such frameworks address what Arnove and Torres (2003) call the dialect of the global and the local. Issues of marginalization have been specifically highlighted by specialists in comparative education within the context of globalization (see, e.g., Stromquist, 2002). Such work can contribute to broader, multidisciplinary analysis beyond that specifically concerned with education.

References

Alexander, R. (2000). *Culture and pedagogy: International comparisons in primary education.* Oxford, United Kingdom: Blackwell.

Arnove, R., & Torres, C. A. (2003). *Comparative education: The dialectic of the global and the local* (2nd ed.). Lanham, MD: Rowman & Littlefield.

Bereday, G. Z. F. (1964a). James Russell's syllabus of the first academic course in comparative education. *Comparative Education Review, 7*(2), 189–196.

Bereday, G. Z. F. (1964b). *Comparative method in education.* New York: Holt, Rinehart & Winston.

Berrio, J. R. (1997). 'Presentación'. issue on 'concepto, métodos y técnicas en educación comparada: Homenaje a jullien de París en el 150 aniversario de su fallecimiento'. *Revista Española de Educación Comparada, 3,* 7–11.

Bray, M., & Gui, Q. (2001). Comparative education in greater China: Contexts, characteristics, contrasts, and contributions. *Comparative Education, 37*(4), 451–473.

Bray, M., & Thomas, R. M. (1995). Levels of comparison in educational studies: Different insights from different literatures and the value of multilevel analyses. *Harvard Educational Review, 65*(3), 472–490.

Burbules, N. C., & Torres, C. A. (Eds.). (2000). *Globalization and education: Critical perspectives.* New York: Routledge.

Carnoy, M., & Rhoten, D. (2002). What does globalization mean for educational change? A comparative approach. *Comparative Education Review, 46*(1), 1–9.

Cowen, R. (2000). Comparing futures or comparing pasts? *Comparative Education, 36*(3), 333–342.

Crossley, M. (1999). Reconceptualising comparative and international education. *Compare: A Journal of Comparative Education, 29*(3), 249–267.

Crossley, M. (2000). Bridging cultures and traditions in the reconceptualisation of comparative and international education. *Comparative Education, 36*(3), 319–332.

Delanty, G. (2000). *Citizenship in a global age: Society, culture, politics.* Buckingham, United Kingdom: Open University Press.

Epstein, E. H. (1981). Toward the internationalization of comparative education: A report on the world council of comparative education societies. *Comparative Education Review, 25*(2), 261–271.

Epstein, E. H. (1994). Comparative and international education: Overview and historical development. In T. Husén & T. N. Postlethwaite (Eds.), *The international encyclopedia of education* (2nd ed., pp. 918–923). Oxford, United Kingdom: Pergamon Press.

Gu, M.-Y. (2001). *Education in China and abroad: Perspectives from a lifetime in comparative education.* Hong Kong: Comparative Education Research Centre, The University of Hong Kong.

Halls, W. D. (Ed.). (1990). *Comparative education: Contemporary issues and trends.* London: Jessica Kingsley.

Hans, N. (1948). *Comparative education: A study of educational factors and traditions.* London: Routledge & Kegan Paul.

Havighurst, R. J. (Ed.). (1968). *Comparative perspectives on education.* Boston: Little, Brown & Co.

Hayhoe, R. (1999). *China's universities 1895–1995: A century of cultural conflict.* Hong Kong: Comparative Education Research Centre, The University of Hong Kong.

Hayhoe, R. (2001). Lessons from the Chinese academy. In R. Hayhoe & J. Pan (Eds.), *Knowledge across cultures: A contribution to dialogue among civilizations* (pp. 323–347). Hong Kong: Comparative Education Research Centre, The University of Hong Kong.

Held, D., & McGrew, A. (2000). The great globalization debate: An introduction. In D. Held & A. McGrew (Eds.), *The global transformations reader: An introduction to the globalization debate* (pp. 1–45). Cambridge, United Kingdom: Polity Press.

Held, D., McGrew, A., Goldblatt, D., & Perraton, J. (1999). *Global transformations: Politics, economics and culture.* Cambridge, United Kingdom: Polity Press.

Jullien, M. (1817). *Esquisse et vues préliminaires d'un ouvrage sur l'Éducation comparée.* Paris: Société Établie à Paris pour l'Amélioration de l'Enseignement Élémentaire. Reprinted 1962, Genève: Bureau International d'Éducation.

Kandel, I. L. (1935). *Studies in comparative education.* London: George G. Harrap.

King, E. J. (1958). *Other schools and ours.* New York: Rinehart & Co.

King, E. J. (1997). A turning-point in comparative education: Retrospect and prospect. In C. Kodron, B. von Kopp, U. Lauterbach, U. Schäfer, & G. Schmidt (Eds.), *Vergleichende Erziehungswissenschaft: Herausforderung, Vermittlung, Praxis. Festschrift für Wolfgang Mitter zum 70 Geburtstag* (pp. 81–90). Köln: Bohlau.

Leclerq, J. (Ed.). (1999). Première partie: Marc-Antoine Jullien de Paris, d'hier à aujourd'hui'. In *L'Éducation Comparée: Mondialisation et Spécificités Francophones. Paris and Sèvres* (pp. 11–103). Association Francophone d'Éducation Comparée and Centre National de Documentation Pédagogique.

Lee, F. J. E. (1999). Comparative education in Taiwan: Retrospect and prospect. In S. K. Yang (Ed.), *Educational sciences: Internationalization and indigenization* (pp. 431–471). Taipei: Yang-Chih Book Co. [in Chinese]

Marginson, S., & Mollis, M. (2001). "The door opens and the tiger leaps": Theories and reflexivities of comparative education for a global millennium. *Comparative Education Review, 45*(4), 581–615.

McIntosh, C. (2002). International review of education: A journal of many incarnations. *International Review of Education, 48*(1/2), 1–20.

Nakajima, N. (1916). *Comparative study of national education in Germany, France, Britain and the USA.* Tokyo: Kyouiku-shicho Kenkyukai. [in Japanese]

Noah, H. J., & Eckstein, M. A. (1998). *Doing comparative education: Three decades of collaboration.* Hong Kong: Comparative Education Research Centre, The University of Hong Kong.

Paulston, R. G. (Ed.). (2000). *Social cartography: Mapping ways of seeing social and educational change.* New York: Garland.

Psacharopoulos, G. (1990). Comparative education: From theory to practice, or are you A:\neo.* or B:*.ist?'. *Comparative Education Review, 34*(3), 369–380.

Rust, V. D., Soumaré, A., Pescador, O., & Shibuya, M. (1999). Research strategies in comparative education. *Comparative Education Review, 43*(1), 86–109.

Sadler, Sir M. (1964). How can we learn anything of practical value from the study of foreign systems of education? *Comparative Education Review, 7*(3), 307–314. (Original work published 1900)

Sandiford, P. (Ed.). (1918). *Comparative education: Studies of the educational systems of six modern nations.* London: J. M. Dent and Sons.

Sanz, F. (1998). Perspectivas de la educación de adultos en una sociedad globalizada. *Revista Española de Educación Comparada, 4*, 69–100.

Stromquist, N. P. (2002). Globalization, the I, and the other. *Current Issues in Comparative Education, 4*(2), 87–94.

Tickly, L. (2001). Globalisation and education in the postcolonial world: Towards a conceptual framework. *Comparative Education, 37*(2), 151–171.

Van Daele, H. (1993): *L'Éducation comparée.* Paris: Presses Universitaires de France.

Watson, K. (2001). Comparative education research: The need for reconceptualisation and fresh insights. In K. Watson (Ed.), *Doing comparative education research: Issues and problems* (pp. 23–42). Oxford, United Kingdom: Symposium.

Welch, A. R. (2001). Globalisation, post-modernity and the state: Comparative education facing the third millennium. *Comparative Education, 37*(4), 475–492.

Wilson, D. N. (2003). The future of comparative and international education in a globalised world. In M. Bray (Ed.), *Comparative education: Continuing traditions, new challenges, and new paradigms* (pp. 15–33). Dordrecht, Netherlands: Kluwer Academic Publishers.

Yu, J. (Ed. and Trans.). (1917). *Comparative Study of National Education in*

Germany, France, Britain and the USA. Shanghai: China Book Company. [in Chinese]

Yung, C. S. S. (1998). *A comparison of comparisons in the field of comparative education: A content analysis of English-medium and Chinese-medium journals*. Unpublished master's thesis, The University of Hong Kong.

Zhang, R. F., & Wang, C. X. (Eds.). (1997). *Short history of comparative studies of Chinese and foreign education* (Vols. 1–3). Jinan: Shandong Education Press. [in Chinese]

4

Globalization and Higher Education Reform in China

Kinglun NGOK

—⁓⁓—

Abstract

The market-oriented reform, economic globalization and the emerging knowledge society have brought about fundamental changes in the context of and conditions for higher education in China since the mid-1980s. Put Chinese higher education reform in the context of globalization, this chapter aims to examine how globalization affects higher education reform in China. The discussion focuses on educational governance, educational financing and provision, curriculum change, and educational competition. The author argues that the impacts of globalization on the Chinese higher education are multiple facets. After about two decades of restructuring and transforming, the unified, centralized, closed, and static higher education system of China has now becoming more diversified, decentralized, open, and dynamic. Massification of higher education brought by the rapid expansion of the public tertiary institutions and the development of private education institutions have satisfied to a large extent the huge education demand of the people. On the other hand, marketization of higher education has also led to the further inequality in education opportunity and quality. While decentralization has stimulated the involvement of local governments and other non-state sectors in higher education development, regional inequality in the area of higher education has deteriorated. International exchange and cooperation has no doubt benefited Chinese higher education sector; however it has also exposed Chinese universities to the severe international competition. Along with the further opening of Chinese higher education sector after China's accession to the WTO, international competition and pressure facing Chinese higher education sector will be intensified. Therefore, it is reasonable to predict that further restructuring and transforming will be introduced in Chinese higher education system.

Introduction

Since the mid-1980s, higher education has undergone major transformations in China. The market-oriented reform, economic globalization and the emerging knowledge society have brought about fundamental changes in the context of and conditions for higher education (Agelasto & Adamson, 1998; Hayhoe, 1996). Representing a new set of ideas, rules, and practices that may affect education policy-making (Dale, 1999), economic globalization has become an important driving force for the transformation of Chinese higher education. China's participation in the global economy has led her to reassess the nature, function, and role of higher education. A new perception of higher education has gradually taken shape in the post-Mao era in line with the development of the market-oriented economy and its increasing integration with the global market.

Along with the implementation of economic reforms and the "open-door" policy, post-Mao Chinese leaders began to realize the important contributions that education can make to both economic growth and social development. For the purpose to produce enough educated human resources for economic modernization, an "economic ideology of education" was developed by post-Mao Chinese leaders. Under this ideology, educational and economic developments are inseparable and interactive. In the views of Chinese leaders, education is the essential tool for economic modernization, and must meet the needs of China's modernizing economy and its future development (Chen, 1999, p. 8).

Like the governments of many nations and regions in East Asia, the post-Mao Chinese government has been increasingly concerned with the role of higher education in improving China's economic competitiveness and its place in the regional and global markets. With China's further integration with the world economy, the Chinese leadership has realized that China's future is based on a high technology knowledge economy, and that the international competitiveness of the state will depend upon educational development and scientific technology as well as the degree of knowledge innovation (The Ministry of Education, 1998). In the late 1990s, Chinese leaders made the decision to "revitalize China through developing science and education" (*kejiao xingguo*). In May 1998, in his speech at the conference celebrating Peking University's centenary, President Jiang Zemin claimed that China must have quite a few first-rate universities of international advanced level. Jiang's wish was soon developed into national higher education policy in December 1998 when the Ministry of Education promulgated its policy document entitled "The Action Plan to Revitalize Education in the 21st Century." In this document, a national plan named "985" was finalized to uplift a few universities to the world class level.

In the "Resolutions on the Further Development of Educational Reform and Quality Education" passed at the Third National Education Working Meeting on 13 June 1999, the Chinese government explicitly stated that education will develop in the context of economic globalization. Higher education reform has to centre on such notions as "excellence," "enhanced international competitiveness," and "quality." The focus is to develop skilled human resources. At the same time, the concept of "lifelong learning" has been put on the policy agenda. The "Action Plan to Revitalize Education in the 21st Century" issued in December 1998 aims to establish a new educational system as well as a lifelong learning system. Lifelong learning and lifelong education are regarded as the foundation of the "knowledge society," and the knowledge society is necessary to increase the national quality of education and to maintain the nation's competitiveness. China's accession to the WTO in 2001 has accelerated its integration with the global community. Against this background, Chinese leaders have realized that Chinese higher education must adapt to the requirements of economic globalization. So reforms must be conducted in Chinese higher education sector to make it more open, more competitive and more internationalized. Otherwise, China cannot produce sufficient talents capable for international competition and meet the international challenges (Zhou, 2001).

This chapter aims to examine how globalization affects higher education reform in China. The discussion will focus on educational governance, educational financing and provision, curriculum change, and educational competition. The main findings include: (1) The Chinese state has reduced its monopolization over higher education due to the limited state financial capacity and the huge demand for higher education; (2) the role of local governments in higher education has increased and the trend of localization of higher education has emerged; (3) new structures of higher education financing and provision have developed due to the introduction of multiple channels of educational financing and the increasing diversity of educational provisions; (4) competition in the higher education sector has been fostered in order to enhance the efficiency and effectiveness of the utilization of educational resources and to catch up the international level of teaching and research; and (5) international cooperation has been extended and strengthened.

Globalization and Changing Governance in Higher Education

Chinese higher education system was developed in the 1950s, which was characterized by unified planning, unified administration, unified syllabus, unified curricula, unified textbooks, unified enrolment, and unified allocation of university places. Under this centralized system of higher education, the state assumed the responsibility for formulating educational policies, allocating educational resources, exerting administrative controls, employing teaching staff, deciding on curricula and textbooks, and recruiting students and assigning graduates. In a nutshell, the state monopolized the provision, financing, and governance of higher education. On top of the strict state control over higher education, another main feature of Chinese higher education governance was the heavy involvement in higher education sector of a certain number of central ministries in charge of economic management. In terms of governance pattern, three basic types of higher education institutions could be identified in terms of governance under the planned economy: (1) those under the direct administration of the Ministry of Education (the previous State Education Commission); (2) those under the non-educational central ministries; and (3) those under various local authorities.

The planned economy justified strict state control over higher education and the great role of central departments in running and managing their own universities and colleges. Owing to the separate establishment and administration of university/college by the Ministry of Education, the non-educational central departments and other local authorities (including educational and non-educational departments), this governance structure was notorious for the "single leadership relationship" (*danyi lingdao guanxi*) and "matrix fragmentation" (*tiao/kuai fenge*). This consequently led to functional overlapping, resources wastage, low economy and efficiency. Under such a governance structure, many issues occurred in the relationships between the central government and local governments, between the superior central departments and the institutions, and between the government and the institutions. Since the central ministries monopolized all the authorities and resources in higher education sector, the incentives of local governments in developing higher education was stifled. Responsibilities and authorities between the leading departments and the institutions were not distinctively identified. Individual institutions were lack of institutional and academic autonomy, and failed to provide education geared to the needs of society and the economic development.

As the market reform proceeds, limitations and weaknesses of such a governance structure of higher education have exposed, and its incompatibility with the market economy has emerged. Meanwhile, the rapid expansion of both higher education institutions and the number of students also necessitated a better governance model to run and monitor the higher education sector in China. Reforms in the governance structure of higher education have been introduced and implemented gradually and incrementally since the mid-1980s. The first critical step to restructure Chinese higher education governance took in May 1985 when the Central Committee of the Communist Party of China issued the "Decision on the Reform of the Educational System" (hereafter referred to as "1985 Decision"). In the "Programme for Education Reform and Development in China" (hereafter "1993 Programme") promulgated in 1993, the central government re-affirmed its 1985 commitment to refrain from direct control of education to one of managing schools through legislation, funding, planning, and advising. The 1985 Decision and the 1993 Programme marked the change in government orientation in educational administration. The basic aim of the Chinese government is to set up a new governance system which is characterized by the two-tier management structure, based on the division of labour between the central and provincial governments, and dominated by the coordinated management of the provincial government.

New governance model of higher education in China has been taking shape since the mid-1990s. Under the new governance model, while non-educational central departments have retreated from the higher education sector, the role of provincial governments in higher education has been increased greatly. Meanwhile, the institutional and academic autonomy of higher education institutions have been increased. By giving more autonomy to the higher education institutions and with lessened state control over the educational realm, it is obvious that higher education institutions have become far more intellectually independent; while educational practitioners and professionals have become increasingly autonomous and they are in better position to negotiate with the state about the course of educational development (Mok, 1999, 2000).

Increasing Role of Local Government and the Localization of Higher Education

The system of "unified leadership by the centre and two-tier administration by the central and provincial (municipal and autonomous regional) governments" has been in force. The new pattern of educational governance changed the relationship between the central and local governments. The role of provincial governments in higher education has been increased largely in terms of financing and management. Provincial governments were encouraged to cooperate with the central government via the Ministry of Education (MoE) to run and fund all MoE-led universities located in the provinces. With the increasing role of the local government in higher education, a new trend of localization of higher education emerged in China.

Take Shanghai for an example. As one of the higher education centres in China, there were about 50 full-time colleges and universities in Shanghai in early 1990s. Among them, more than half were run and funded by the Ministry of Education and other departments at the central level, while others were run and funded by the Shanghai municipal education department and other municipal departments. Such a system for administering higher educational institutions led to the separation of the centre and the locality, the segmentation of universities, resource wastage, and functional overlapping, and thus could not achieve economy of scale and the better use of the limited resources. With decentralization policies being pursued by the central government, the Shanghai municipal government planned to strengthen its coordinating function in relation to the universities that are located in Shanghai. The municipal government began to make adjustments for the universities and colleges, which were previously under the control of the various departments of the municipal government, by transferring them to be under the jurisdiction of the Municipal Commission for Education. At the same time, many universities and colleges which have similar functions were merged and combined together. For example, in May 1994, the original Shanghai University was merged with the Shanghai University of Industry, Shanghai Science and Technology University and Shanghai Higher Vocational College of Science and Technology to form the new Shanghai University. In October 1994, the Shanghai Normal University and Shanghai Technical Normal Colleges were also merged. Resources have been concentrated and directed to a few key universities and key disciplines so as to enhance investment efficiency. For instance, starting from 1999, Shanghai decided to pull financial resources together to fully develop Fudan University and Shanghai Jiaotong University, the two key universities that are under the Ministry of Education but are located in Shanghai, aiming to build them into "world-class" universities. Meanwhile, the municipal government started to cooperate with the Ministry of Education to run and fund all the seven MoE-led universities located in Shanghai. Besides two special colleges, all the higher educational institutions originally run and administrated by central departments and located in Shanghai have now been taken over by the municipal government (Chan & Ngok, 2001).

Retreat of Non-educational Central Departments from Higher Education

In response to the problems caused by "matrix fragmentation" (*tiao/*

kuai fenge) and the heavy involvement of specific central economic management departments in higher education, a new wave of readjustment of higher education institutions was launched since early 1992. Main forms of readjustments include joint investment (*gongjian*), cooperation, merger, and even abolition. From 1992 to 2000, 387 regular universities were merged and readjusted into 212 universities. In the year of 2000, 53 universities under the ministries of the central government were merged into 22 universities (*People's Daily*, 1 November 2000).

The 1998 administrative reform of the central government, which abolished the bulk of central ministries in charge of economic management, has brought about the great wave of readjustments of universities and colleges that were previously under the control of the various non-educational departments of the central government. As a result of this reform, the bulk of the central departments in charge of specialized economic management was abolished, including Ministry of Coal Industry, Ministry of Machine-Building Industry, Ministry of Metallurgical Industry, Ministry of Internal Trade, Light Industry Council and Textile Industry Council, Ministry of Posts and Telecommunications, Ministry of Electronic Industry, Ministry of Radio, Film and Television, Ministry of Electric Power Industry, Ministry of Chemical Industry, and Ministry of Forestry. Before the proposed restructuring there were more than 90 regular higher education institutions directly under these ministries. With the abolition of these central ministries, the management structures of 91 universities were under the readjustment. It has been the largest scale of management reform of higher education institutions in China since the early 1990s. Among the 91 regular higher education institutions, 10 leading universities are under the joint investment (*gongjian*) by the central and local governments with the former prevailing in major decision-making and the latter prevailing in the daily management of the universities. The other 81 universities are jointly administered by the central and local governments with the latter prevailing in the management. Local governments will manage their state assets, and be responsible for the management of their staff establishment, labour and wage. The development of these universities will be placed under the local economic and social development plans. The provincial governments have the responsibilities to take measures to allow these institutions to play a more distinct role in the promotion of local economic and social developments. Preferential treatment available usually to local institutions must be made available to these institutions.

Now, with few exceptions, non-educational central government ministries have retreated from running higher educational institutions. Most of the higher educational institutions originally run and administered by the central ministries located in the provinces have been taken over by the provincial governments.

University Autonomy

One central theme of the transformation of higher education governance is the academic and institutional autonomy of universities. With the effects of marketization and decentralization in higher education sector, the autonomy of higher education institutions has been increased. Instead of the government directly intervening in the everyday operation of individual universities, the government tended to manage universities through legislation, funding, planning, provision of information, advice and other necessary administrative means.

The autonomy of universities was first legally enacted in 1998 with the passage of the first Higher Education Law in China. Under the ìPresidential Responsibilityî system, university presidents are held responsible for the formulation of policies and long-term development plans as well as objectives. Universities have autonomy in the organizing of teaching and research, in personnel decisions, and in the distribution of funding and materials. Specifically, universities have the power to formulate annual recruitment plans, to adjust the quota of students among different departments and programmes, to restructure and establish programmes, to determine the internal structure, to hire and fire teachers and staff, to raise and use funding, and to distribute bonuses and benefits to staff. Within the university, colleges and departments also enjoy greater autonomy and powers in matters relating to teaching and research, management of personnel, and resource allocation (Mok, 1997). Although it is reasonable to argue that universities have been granted more autonomy, the fact that university is treated as the appendix of the state has not changed to a great extent.

Role of Law in Higher Education Governance

The Chinese government attached more importance of the role of law in administering education. Law has become an important form of educational governance. More and more laws on education have been enacted since 1980 when the "Regulations on Academic Degrees," the first educational law was promulgated. In 1985, the Decision on Educational System Reform called for speeding up the work on educational legislation. The 1993 Programme proclaimed to make use of legislation as a main means of educational management. From 1993 to 1998, four laws on education were enacted, which were the Teacher Law (1993), the Law on Education (1995), the Law on Vocational Education (1996), and the Higher Education Law (1998). With the promulgation of these laws, a preliminary legal system of education was established in China (Sun, 1999, pp. 62–84).

Institutional Amalgamation and the Establishment of Cross-institutional Consortiums

In order to make better use of the limited higher education resources and increase the competitiveness of higher education sector, the Chinese government has made attempts to optimize educational funds through institutional mergers and cooperation between institutions in sharing resources, with the intention of raising student-staff ratios and cost-effectiveness. Institutional merger is also seen as a way to readjust the strategic structure of higher education institutions. Since the mid-1990s, institutional amalgamation has been a remarkable trend in China's higher education sector (Chen & Lin, 2001). By 1998, 207 institutions had been merged into 84 (*China Education Daily*, 2 May 1998).

Through merger, the number of higher education institution has been decreased. At the same time, cross-institutional consortiums or super-universities were established by merging mono-disciplinary universities/colleges and the alliance between universities. The establishment of new Zhejiang University in 1998 was a significant case for the restructuring of higher education institutions in China. It was established on the basis of the merger of Zhejiang University, Hangzhou University, Zhejiang Agricultural University and Zhejiang

Medical University. As a multidisciplinary university, its programmes cover arts, humanity, education, economics, management, law, agriculture, sciences, engineering and medicine. In addition, there are national laboratories, research centres, post-doctoral stations at the university. The merger was successful in making Zhejiang University one of the leading universities, both in terms of size and diversity (Zhou, 2000, p. 16).

Changes in Educational Financing

Educational financing is a major aspect of higher education reform. In China, investment in education is gravely insufficient. While the developed countries spend 5% of GDP on education on average, China spends less than 3% of GDP. As a result, the state has never satisfied the pressing demand for education among the population. In order to improve the financial situation, the state searched for "multiple channels" of educational financing instead of solely relying upon the state's support. As a result, a new system of educational investment has taken shape in China. Besides relying on the central governmental educational budget, an increasing portion of the financial resources to run universities comes from local taxes, tuition fees, loans from state banks, overseas donations, local fund raising, and income from enterprises. Since the early 1980s, state funding in higher education has been gradually reduced while grants, funds and loans generated from other non-state sectors have become increasingly important. Tuition fees are a growing source of income, sometimes representing 50% of a student's direct education expenditure. For private universities, fees may account for more than 90% of revenues.

Fee-charge Principle

In line with the growing tolerance of the individualism associated with a market economy, the idea of education for personal advancement and personal fulfilment is no longer condemned. Higher education is increasingly seen as a channel for social mobility and personal development. The government has begun to see higher education as consumption and a private good benefiting primarily the individual even though the nation may stand to gain in the long run. This orientation opens a new official stand on education financing. Since higher education is a consumption item, the consumer has to pay; and thus the fee-charge principle is introduced in Chinese higher education system.

Throughout the 1980s and 1990s, the majority of students in colleges and universities were financed by the state, but new types of fee-paying students emerged. These are the commissioned students and the self supporting-students. The former are students enrolled as a result of contracts universities have signed with enterprises and other employing units, or even individual employers; the latter refers to those who have to pay out of their own pockets (Yin & White, 1994). Since 1997, all students enrolling in higher education have to pay tuition fees. Tuition figures more prominently in the income of higher educational institutions which are suffering from the poor inputs from the government. With the increase of tuition fees, many students from poor families can hardly afford higher education service (Yang, 2002). High tuition fee has been a major concern for many parents.

Revenue Generating Activities

Financial constraint is the main problem confronting Chinese higher education institutions. The government cannot provide sufficient funding to universities; instead it implements favourable policies, encouraging universities to make money on their own. As a result, educational institutions at all levels engage in different revenue generating activities to find additional funds to sustain their institutes, and to improve the living and working conditions of faculty members. Schools offering commissioned courses, running adult classes and evening courses to attract more students, or charging consultant fees are becoming more and more popular (Mok, 1999).

To attract more grants and funds, Chinese universities establish and maintain close links with the business and industrial sectors (Mok, 2001; Zhou & Cheng, 1997). They promote technology transfer and commercialize the results of their academic research; some even set up their own businesses and enterprises (Kwong, 1996). To raise income, universities are increasingly spinning off research activities to the private sector.

WTO Accession and New Methods of Educational Financing

With China's WTO accession, more foreign universities and colleges will enter into the Chinese market and have an impact on domestic higher education institutions, including the opening of its higher education sector to various investors. The Chinese government is considering issuing treasury bonds and inviting investment from international financial institutions, foreign government and individual investors to foster the country's education (*Beijing Evening News*, 8 November 2001).

Changes in Higher Educational Provision

With the promulgation of the Program for Education Reform and Development in China in 1993 (hereafter 1993 Program), the trend of decentralization and marketization of higher education was further strengthened. The 1993 Program identified the reduction of centralization and government control in general as the long-term goals of reform. The government began to play the role of "macro-management through legislation, allocation of funding, planning, information service, policy guidance and essential administration", so that "universities can independently provide education geared to the needs of society under the leadership of the government" (CCPCC, 1993). Thereafter, we have witnessed a large-scale development of higher education in the 1990s and different types of tertiary institutions have evolved in China, including both national (public) and private (*minban*) higher education institutions.

Rapid Expansion of Higher Education

The huge gap between demand and supply of higher education service is a salient feature of Chinese higher education development. Although the scale of Chinese higher education has been expanded steadily since the late 1970s, it cannot meet the huge demand for higher education of the people. To spur the weak domestic economy, to ease up unemployment pressure, and to meet the increasing demand for higher education scale, the Chinese government decided to expand rapidly the higher education sector in the late 1990s.

In 1997, the gross enrolment ratio of China was 9.1%, but it increased to 9.8%, 10.5% and 11% respectively in 1998, 1999 and 2000 (National Centre for Education Development Research, 2001, p. 11). In 1999, the intake of regular higher education institutions was 1.53 million, representing a 42% increase from 1.08 million in 1998. In the following years, quantitative growth continued. In 2000, the intake of higher education institutions reached 2.2 million, almost double of the intake in 1998. In 2001, a total of 2,682,800 first year students enrolled in 1,225 regular tertiary institutions. The expansion continued, and the number of new students reached 4.47 million in 2004 (see Table 4.1). The goal to reach a gross enrolment ratio of 15% was fulfilled in 2002, eight years earlier than the original schedule set in the *Action Plan to Vitalize Education towards the 21st Century* (Ministry of Education, 1998). In order to boost economic development, the Chinese central government lifted the longstanding restrictions on marital status (required to be single) and age (below 25 years of age) of student examinees.

Significant changes have also taken place in the area of a tightly controlled job-assignment system for graduates. In the past, university graduates in China were assigned jobs only according to

Table 4.1   **Numbers of Regular Higher Education Institutions and Student Enrolment**

Year	No. of Institutions	New Students	Graduates	Students Enrolled
1990	1,075	609,000	614,000	1,206,300
1995	1,054	926,000	805,000	2,906,000
1998	1,022	1,084,000	930,000	3,409,000
1999	1,071	1,597,000	848,000	4,134,000
2000	1,041	2,206,072	949,767	5,560,900
2001	1,225	2,682,800	1,036,300	7,190,700
2002	1,396	3,205,000	1,337,300	9,033,600
2003	1,552	3,821,700	1,877,500	110,856,000
2004	1,731	4,473,400	2,391,200	13,335,000

Source: Figures from 1990 to 1999 are cited from *China Statistical Yearbook 2000*. Figures from 2000 to 2004 are cited from the annual *National Education Development Statistical Bulletin* issued by the Education Ministry.

the government centralized planning; there was no prior meeting between the employer and employee (Williams, Liu, & Shi, 1997, pp. 152–153). As a result, mismatch between job requirements and students' expertise and preference were common. In the late 1980s, this practice changed to one of "mutual selection" between employers and graduates with employers specifying their job requirements and graduates their job preferences. The purpose was to allow graduates greater freedom in choosing jobs of their preferences and to ensure a more effective job allocation mechanism, so that the needs of the socialist market economy could be better met. At the beginning, the government allowed only a certain proportion of graduates to contact prospective companies directly prior to graduation (Williams et al., 1997, pp. 152–153), but the proportion of graduates being "assigned" to jobs has gradually decreased.

The Development of Non-state Higher Education

For a long time, all universities in China had been under direct governmental control, such that they were run, funded, and managed by the government. To increase educational facilities, non-state sectors, such as mass organizations, business enterprises, private institutions, private individuals, and even foreign institutions are encouraged to support academic programmes in existing educational institutions or to sponsor educational institutions in post-Mao China (Ren, 1996; Zhou & Cheng, 1997). Since the mid-1980s, different types of schools and colleges run by the non-state sector have emerged, and their number has grown steadily. Officially, these schools are registered as *minban* (lit. "people-run") schools, which include a wide variety of schools run by different non-state bodies (*shehui liliang*)—collectives, mass organizations, business enterprises and private entrepreneurs (Peng, 1997). This so-called "non-state-sponsored" education can realize multiple channels of financing, encourage diversification in the provision of educational services, and the like. Moreover, it can also encourage competition, and thus increase effectiveness and efficiency in the provision of educational services.

As of 2004, there were 1,415 *minban* higher learning institutions of all kinds in China, most of which provided instructions for those who were preparing for the state examinations. Among them, 228 were regular *minban* higher education institutions which could offer diploma or degree programmes recognized by the government. Most of them were occupation-oriented. In 2004, there were 1.39 million students registered in the *minban* higher learning institutions in the whole country (Ministry of Education, 2005).

Market-driven Curricula and Programmes

Before the 1980s, the curricula in universities were very specialized, and students were locked into narrow fields of study. The highly specialized nature of the curricula made graduates quite inflexible in adapting to new technologies and the changing labour market; it sometimes even resulted in a mismatch between the demand for the trained, specialized labour and the supply. Increased institutional autonomy has given universities more power to run institutions according to labour market needs, to revise curricula and syllabi, and to introduce new courses of study.

Since 1985, higher institutions have been able to participate in the definition of curriculum. They were given power to modify teaching objectives in different disciplines, formulate teaching plans and programmes, and compile and select teaching materials (Hayhoe, 1989, p. 41). Many universities have taken the initiative to broaden the over-specialized curricula by combining several narrowly specialized academic programmes into broader ones. With the greater power in formulating teaching plans and materials, universities have designed their courses to make their graduates employable and to suit employers' demands. University courses and curricula are "market-driven," stressing practical and applied values of the curriculum (Johnes & Taylor, 1990; Mok, 1998). Specialities that fail to attract students are phased out.

With China's accession to the World Trade Organization (WTO), significant changes in the curricula of colleges and universities are expected. It was reported that some Chinese universities are restructuring their curricula. By 2004, 5% to 10% of major courses at local colleges and universities will be given in English, including information technology, bio-technology, finance and law (*Beijing Evening News*, 8 November 2001). Nowadays, most of the key universities in China offer English-taught courses. For example, in 2003, 10% of courses in Tsinghua University were taught in English. The University plans to teach 30% of all its causes in English up to 2010 when it reaches the level of world class university (*Mingpao Daily*, 10 August 2003). Meanwhile, the Ministry of Education has stepped up efforts to compile English textbooks and introduce original versions of textbooks from English-speaking countries into Chinese universities. In fact, the use of English textbooks is very popular in Chinese universities, especially in the disciplines of medicine, engineering, business management, and public management.

Competition as Means to Enhance Efficiency, Effectiveness and Quality

Though the Chinese government has tended to reduce per capita public funding to higher education, it has taken various administrative and financial initiatives to influence researches and teaching curricula of higher education. It has, in fact, played an important role in promoting educational competition, with the belief that China's education and technology profile can thus be elevated. Since the 1990s, the government has taken various measures to encourage competition among higher education institutions, such as competitive allocation of operational funds, and government-initiated projects, for instance, the "211 Project" (which will be explained below). The central government has launched new initiatives, pooling limited resources to fund key disciplinary areas. These initiatives include, for example, the plan to build up key national bases for humanities and social sciences research and key national laboratory for science in regular universities. In this regard, the role of the government in education is still in the context of globalization. All these developments echo the international trend in educational restructuring: ongoing devolution in finance and administration with increasing central government influence in curriculum development.

The "211 Project"

"The 211 Project," launched in the mid-1990s, represents the Chinese government's most ambitious goal in higher education development. The aim of the project is to strengthen about 100 higher education institutions and key disciplinary areas as a national priority for the 21st century. Primarily aiming at training high-level professional manpower to implement the national strategy for social and economic development, the project has impact on the following areas: improving higher education; accelerating national economic progress; pushing forward the development of science, technology and culture; enhancing China's overall capacity and international competitiveness; and laying the foundation of training high-level professional manpower mainly within the educational institutions at home. It is envisaged that after several years' efforts some of these universities will have greatly improved their quality of education, research, management and institutional efficiency. In addition, these institutions will also have made remarkable progress in reforming their management and thus become bases for training high-level professional manpower and for solving major problems for the country's economic construction and social development (*China Education Daily*, 7 December 2001). As a result of such efforts, the group of institutions will set up national standards in overall quality, with some of the key universities and disciplinary areas approaching or reaching the advanced international standards.

Since its launching in the mid-1990s, the "211 Project" has been carried out smoothly. In its first phase, 98 institutions of higher learning nationwide have gone through sector preliminary examination as scheduled. A total of 602 key disciplinary areas have been identified. Among them, 62 (10.3%) are from social sciences and humanities, 57 (9.5%) from economics and law, 89 (14.8%) from basic science, 42 (6.9%) from environmental resources, 255 (42.4%) from industry and high-tech, 66 (10.9%) from medicine and nursing, and 31 (5.1%) from agriculture. The second phase of the project will focus more on the establishment of world-class universities in China (*China Education Daily*, 8 February 2001).

Building up World-class University

"World-class university" has become a buzzword in China since the end of the last century. In May 1998, Li Lanqing, then Vice Premier in charge of education policy, expressed explicitly for the first time that China should build up a batch of world-class universities. Two days later, Li's words were echoed by President Jiang Zemin when he made a speech at a ceremony celebrating the centenary of Peking University. Jiang asserted that China must have quite a few first-rate universities of international advanced level. Immediately, building up world-class university became a national policy when the Ministry of Education promulgated the *Action Plan to Vitalize Education towards the 21st Century* in December 1998. One policy option included in the Plan is to lift a few universities and some key disciplinary areas in China to the level of world class within 10 or 20 years in the 21st century. As President Jiang first made such the proposal of building up world-class university in May 1998, such a policy was also named "985 Plan." Since then, Peking and Tsinghua have been handpicked by the central government to make as world-class institutions. As a result, a huge number of extra money has been invested in these two universities to promote their teaching and research quality. Renmin University, the key university in social sciences in China, has determined to develop itself as the world-class university in the field of social sciences (Field interview in Beijing, 2001).

If financial resources were available, individual provinces and municipalities could allocate additional funds to develop one more key university in their own regions. For example, Shanghai municipal government identified Fudan University and Jiaotong University in 1998 as the two "key universities" in the region, and additional resources were given to the two universities to make them the best institutions in the whole region (Field Interview in Shanghai, 1999). Universities that are less well-endowed can merge with other local colleges to become a comprehensive university to increase their strengths and competitiveness.

Building up Key National Bases for Humanities and Social Sciences Research

As China's integration with the international community deepens, the poor performance and quality of Chinese humanities and social sciences become salient. In order to improve this situation, the Ministry of Education issued the Plan to Build up Key National Bases for Humanities and Social Sciences Research in Regular Higher Education Institutions in June 1999. The plan included a selection of about 100 leading research centers in universities nationwide.

Universities which host these research centers are given extra funds and grants to launch new research projects so as to enhance their overall research capacity and improve their international reputation in the fields of humanities and social sciences. The key national bases have become the focus of university competition. More such key bases are hosted, higher reputation a university enjoys. In fact, top universities, such as Peking University, Renmin University, and Fudan University have hosted more such bases. On the whole, such a policy initiative has exercised great impacts on the development of the humanities and social sciences in China.

A More Open Higher Education Sector

Increasing International Exchange and Cooperation

International cooperation is an important aspect of China's educational development under the impacts of globalization. The open door policy adopted in 1978 ended the self-isolated situation of China's education, and started a new stage of international communication and cooperation in the education sector. Chinese students were sent abroad for further studying, and foreign students were hosted in China. Meanwhile, cross-border academic communications were resumed and expanded. International communication and cooperation has become the new dynamics of China's education reform and development.

Since 1979, more than 320,000 Chinese students have been sent to more than 100 countries and regions. Meanwhile, China has hosted 340,000 students from more than 160 countries and regions. In addition, some 40,000 foreign experts and teachers have been imported into China. A huge number of Chinese experts and academicians were invited to take part in international conferences held abroad and to make presentations. In 1996 alone, China sent out more than 10,000 students to nearly 100 countries and regions and hosted nearly 33,000 international students from 160 countries and regions ("The development of education in China," 2001).

On top of student exchange and academic cooperation, China has also launched joint educational institutions and programmes with other countries and regions, especially the developed economies. In 1995, China established about 80 joint educational institutions and programmes with countries and regions, such as the United States, Australia, Canada, and the United Kingdom. This figure grew fast to 712 by the end of 2002. Although most of the provinces in China are involved in the Sino-foreign joint education undertaking, most of the institutions and programmes are concentrated in Shanghai, Beijing and the prosperous coastal regions. Joint institutions and programmes cover almost all aspects of education sector, from kindergarten to post-graduate school. The most popular joint education programmes include business administration, foreign languages, computer science and economics and finance ("Sino-foreign joint education," 2003).

In addition, China has extended its connections with international organizations, such as UNESCO, UNICEF, United Nations Population Fund (UNFPA), United Nations Development Programme (UNDP), the World Bank and many other international or regional organizations. China has benefited greatly from the educational aids offered by these organizations. Making use of the loans from the World Bank has become a constituent component of China's educational development strategy and planning ("The development of education in China," 2001).

Wide Use of Modern Educational Technology

The wide use of modern educational technology is one the main features of China's educational development in the post-Mao period. The use of television injected new forces in China's education development. Earlier in 1978, the Chinese government decided to set up the Central Radio and Television University (CRTVU) and the Central Audio-visual Centre in Beijing with their extensions all over the country. In order to maximize the role of television in education, the China Educational Television Station was set up in 1986. Local governments also established their own educational television stations. The 1980s witnessed the rapid development of the broadcast/TV-based distance education in China.

Since the 1990s, the popularity of information and Internet technologies became the new driving force of China's educational development, especially the distance learning. Universities have played the key role in developing cyber education. At the end of 1994, with the financial support from the central government,

Tsinghua and other nine universities completed the China Education and Research Network (CERNET) Pilot Project, the first TCP/IP-based public computer network in China. In 1997, Hunan University, through cooperating with Hunan Telecom, established China's first on-line university. In 1998, Tsinghua University launched on-line master programmes. Tsinghua University, Beijing University of Post and Telecommunications, Zhejiang University and Hunan University are among the first batch of higher educational institutions pioneering distance learning. To regulate the development of distance learning, the Ministry of Education promulgated a document entitled "Opinions on Developing Advanced Distance Learning in China" in 1999, which expatiates the guidelines, aims and tasks of distance learning in China. In August 1999, Peking University and the Central Broadcast and TV University joined the pioneer list for distance learning ("The development of education in China," 2001).

The year of 2000 witnessed leaping progress of cyber education and distance learning in China. In July, the Ministry of Education promulgated "the Several Opinions on Supporting Some Universities and Colleges to Set up Internet Education Schools and Pioneer Distance Learning." According to the document, 31 universities and colleges were granted substantial autonomy in their distance learning initiatives. They may set the admission gateway and determine the admission quota, offer programmes outside the subject catalogue, and award degree certificates. In September and October, some of the above-mentioned higher education institutions kicked off their on-line campus programmes. On October 31, China Advanced Distance Learning Satellite Broadband Multimedia Transmission Platform got into operation, allowing simultaneous transmission of decades of video and multimedia channels at different rates. Moreover, the Internet access service provisioned on the platform enables high-speed interconnection with CERNET, forming a satellite-land consolidated bi-directional education network. Operation of this platform thoroughly changes the situation of one-way transmission over satellite TV network in China. According to the statistics revealed by the Ministry of Education, by the end of 2000, the 31 higher education institutions had offered seats to nearly 190,000 users, most of them were pursuing degree programmes (Liu, 2001).

Discussion and Conclusion

Since China opened its door to the outside world in the late 1970s, China's education has experienced great changes due to the impacts of globalization and other developments. Integrating with the international economy has not only attached great importance to the role of education in national economy, but also stimulated the educational demand of the people. The Chinese government may not be fully committed to the ideology underpinning the global economy; she was driven to it by more pragmatic considerations of financial stringency and the desire for economic advancement. Nevertheless, integration into the world economy has led to a redefinition of the role of higher education in China. The central government began to see higher education more as an instrument to impart the scientific and technological knowledge needed in the global economy. This change of priorities prompted the state to relinquish its monopolistic role in higher education and to allow room for non-state social forces to become involved.

The use of the strategies of decentralization and marketization in the Chinese context is highly instrumental. The Chinese government intended to use these strategies to improve its financial situation and enhance the efficiency and effectiveness in the use of its resources in the face of financial stringency. The adoption of these policies reflected an attempt to make use of market forces and new initiatives from the non-state sectors to mobilize more educational resources and create more learning opportunities for its citizens. Nevertheless, the educational changes resulting from economic globalization are far-reaching. The trends of decentralization and marketization have considerably affected education policy and structure with changes ranging from administration, financing, programming, and student intake, to graduates' employment. More importantly, these changes have changed the relationship between the central and local governments, the state and universities, and also the role of the state in higher education.

The increasing responsibility of local governments for educational investment has reduced the role of central government and increased the power of the provincial and county governments in educational planning and administration. The introduction of fees and the adoption of multiple-channels of funding have diminished the central and local governments' responsibilities for educational financing and increased university autonomy. It has ushered in a new administrative relationship between universities and the government. Direct state control and management in universities were abandoned; instead the state relies on regulative and financial tools to manage universities.

While educational opportunities in the higher education sphere have been expanded rapidly, and the gap between demand and supply of education has been narrowed, not all Chinese people have equally benefited from the rapid expansion. The inequality of educational opportunity has been deteriorated rather than improved. First of all, there is an increasing rural-urban disparity in terms of educational opportunity. Rural-urban disparity is a longstanding problem in China's social development. Educational disparity between rural and urban regions has being widened since the late 1970s. Second, the economic reform has also contributed to regional disparity of education. The rapid expansion of higher education in recent decade benefited mainly people in the coastal provinces and large cities. In Beijing, higher education enrolment rate of senior high school graduates reached 70% in 2001. In Shanghai, 38.8% of a cohort aged between 18 and 22 has been recruited by higher educational institutions. In Jiangsu, the gross enrolment ratio of higher education has reached 15% in 2001 (Yang, 2002). More badly, the huge change in social stratification has led to great disadvantaged social groups in China, which include the unemployed, laid-off workers from the ailing state-owned enterprises, and other people suffering economic vulnerabilities. Students from these poor families are found difficult to afford the soaring educational costs, especially the higher education services. Access to higher education of some students from poor rural areas and urban poor families is denied due to their financial difficulties.

The impacts on Chinese higher education are multiple facets. After about two decades of restructuring and transforming, the unified, centralized, closed, and static higher education system of China has now becoming more diversified, decentralized, open, and dynamic. Massification of higher education brought by the rapid expansion of the public tertiary institutions and the development of private education institutions have satisfied to a large extent the huge education demand of the people. On the other hand, marketization of higher education has also led to the further inequality in education opportunity and quality. While decentralization has stimulated the involvement of local governments and other non-state sectors in higher education development, regional inequality in the area of higher education has deteriorated. International exchange and cooperation has no doubt benefited Chinese higher education sector; however it has also exposed Chinese universities to the severe international competition. Along with the further opening of Chinese higher education sector after China's accession to the WTO, international competition and pressure facing Chinese higher education sector will be intensified. Therefore, it is reasonable to predict that further restructuring and transforming will be introduced in Chinese higher education system.

References

Agelasto, M., & Adamson, B. (1998). *Higher education in Post-Mao China.* Hong Kong: Hong Kong University Press.

Chan, D., & Ngok, K. L. (2001). Centralization and decentralization in educational development in Shanghai. *Education and Society, 19*(2), 29–78.

Chen, W., & Lin, W. (2001). Yi hebing wei qiji shixian xuexiao kuayueshi fazhan [Making use of merging as an opportunity to expand higher education development]. *Zhongguo gaodeng jiaoyu* [China Higher Education], *12*, 35–36.

Chen, Z. L. (1999). Fifty-year of education in the People's Republic of China. *Jiaoyu yanjiu* [Education Studies], *9*, 3–15.

Chinese Communist Party Central Committee (CCPCC). (1993). *Zhongguo jiaoyu gaige gangyao* [The program for reform and development of China's education]. Beijing: People's Press.

Dale, R. (1999). Specifying globalization effects on national policy: A focus on the mechanisms. *Journal of Education Policy, 14*(1), 1–17.

The development of education in China: A review [*Zhongguo jiaoyu fazhan gaikuang*]. (2001). Retrieved November 25, 2004, from http://www.edu.cn/20010823/207269.shtml

Hayhoe, R. (1989). *China's univeisities and the open door.* New York: M. E. Sharpe, Inc.

Hayhoe, R. (1996). *China's universities 1895–1995: A century of cultural conflicts.* New York: Garland Publishing.

Ji, P. (2000). 1999 nian Zhongguo gaodeng jiaoyu fazhan fenxi [An analysis of China's higher education development in 1999]. In Yuan Zhenguo (Ed.),

Zhongguo jiaoyu zhengce pinglun [A review of Chinese education policy] (pp. 147–152). Beijing: Educational Science Press.

Johnes, J., & Taylor, J. (1990). *Performance indicators in higher education: UK universities.* Buckingham, United Kingdom: Society for Research into Higher Education and Open University.

Kwong, J. (1996). The new educational mandate in China: Running schools, running business. *International Journal of Educational Development, 16*(2), 185–194.

Liu, J. (2001). Advanced distance learning. Retrieved November 25, 2004, from http://www.edu.cn/20010830/200786.shtml

The Ministry of Education. (December 24, 1998). *The Action plan to vitalize the education towards the 21st Century.* (government document)

The Ministry of Education. (2005). *2004 nian quanguo jiaoyu shiye fazhan tongji gongbao* [*2004 National education development statistical bulletin*]. Retrieved April 10, 2006, from http://www.moe.gov.cn/edoas/website18/info14794.htm

Mok, K. H. (1997). Marketization and quasi-marketization: Educational development in post-Mao China. *International Review of Education, 43*(5–6), 547–567.

Mok, K. H. (1998). The cost of managerialism: The implications for the "McDonaldisation" of higher education in Hong Kong. *Journal of Higher Education Policy and Management, 20*(1), 77–87.

Mok, K. H. (1999). Education and the market place in Hong Kong and Mainland China. *Higher Education, 37*, 133–158.

Mok, K. H. (2000). Social and political development in post-reform China. Basingstoke, United Kingdom: Macmillan.

Mok, K. H. (2001). From state control to governance: Decentralization and higher education in Guangdong, China. *International Review of Education, 47*(1), 123–149.

National Centre for Education Development Research. (2001). *2000 nian Zhongguo jiaoyu lupishu* [Green Paper on China's Education 2000]. Beijing: Educational Science Press.

Peng, D. (1997). *Private education in modern China.* Westport, CT: Praeger.

Ren, L. S. (1996). Exploration of the market effects of schools run by societal forces. *Chinese Education and Society, 29*(5), 15–19.

Sino-foreign joint education undertaking: Its status [*Zhong wai hezuo banxue jiben qingkuang*]. (2003). Retrieved October 20, 2004, from http://www.edu.cn/20030407/3081628.shtml

Williams, G., Liu, S., & Shi, Q. H. (1997). Marketization of higher education in the People's Republic of China. *Higher Education Policy, 10*(2), 151–157.

Yang, R. (2002, April). *Progresses and paradoxes: New developments in China's higher education.* Paper presented at the Department of Public and Social Administration, City University of Hong Kong.

Yin, Q., & White, G. (1994). The marketization of Chinese higher education: A critical assessment. *Comparative Education, 30*(3), 217–237.

Zhou, Y.-Q. (2001, February 16). 21 shiji: Jianshe yige shenmo yang de gaodeng jiaoyu? [What kind of higher education should be constructed in the 21st century?] *Zhongguo jiaoyubao* [China Education Daily], p. 1.

5

Quality Assurance in the Context of Globalization and Its Impact on Higher Education

David GAMAGE & Jaratdao SUWARNABROMA

—ɯ—

Abstract

In the 1970s the Japanese manufacturers were the first to institute quality mechanisms, receiving world-wide acclamation and recognition for their products and services. In the 1990s globalization, IT and the spread of democracy brought down the barriers to trade and education. Increased costs to producers, customers, and nations due to poor quality resulted in renewed appreciations of quality. Until the 1980s, universities were resting on their laurels. But, the development of higher education as an industry and increased competition forced institutions to institute mechanisms for monitoring and enhancing the quality of their services. Globally, governmental concerns for quality, declining public funding and the need to attract and retain increasing numbers of students are the key factors which require higher educational institutions to maintain a competitive edge.

Total Quality Management (TQM) enhances the ability to face the challenges of the 21st century. Now, the universities explicitly through visions and missions acknowledge their obligation to meet the needs of a range of stakeholders. The higher education industry is a unique one and its principles do not often apply to other business enterprises. In higher education, customer's perceptions and opinions on quality of services are of paramount importance. TQM in higher education needs to cover a wide range of campus-based services along with the traditional academic aspects. In the new millennium, the adoption of quality assurance measures in higher education in particular is no longer an option. Currently, the issue of quality emerges as an important high priority whereby the students' opinions on all aspects of their experiences

in higher education are now being canvassed widely and are regarded as
essential to effective monitoring of quality in universities. This chapter focuses
on the impact of quality assurance in higher education.

Introduction

Currently, the higher education systems around the globe have two
dominant characteristics. The first is that in spite of the fact that we
have entered the 21st century with a highly advanced technology in
various spheres of human endeavour; higher education is still very
much in demand and is correlated with personal and economic
development. Most governments around the world believe that
higher education enables the development of its human resources
leading to higher levels of long-term national development. To prove
this point economists and scholars refer to the examples of the
United States and Japan who have been able to build the world's first
and second biggest economies as against the countries such as Brazil
and Russia with vast natural resources. The second characteristic is
that higher education systems throughout the world appear to be in
crisis because of the keen competition for funding, students and
faculty in the midst of increasing costs and declining public funding
with stringent needs to ensure accountability and consumer
orientation. This second characteristic has become a cause of much
concern to most higher educational institutions, forcing them to
embrace the concept of total quality management (TQM) with a
high degree of customer orientation if they are to survive in a highly
competitive environment. This chapter attempts to discuss what
TQM is, how it started, what it means in the context of higher
education, how it could be approached, difficulties that needs to be
confronted, its impact on higher education, global trends and the
possible advantages in adopting quality assurance measures.

Total Quality Management (TQM)

Many organizations have come to the conclusion that quality is
critically important. Some see quality as a requirement for survival in
the 21st century. Many scholars (Bonstingl, 1992; Deming, 1986;
Newby, 1999; Owlia & Aspinwall, 1996) have emphasized the
importance of quality in organizational products and services. Chen,

Chou, and Hsien (2002) state that in the contemporary world, the most important issue in business and industry, in education and the government sector is quality of their products and services. In order to study the application of TQM in higher education, an understanding of the definition of TQM is of primary importance. There are many definitions for TQM as well. Dahlgaard, Kristensen, and Kanji (1994) define TQM as a management process which any organization can implement through long-term planning, by using continuous quality improvement plans leading to the accomplishment of the organizational vision by developing an organizational culture characterized by increased customer satisfaction through continuous improvements with the efforts of all employees. Wilkinson and Witcher (1991) define TQM by taking a hierarchical approach. Quality is to satisfy customers' expectations continuously by achieving total quality at low cost with the objective of achieving TQM through everybody's participation. A more pervasive definition of TQM proposed by Miller (1996) and currently being widely used reads:

> An ongoing process whereby top management takes whatever steps necessary to enable everyone in the organization in the course of performing all [types of] duties to establish and achieve standards which meet or exceed the needs and expectations of their customers, both external and internal. (p. 157)

TQM can be defined as a holistic approach, a philosophical perspective that provides guidance for day-to-day actions. Its philosophy is driven by the force of quality and focuses on the never ending improvement of all processes. Its definition includes a goal and a process that accepts feedback from all stakeholders to define the "product and service" quality level and the specifications to be met. Fields (1993) asserted that total quality management is a culture of total commitment to customer satisfaction through continuous improvements and innovations in all aspects of the business. According to Bonstingl (1992), TQM requires consistent efforts by the entire group of the team, working together towards the achievement of the set goals based on an agreed vision and a mission. It is also important to use both quantitative and qualitative data in measuring how well the needs of all the relevant stakeholders are met.

Firms in many industries have attempted to enhance their customers' perceptions of quality through adoption of TQM systems. Variation of the TQM framework, including total quality service (Albrecht, 1991) and the total quality process have been adopted by educational institutions to bolster eroding competitive positions amongst them. TQM has become operational in many institutions and systems in response to the calls for reforms and restructuring. According to Cannon and Sheth (1994), the perspective of TQM in educational offerings should be improved continually in order to reflect the latest methods and trends to satisfy the needs of customers. To that end, Brown and Koenig (1993) recommend that customer evaluation of the quality of their education should be an integral part of TQM. Indeed, a better understanding of how customers perceive quality can provide valuable information to management for designing service delivery systems that enhance customer satisfaction (Seymour, 1992). The key theoretical linkage here is that customer satisfaction is affected by perceived quality (Anderson & Sullivan, 1993; Cronin & Taylor, 1992). What is clear from the literature is that perceived quality of service in higher education is of paramount strategic importance (Bemowski, 1991; Peter, 1992). There are a number of markets that a higher educational institution must consider when assessing perceived quality.

History of Quality Management

The concept of "quality" has been contemplated since the Industrial Revolution and continues to be a topic of intense current interest. Quality management finds its roots in the 1930s and in the elements of statistical process analysis created by Walter Shewhart of Bell Laboratories. Shewhart posited that manufacturing could be improved through a focus on identifying and correcting problems during the manufacture of products. Subsequently, William Edwards Deming, a protégé of Shewhart at Western Electric, and others utilized statistical process control to improve the quality of military armaments during World War II. Deming's teaching on statistical control to engineers and inspectors, was based on Shewhart's concepts but with significant improvements. Following the World War II, Deming tried to promote his ideas about quality to Americans but found that the Americans were not interested. However, post-war Japan showed a keen interest on the Deming's overtures as Japan faced two challenges blocking her economic advancement: one, that Japan was decimated in the war and second that whatever industries existed were shoddy and of poor quality. As Cole (1998) notes "the new quality paradigm which was developed by Deming in Japan from 1955–1980 emerged from the sense of crisis following the devastations at the World War II" (p. 45).

The systematic use of TQM principles and methods applied in the production sector made a significant contribution to enable Japan to develop the second biggest economy in the world by the 1970s. The subsequent adoption of TQM by Japanese industry and commerce, but not by the United States, was widely credited as a significant factor for Japan's miraculous post-war economic reconstruction and the current massive trade imbalance between the two countries. This particular event aroused the interest of U.S. industries and although a few of them had begun to work with quality circles in the 1970s, many were ready to accede to the need to reinvest in quality. Driven by such forces as increasing global competition and the struggle to survive, increasing costs, demands for accountability and rising customer expectations about quality, a number of U.S. corporations undertook quality management initiatives. While many of the preceding efforts on creating quality outcomes have focused on manufacturing and traditional service-oriented businesses, there is a growing concern that the concepts relating to quality need to be addressed and infused into the educational process. Bemowski (1991) suggests that academic institutions are experiencing competitive pressures and the application of TQM concepts may be necessary for them to survive in the future.

TQM Applied to Higher Education

Attempts to introduce industrial quality concepts such as TQM into higher education began in the late 1980s (Sallis, 1993). This was prompted by the successful implementation of quality strategies into many of the manufacturing and service organizations on the one hand and a growing need to improve the value of higher education for its stakeholders on the other (Vazzana, Elfrink, & Bachmann,

2000). Currently, TQM has become an industry recognized by a common model of quality management in the contexts of world's two economic super-powers, the United States and Japan. TQM is clearly emerging within education as a live issue. On the basis of demands for increased quality, to date many institutions have introduced the principles of TQM into various aspects of the educational arena (Bonser, 1992; Muller & Funnell, 1992; Yorke, 1992) as a step towards bringing better management to higher education.

Problems Confronted by Universities in Implementing TQM

The application of the concept of TQM to the service sector has not been an easy task. From the review of literature on the field and my own experience in working in many universities around the globe, it is evident that there are a number of barriers or perceived barriers to the adoption of TQM. These include:

1. the concept of academic freedom and the tradition of individual rather than collective responsibility for quality;
2. the tradition of paternalism rather than customer focus;
3. the claim to professionalism and the rejection of industrial models and vocabulary;
4. the long and tedious process of changing the culture within academic institutions; and
5. the difficulties experienced in measuring quality.

Academic Freedom and the Tradition of Individual Responsibility

Higher education is a very humanistic area where institutional autonomy and academic freedom are highly valued, where specialized faculties avidly protect their turf, and where tradition bound professors are unlikely to adopt a paradigm that proposes continuous improvements. Seymour (1992) noted that though TQM tries to bring people together to work cooperatively, the universities are largely decentralized into separate departments, schools and/or faculties, that have a history of turfman-ship and win-lose interactions. The core of professionalism in teaching has always been connected with the autonomy of professionals in their arenas, such as the teacher in his or her own classroom. Quality in these instances has been defined by each professional, based on his or her own individual dealings with students (Morgan & Murgatroyd, 1994). This approach differs from TQM because although TQM encourages the individual to take responsibility for the standards and quality of his/her work, it only does so in the context of a system which has a commonly agreed purpose and a collective view on the dimensions of quality.

Tradition of Paternalism as Against Customer Orientation

Traditionally it is the teacher who determines what the needs of the students are. This "top-down" approach to quality is different from the customer focus of TQM which stresses the importance of discovering what a range of stakeholders, including students, want and then aligning the service to their requirements (Dahlgaard, Kristensen, & Kanji, 1995). Very often, the students are at the receiving end of the continuum even though the concept of TQM expects them to reverse the roles with emphasis on customer orientation. In 1999 when the first author gave some lectures to graduate students at an overseas university, which included sources drawn from 1999 publications, some of the students who were school leaders told him that the latest publications that they had in the library were 1987. In this context, when he asked them "Why don't you ask your professor to order latest publications to the library?" they responded by saying, "We don't want to do that as we could be victimized." This particular incident illustrates the difficulties in changing the perceptions of both the students and academics because of past precedents.

As against this proposition, the students (mostly professionals) who are enrolled for the Master of Leadership and Management in Education (MLMEd) Programme at the University of Newcastle in Australia are strongly encouraged to come up with constructive suggestions to improve the programme even to the extent of challenging the lecturers. This policy has encouraged the graduate students to express their frank opinions, both positive and negative, on all aspects of the programme. This type of customer orientation has enabled the University of Newcastle to increase its student numbers consistently from all the Australian school systems as well as many different overseas destinations.

Claim for Professionalism and Rejection of Industrial Models

The industrial models and vocabulary can be rejected as inappropriate to the cultural tradition of education. The terms "customer" and "market" have met with resistance from some educators, who argue that they are applicable only to commercial environments (Corts, 1992; Sallis, 1993). Higher education institutions may differ from business organizations in that, for many of their members, satisfying the needs of the students by treating them as customers is not the most important form of excellence. Quality of output and reputation in academic research are most likely to be highly valued in many higher education institutions. Even if the concept of the customer were agreed, many academics would be uncomfortable with the priority that TQM places on the needs of the customers.

It is important to point out that the definition of customers in a university is quite broad. While students are accepted as the primary customers by many, other potential customers like parents, employers, government and society need to be considered. The plurality of the university's customer means that sometimes the products or goals of the university are in conflict. Thus universities have a role in moderating competing needs and expectations and in taking responsibility for final judgments (Harvey, 1995).

Long and Tedious Process of Changing Organizational Culture

A university is not simply a version of a manufacturing environment. The unique skills of its staff, its management structure, and its traditional autonomy have significant impact on the process of implementing TQM. Sometimes, TQM is seen as resulting in increased layers of management enabling many staff to resist the change under the pretext of referring to it as another ploy that increases managerial control and undermines academic autonomy. Indeed, in most organizations there is a clear line of authority. Each manager is responsible for directing and monitoring the activities of his/her subordinates and is in turn accountable for the performance of the subordinates.

In a university, this line of authority is much less real and difficult to enforce. A faculty or a school will have a dean and heads of departments with responsibilities on administrative matters rather than academic, but beyond this there is no clear management structure. Academics are expected to operate with a considerable degree of autonomy as most of them are supposed to be specialists in their own fields of study. This has implications for the implementation of TQM within a university. The collegiate structure leads to an emphasis on individual work, which may impede effective teamwork both in specific quality-improvement teams and in the general development of TQM within the operations of the university.

Difficulty in Measuring Quality

A major aspect of TQM which is being resisted is the measurement of quality and difficulty in identifying tangible results as well as to get people to be accountable. One central tenet of TQM is the need and ability to measure the effect of improvements in quality. More specifically, many organizations would seek to set the cost of a quality programme against savings arising from improvements in quality (Rowley, 1997). This can be difficult to implement in an educational environment. It is obvious that introducing TQM in a university is not a trivial exercise as there are many complex issues that increase the difficulty. The variety of customers and their different needs, the loose management structures, difficulties in identifying tangible results and the nature of academic work, all having the potential to inhibit the implementation of TQM.

Nevertheless, beyond the issue of decreasing funding and more scrutiny from external authorities, it is the realization that TQM offers opportunities for universities to enhance performance both in their academic and service areas have led to the adoption of TQM. Bailey and Dangerfield (2000) express the opinion:

> Proponents of TQM can hardly be ignored in HEIs. Problems in higher education require attention. Teaching and learning need to be improved and assessed. Processes should be adopted to improve the quality of education, increase constituent involvement, empower faculty and focus on the customer. (p. 3)

How Did TQM Impact on Higher Education?

The forces of globalization, advancement of telecommunication and IT, democratization of the former Soviet Block countries in Eastern

Europe and the emergence of the knowledge society have affected almost all organizations around the world. These forces call for changes, especially in relation to improvements in the quality of their products, to compete for survival in a global market. Increased cost to producers, customers, and nations due to poor quality has prompted renewed appreciation of the quality assurance function. Crosby (1979) asserts that the Japanese manufacturers were the first to initiate a quality revolution in the 1970s and have since received worldwide acclamation and recognition for their achievements. The United States joined the race for quality in the mid 1980s, perhaps with the release of William Ouchi's (1981) study on the best run Japanese and American companies and has made rapid advances (Walton, 1986). Following this, Europeans launched cooperative efforts to improve quality. In addition to manufacturers, education systems and government organizations all over the world are instituting quality audit or inspection systems.

Since the 1990s many universities also have started to strengthen their mechanisms for monitoring and enhancing the quality of their services. This is particularly due to an increasing concern on the part of governments around the world to ensure that higher education systems maintain their competitive edge. Accordingly, national approaches to extra-institutional scrutiny have been established with particular approaches that reflect different national styles. However, the growth of the "quality industry" in universities has generated a lively debate about what constitutes "quality," impacting enormously on all academics. Many academics have noticed that quality has become a high priority issue.

During the last decade of the second millennium, education systems around the globe were faced with pressures associated with financial constraints, demands for public accountability and the need for defense of institutional autonomy. One of the major areas of common interest which will remain to the foreseeable future is the growth of quality assurance mechanisms. As we enter the third millennium a range of issues are beginning to emerge that question the effectiveness of current policies and practices. Hudson and Thomas (2003) assert that it is evident that the nature of higher education in the years beyond 2000 will be quite different from the last decade of the second millennium. In many respects the key word will be a customer-driven market. So from this fact, the customer-focused evaluation has pushed the quality assurance into new heights where it has become essential for committing its role in ensuring that higher education institutions maintain quality through the adherence to agreements upon consumer-based standards.

As it is, higher education is evolving from a loosely federated system of colleges and universities serving students of the local or regional community into a global knowledge and learning industry embracing many features of industrial organizations. Because of the keen competition from other tertiary institutions, higher education is evolving as a deregulated industry similar to healthcare and communications. Thus, the global knowledge-learning industry is likely to be unleashed by the rapidly advancing information technology freeing it from the constraints of space, time and the need for accreditation. Perhaps, in the future learning could be made available for everyone, every place all the time implying continuous improvements of the products and services to attract the customers (Gamage & Ueyama, 2001). In fact, currently, the Master of Leadership and Management in Education (MLMEd) Programme of the University of Newcastle has attracted enrolments from countries such as Bhutan, Botswana, Brazil, Bangladesh, Canada, China, Hong Kong, Indonesia, Japan, Kuwait, Malaysia, Maldives, Mali, New Zealand, PNG, Samoa, Singapore, South Korea, South Africa, Philippines, Taiwan, Thailand, the United Kingdom, the United States, Vietnam and Zambia through the Internet.

In the circumstances, several universities have followed the industry's strategic orientations for working towards customer satisfaction and have initiated working with the dimensions of TQM to improve the quality of their programmes and services. Universities chose TQM to distinguish themselves better from their competitors and to compete better in the market place (Mergen, Grant, & Widrick, 2000). The prime focus of the TQM effort is directed towards achieving customer satisfaction. This involves defining customers and their requirements, improving the processes used to deliver services to customers and measuring customer satisfaction (Mergen et al., 2000). Thus universities, through mission statements, now explicitly acknowledge their obligations in meeting the needs of a range of stakeholders (Macfarlane & Lomas, 1999). This new emphasis is supported by the Dearing Report (National Committee of Inquiry into Higher Education in the UK, 1997), which makes a significant number of references to the importance of meeting stakeholders' interests. However, there is a difficulty in the definition of customer and the problem of actually determining the customers' requirements in relation to their particular product or services (Harvey & Green, 1993).

In higher education, the definition of customer is quite different from that in manufacturing or general services since groups such as students, employers, academic staff, government and families are all customers of the education system and they have diverse needs. Erwin and Knight (1995) have identified a range of stakeholders to whom higher education should be accountable including government (at all levels), employers, educational institutions themselves and their students and the public who need to know what higher education offers and to be able to place their trust in such institutions. Welsh, Alexander, and Dey (2001) suggest that this new way of looking at "customers" of education has created a need for a systematic review of how students, alumni, employers, faculty and staff perceive the quality and effectiveness of the programmes and services. Thus, it is clear that quality is in the eyes of the customer even if it has not yet been realized what actually the need is (Yorke, 1999).

Within this context, quality is a highly contested concept and has multiple meanings to people who consider higher education and quality differently. One definition of quality that is relevant to the issue of quality assurance is fitness for purpose (Harvey & Green, 1993). Vroeijenstijn (1995) defines quality assurance as the systematic, structured and continuous attention to quality in terms of quality maintenance and quality improvements. This definition captures the dual nature of quality assurance, but pressures at the end of the second millennium tended to focus attention on those elements of the definition that emphasized "fitness for purpose" rather than continuous enhancement. If quality is judged on a fitness-for-purpose basis, the purposes of student experiences and the variations in the perspectives of the relevant stakeholders need to be identified. In other words there are different stakeholders in the process and it is important to provide them with an opportunity to articulate their views (Barnett, 1997).

In the contemporary world, because of the advancement of IT and telecommunication, the students have many options to undertake their studies either on campus, off-campus or off-shore. These options enable the educational institutions to attract and retain students. For this purpose, it is imperative for universities to identify and deliver what is important to students. Higher education is increasingly recognized as a service industry and is placing greater emphasis on meeting the expectations and needs of students (Cheng & Tam, 1997). As the views of the customers assume paramount importance in a service set-up, the service quality literature has recognized the "customers' perception of service quality" and their overall satisfaction as the key determinants of institutional performance and standing (Shemwell, Yavas, & Bilgin, 1998; Spreng & Mackoy, 1996). The object of assuring customer satisfaction may be seen as two-fold. One, institutions need to attract and retain students in an efficient and an effective manner in order to stay viable. Two, the external environment demands accountability and performance measures. This has led to an increased attention to studies on measurement of students' satisfaction and their perceptions of service quality in higher education (Rowley, 1997). On the other hand, if a particular institution wants to rest on its past achievements and reputation, with no efforts to undertake continuous improvements to its programmes and services is likely to lose its place in the higher education ladder.

A study by Soutar and McNeil (1996) addressed the similarities between many service industries in the business sector and higher education and suggest that the business world's research on the assessment of service quality may be applicable to higher education. Specifically, service marketing concepts borrowed from the business and industry sector may be useful. Marketing services have developed a large body of knowledge, with a substantial proportion of it in the areas of service quality and satisfaction with services (Szymanski & Henard, 2001).

In recent years, numerous studies have been conducted on the relationship between service quality and satisfaction. Practitioners and academics alike are keen on accurately measuring service quality in order to better understand its essential antecedents and consequences, and ultimately, establishing methods for improving quality to achieve competitive advantages (Rust & Oliver, 1994). Service quality is commonly noted as a critical prerequisite for establishing and sustaining satisfying relationships with customers. In this way, the association between service quality and customer satisfaction has emerged as a topic of significant and strategic concern (Cronin & Taylor, 1992). Since then there have been many attempts to establish the nature of the relationship between service quality and customer satisfaction.

A basic agreement emanating from a wide range of literature on service quality and customer satisfaction is that service quality and customer satisfaction are conceptually distinct but closely related constructs (Dabholkar, 1995; Shemwell et al., 1998). In general, research in this area suggests that service quality is an important indicator of customer satisfaction (Spreng & Mackoy, 1996). However, it is difficult to separate the actual service quality and perceived service quality from a customer's viewpoint. Therefore, most researchers only measured perceived service quality and suggest that higher levels of perceived service quality give more satisfaction to consumers. Cronin and Taylor (1992) assert that service quality was the antecedent of consumer satisfaction when they examined four service industries of banking, pest control, dry-cleaning and fast food to investigate the relation of service quality to consumer satisfaction. The same conclusion also appeared in other studies in this area (Anderson & Sullivan, 1993; Cronin, Brady, & Hult, 2000; Fornell, 1992). In order to investigate the link between perceived service quality and customer satisfaction, operating aspects of service quality are required. It is important to recognize what aspects of service quality are important in their judgments which will ultimately lead to positive perceptions of quality and overall satisfaction.

By taking a customer-oriented approach, the role of student voice in achieving quality in higher education, becomes more important. Doherty (1994) claims that the experience of satisfaction creates the perception of good quality and good quality is satisfaction resulting from product or service fitness to purpose. In taking customer satisfaction into consideration, knowledge and better understanding of the processes and various characteristics, qualities and attributes, which underline students' perceptions of quality, are warranted. The anticipated outcome of this approach is the identification of which components of the service delivery processes are more important in their judgments which will provide clarification of the core criteria for quality assurance employed by students when evaluating quality of services.

This approach can offer us a more rounded, and in the long term more robust, view of what "quality" means in a university setting. It provides a framework for identifying students' perceptions in quality. Hill (1995) suggests that the opinions expressed by the students should be taken seriously in any discussion about quality in higher education. Despite the importance of perceived service quality as a major form of student evaluation services, the literature reveals that there has been limited research on the dynamics of the relationship between student satisfaction and service quality (Taylor & Backer, 1994).

Service Quality and Customer Satisfaction

Marketing research has also been used to identify criteria by which the students select academic programs and educational institutions. Kotler and Fox (1985) argue that the marketing concept and marketing management techniques are applicable to all colleges and universities, especially in a changing environment. The central philosophy of marketing is built on the notion of service quality and consumer satisfaction. Service quality and customer satisfaction are arguably the two core concepts that are at the crux of the marketing theory and practice (Spreng & Mackoy, 1996).

The effect of evaluative criteria in forming perceived service quality can be influenced by factors like consumers' individual characteristics such as age, gender, education and occupation (Bettman & Park, 1980; Oliver, 1980). As a consequence, when higher educational institutions undertake marketing of their programs to prospective students, it is important to consider the impact of demographics and other related variables on customers' evaluation of service quality and judgments. The satisfaction and other plausible mediating roles of perceived service quality on the effect of consumers' individual characteristics contribute towards overall satisfaction. For instance; a distance learning student of the MLMEd programme of the University of Newcastle, on the completion of his course on "Introduction to Educational Administration" after marking the student evaluation sheet at "5," that is, highest level of satisfaction has commented on the quality of the subject as follows:

> I believe this is an excellent subject and the [assessment] tasks require students to demonstrate an understanding of the contents in relation to their own personal context. I firmly believe that this subject has improved my capacity to be an effective educational leader in my school. The readings and lecturer knowledge is outstanding. Thank you. (MLMEd student, Semester 1, 2004)

A distance learning student who completed another subject (course) on "Leadership and Strategic Management" of the same programme, commenting on the quality has stated:

> This is an outstanding subject in preparing aspiring leaders for their future leadership roles. My school community is grateful for the practical nature of the subject and it has provided a long term benefit (a strategic plan and a planning framework) to the school. My only concern was assignment two on [module two].... However, that is only a minor problem. I have enjoyed completing this subject. (MLMEd student, Semester 1, 2004)

A research project involving 1,532 students from nine Thai private universities conducted by the second author in 2002 is a very good example to show that quality can be achieved even without additional resources if the quality of services can be improved with better commitments and dedication. The analysis of the data suggests that the most significant factors which contribute towards the student satisfaction are the quality of relationships between the academic staff & students, and the quality of the academic programmes (Suwarnabroma, 2004).

Global Trends

In the current context, the assurance of quality has become preeminent. As Kerr (1987) has noted, we are not experiencing an evolutionary change in higher education, but a revolutionary change. The well-known management consultant, Peter Drucker (1997) goes so far as to say that "thirty years from now university campuses will be relics, universities won't survive" (p. 1). However, the authors have some reservations on this prediction as student needs and interests vary vastly. This is obvious from the fact that in spite of the introduction of cheaper distance learning courses with identical material for the on-campus and off-campus students, some students prefer the face to face teaching with peer groups for interaction for sharing their knowledge and understanding. Even though the numbers involved in distance learning are increasing, the numbers of those who prefer on-campus teaching are increasing faster.

The expansion of higher education, the new demands for tighter linkages between universities and economic development, and the emerging international competition among universities are the factors, which have led to contemporary concerns for quality in higher education. In countries where higher education facilities are expanding rapidly, developments may take place more quickly than the establishment of monitoring procedures, with a consequent threat to quality and standards. The specific notion of the "return on investment" is invoked, requiring public attention in every country to the relative efficiency of higher education.

In recent years, there has been increasing demands by "stakeholders" in higher education for institutional accountability. These demands have come primarily from governments who argue that the public investment in higher education justifies closer scrutiny of the outcomes achieved by public funded institutions. The students also expect to receive good quality teaching and adequate learning resources to meet their needs. These demands are also driven by fears that the expansion of higher education is threatening quality (Walden, 1996). As public funding declines while the participation rates are increasing resulting in the deterioration of student-staff ratios, it is not unreasonable to ask the question: How can the public be reassured that the quality of higher education is being maintained in the face of these changes? (Porter, 2000).

The trend towards quality assurance in higher education in countries around the world reveals a need for quality systems that not only perform a regulatory function, but also improve the quality of educational experience, providing a developmental function as well. An analysis of the development of quality assurance systems in various countries can help to make an elusive concept more tangible and assist in developing a framework within which action can be taken to achieve, maintain or improve quality.

In the United States, accreditation arose before World War II because of the recognition of the need to establish standards for admission and transferability of credit. Other accreditation initiatives followed, in which specific disciplines and professions began to monitor their own programs to ensure that quality standards were met to guard against unacceptable practices. The Council for Higher Education Accreditation (CHEA) was developed as an umbrella organization for the regional and professional accrediting agencies. Thus, in 1993, CHEA emerged from the dissolution of its predecessor organization, the Council on Postsecondary Accreditation (COPA). The findings of CHEA surveys, as well as anecdotal information from various American accreditors, confirm that there is a keen interest in expanding quality review activities around the world (Eaton, 2001).

In 1990, Ernest Boyer, then President of the Carnegie Foundation for the Advancement of Teaching, in his report: *Scholarship Reconsidered: Priorities for the Professoriate*, advocates the need to place greater emphasis on teaching, generated an enormous interest leading to a number of other publications emphasizing on quality of teaching. These were designed to reflect on academics' work and how quality work is acknowledged and rewarded. Boyer's report was also followed by a companion document authored by several other eminent scholars entitled: *Scholarship Assessed: Evaluation of the Professoriate*. The general theme in these reports was the need for the assessment of scholarly work more broadly (Gamage & Mininberg, 2003).

Regionally, Europe is taking on the challenge of creating a "European education space" and currently exploring the feasibility of European accreditation of institutions and organizations (Eaton, 2001). This would place a "European" stamp on the quality review efforts of various countries. While this comprehensive European approach is attractive to some leaders in European higher education, the idea is of some concerns to others.

In 1986, the Japanese Ministry of Education established a University Council (UC) as an advisory body. The UC comprises of experts including representatives from industry and labour unions and it recommended the introduction of a "self-monitoring and self-evaluation" system in all institutions, whether they are national, local public or private. This recommendation was implemented in June 1991. The Japanese University Accreditation Association (JUAA) has also had a significant impact on these processes. In 1992, the JUAA published its guidelines for self-monitoring and self-assessment and introduced a voluntary external evaluation programme in 1996. In addition, the Ministry of Education encouraged the development of a more systematic evaluation and quality assurance programme. This policy was basically extended to the local, public and private sector universities as well (Yonezawa, 1998).

Yonezawa (2002) asserts that a sociological perspective to quality assurance provides two kinds of distinctions: (1) internal versus external assessment, and (2) centralized versus decentralized assessment. Even though Japan and Germany have similar quality assurance systems comprising of internal orientation while being decentralized, the Japanese model appears to be much better developed, and a unique one. However, as the Government was not happy with the process of voluntary self-evaluation, a new quality assurance body similar to the European quality assurance model was established. Based on a research project involving 586 Japanese universities with a response rate of 71.3%, Yonezawa (2002) has collected data on six categories such as (1) feedback by the students, (2) organizational management, (3) educational activities, (4) research activities, (5) entrant and graduate performance, and (6) contributions for the society and student services.

The data analysis has revealed that the universities with faculties of natural sciences, engineering and agriculture placed more importance on student feedback whereas the universities with social sciences have not depended on student feedback. Again the universities with faculties of medicine, dental and natural sciences, engineering and agriculture have positively correlated with research activities. These findings suggest that competition in research fields have boosted the current self-monitoring and self-evaluation activities in Japan. Further, there has been a big variation in the patterns of evaluation conducted even within the universities with very similar characteristics (Yonezawa, 2002).

In Britain, in response to the demands on quality assurance, there has been considerable growth of quality management through an internal "quality" or "standard" office. Externally, first quality assurance was implemented through the Higher Education Quality Council (HEQC, 1993–1997), and then the Quality Assurance Agency for Higher Education (QAA). The external processes have included departmental subject reviews institutional audits, benchmarking, programme specification and performance indicators (Armstrong, 2000). Therefore, higher education in Britain now operates within a framework for quality assurance, audit and assessment. Quality assurance and control are primarily the responsibility of individual institutions. The checks on whether the policies and procedures operate in practice, is the responsibility of the Division of Quality Audit of the Higher Education Quality Council (HEQC), which is the successor to the Academic Audit Unit of the Committee of Vice Chancellors and Principals (CVCP) (Gordon, 1993).

In Australia, towards the end of 1991, the Federal Minister for Higher Education and Employment Services announced that the government would provide funds for quality assurance and on enhancement programmes for universities with a prize pool of $77, $71, and $50 million from 1992 to 1995. Subsequently in 1993, the Commonwealth government established a quality assurance system to be administered by a Committee for Quality Assurance in Higher Education (CQAHE). The CQAHE conducted reviews of quality in universities from 1993 to 1995 and recommended additional funding to universities in proportion to the effectiveness of quality assurance mechanisms and excellence of their outcomes. Currently, most Australian universities have incorporated quality assurance mechanisms into their internal structures including self-evaluation of faculties and other administrative units followed by external reviews on a rolling basis. The Australian universities such as the University of Newcastle has appointed managers and assistant deans to be in charge of quality assurance at the levels of schools and faculties respectively, to ensure that continuous improvements are effected in the academic programs and services to students and the community. Course Experience Questionnaire (CEQ) and Student Evaluation of Subjects (SES) are instruments which are widely used in Australia to measure students' satisfaction with quality of university courses and services (Gamage, 2002).

In 2000, the Australian Universities Quality Agency (AUQA) was established by the Ministerial Council on Employment, Education, Training and Youth Affairs (MCEETYA) as a "not for profit" organization to:

1. arrange and manage a system of periodic audit of quality assurance arrangements relating to the activities of Australian

universities, other self-accrediting institutions (SAIs) and state and territory higher education accreditation bodies;

2. monitor, review, analyse and provide public reports on quality assurance arrangements in SAIs, and on processes and procedures of state and territory accreditation authorities, and on the impact of those processes on quality of programmes;

3. report on the criteria for the accreditation of new universities and non-university higher education courses as a result of information obtained during the audit of institutions and state and territory accreditation processes;

4. report on the relative standards of the Australian higher education system and its quality assurance processes, including their international standing, as a result of information obtained during the audit process.

The AUQA, which became operational with the appointment of the executive director in July 2001, has created a great deal of international interest. A number of delegations from China, Malaysia, New Zealand, South Africa and Thailand have visited the AUQA and had discussions with the AUQA officials for the purpose of studying the Australian approaches to quality assurance (http://www.auqa.edu.au retrieved on 15.10.2004).

In 1993, the University Mobility in Asia and Pacific (UMAP) consortium, a group of government and nongovernmental representatives of universities in the region, was formed to meet the region's challenges to enhance student and staff mobility. In view of the fact that successful credit transfers are ultimately tied to perceptions of institutional quality, UMAP is being pressured to establish additional quality assurance linkages around the world.

In Norway, the advent of the policy for quality and integration can be traced back to a media controversy in the national daily *Dagbladet* during the spring of 1986. Gudmund Hernes of the University of Oslo, while being a guest professor at the Harvard University, initiated the controversy by contributing an article titled "Is it possible to be ambitious in Norway?" (Hernes, 1986). He criticized the Norwegian universities; especially his own for mediocrity and suggested that one might learn something about academic standards and ambitions from Harvard. In 1987, Hernes, who was also a politician, was appointed to head a commission on higher education reforms and the report was released in 1988.

The policy recommendations of the Hernes Commission were couched in the language of "quality" but "efficiency" was considered a fundamental value. It placed a heavy emphasis on output and the speed with which an output of acceptable quality is produced. The Commission report won immediate approval from university academics as there was something to gain by all affected parties. The report based its recommendations on the premise that research based knowledge of all types was in demand. Its arguments for basic education and graduate education provided a new legitimacy for increased budgets and more teaching positions. The Commission also based its recommendations on the premise that there should be a 5% real annual growth in university budgets in the coming years, so there would be some gain for all academic groups. The concern for quality had a strong appeal to the academics and made it harder for them not to be favourably inclined (Hernes, 1988).

It is important to note that many of the Commission's specific recommendations came from the universities themselves or the major trade unions representing the staff in universities. The report supported the "binary system" with its clear distinctions between the university and college sectors. The devolution of responsibility from the Ministry to the institutions also pleased the administrators. Finally, the consensus culture of the Norwegian political and administrative life enabled the institutionalization of the quality culture within the Norwegian higher education. Once again when he was a guest professor at Harvard in 1990, he was asked to accept the position of the Minister for Education, to which he agreed by expressing concerns regarding the quality in the entire system of Norwegian education. Hernes suggested that university teachers should ask questions such as: How many teachers are actually active researchers? How many teachers do really inspire their students? He also pointed out that students gave the best years of their lives to the university to be cheated because they were not given the opportunity to develop their abilities to full potential. Finally, he called for a new assessment system on teaching and research to improve the quality of teaching and research (Bleiklie, Hostaker, & Vabe, 2000).

In 1989, the Hong Kong government adopted a policy of dramatic expansion of its higher education system in order to double the first year university enrolments from 9% of the age group in 1989/1990 to 18% by 1994/1995. It was believed that amongst the reasons for such a rapid expansion was the demand for a highly qualified workforce and the loss of well trained graduates through emigration prior to 1997 due to the political uncertainty. By then, Hong Kong was able to establish seven universities and two degree awarding institutions and one tertiary level teacher education institution along with one private post-secondary college. However, in Hong Kong, the primary responsibility for quality assurance rests with the individual institutions themselves (University Grants Committee of Hong Kong, 1996).

But, in view of the fact that the University Grants Committee (UGC) has to be accountable for the large public expenditure amounting to HK$14 billion a year, several measures were taken to actively monitor quality assurance to ensure that quality is not missed in the midst of quantity. In doing so the UGC had to balance its public accountability with the institutional autonomy and the academic freedom. In 1990, the Hong Kong Council of Academic Accreditation (HKCAA) was established to advise the UGC on the academic quality and standards of degree programs proposed or offered by the non-university institutions. Recognizing that quality teaching is a primary responsibility of all public funded institutions, the UGC conducted a series of Teaching and Learning Quality Process Reviews from 1996 to 1997 (TLQPRs) in all relevant institutions. According to Young (cited in Tam, 1999) these reviews focused on institutions' teaching and learning quality assurance processes and the appropriateness and adequacy of the processes for maintaining and improving the quality of teaching and learning. Even though the UGC recognized that it is difficult to establish a set of quantitative indicators to measure the quality of teaching and learning in any meaningful way, it was assumed that the introduction of an element of qualitative assessment, through inspections, peer reviews and visits would make such a process more meaningful.

In addition, reviews for the purpose of ensuring that the institutions have instituted appropriate and effective processes to manage the devolved funds and other resources towards the accomplishment of institutional aims and objectives were also introduced. French (cited in Tam, 1999) has pointed out that these management reviews were meant to examine the institutions' allocation of resources, planning and financial processes as well as institutional roles, missions and academic objectives. However, the main aim of the reviews are to assist the institutions in enhancing the quality of their management by promoting the sharing of experiences and best practices towards the achievement of institutional objectives. Apart from the above reviews, since 1994, the UGC introduced the research assessment exercise to assess the proportion of the academics who can be regarded as active in research as an indicator to be factored into institutional funding. The purpose of this exercise is to assess the academic performance through the research output in allocating a portion of research funding with the recurrent grant for the next triennium (University Grants Committee of Hong Kong, 1996).

On the other hand, in Singapore, the quality assurance is managed by the institutions themselves without being centrally directed. The improvement of quality and academic standards is a central goal of universities to achieve a competitive edge in a highly competitive global market. Quality assurance is applied as a means to ensure that universities are well managed in response to pressure for accountability and efficiency in a country dominated by the market philosophy. Singaporean universities have adopted the management concepts, theories and practices from the private sector. Gopinathan and Morris (1997) have pointed out that the purpose of quality assurance and audit in Singapore is to make sure that quality of teaching and research can be improved and resources can be distributed in a more rational manner. According to Selvaratnam (1994), quality assurance and enhancement is partly achieved by the recruitment of talented and outstanding local and overseas scholars. The quality of university education is reinforced by four main strategies: (1) a stringent tenure policy, (2) rewards for good teaching and performance in research with incentives and recognition, (3) favourable staff-student ratio accompanied by well equipped teaching and research facilities, and (4) the provision of staff training to upgrade the skills and performance of university staff.

In Thailand, especially after the Asian financial crisis of the mid-1990s, university enrolments were badly affected and the effect on private universities, were far worse than that of state universities. A government instituted high-powered committee of enquiry blamed the poor quality of education imparted to the students for the country's economic problems. The Committee Report made "the quality" as the key to training students for the purpose of competing in the job market in an era of globalization (Vargo, 1998). The Thai government believed that Thailand's future depends on generating good leaders and citizens, building upon the experience of the past, learning from the circumstances of the present, and preparing for the challenges of the future. In order to realize these goals, Thai government committed itself to promoting high quality education by adopting a quality assurance system.

The Ministry of University Affairs (1998) of Thailand established the Eighth Thai Higher Education Development Plan (HEDP), 1997–2001. The overall purpose of HEDP is to raise the education standards and academic excellence in keeping with the concept of TQM in all public and private universities. In the circumstances, the Ministry of University Affairs, which was responsible for all universities, encouraged the universities to offer a world-class education. In recent times, in a highly competitive management environment in Thailand, the application of TQM measures has become an important strategy for quality improvement. Many colleges and universities in Thailand's educational sector have introduced the TQM concepts and activities (Office of the National Education Commission, 2001). TQM has been described as a management philosophy and a way of thinking that has helped many organizations towards achieving excellence in their core-business.

Reported Benefits of Applying TQM

Since the late 1980s, many tertiary institutions have experimented with many different approaches and types of quality assurance mechanisms. Apart from the institutions themselves, the higher education systems have imposed certain types of quality reviews to improve the quality of higher educational programmes and services. Britain has played a major role in establishing a number of structures for the imposition of quality assurance reviews. Benefits accrued from the pioneering attempts to apply TQM in colleges and universities in different contexts and situations could be identified as:

1. providing the staff with opportunities to engage directly in the improvement of their working environments;
2. a change of attitudes from explaining, to listening to their customers;
3. improved organizational cultures, attitudes and morale;
4. more emphasis on collection and analysis of data and data-based decision making;
5. effective communication and better working relations between people in different departments, schools and faculties with related functions;
6. the development of a common language on issues relating to quality, irrespective of the organizational components;
7. increased knowledge and understanding on organizational visions, goals and strategies towards the accomplishment of the shared vision; and
8. direct savings in ongoing expenses and indirect savings in potential expenses.

The above benefits that could be gained through the application of TQM in organizational settings and recent emphasis on quality in higher education should lead to positive effects resulting in the expansion of the implementation of TQM in universities. Sallis (1993) asserts that TQM is a quality culture which has moved beyond notions of quality control and quality assurance to provide a philosophy and methodology which help institutions to manage change and to set their own agendas for dealing with the external world. The quality culture is one "where the aim of every member of staff is to delight their customers." To implement TQM fully, it is necessary to build a firm focus on customers as the definers of quality. The complex array of customers and their needs make this a challenging activity for a university. Thus, it is necessary to examine higher education institutions in terms of all stakeholders and their perceptions on the quality of education.

Conclusion

The adoption of quality assurance measures by the higher educational institutions in particular and other educational institutions in general is no longer an option; it is a necessity for survival in a competitive world. The increasing costs and decreasing public funding and its inability to compete with areas such as health and basic education have encouraged governments to support privatization of higher education. This measure is forcing the existing institutions to resort to continuous improvement of the quality of programs and services for their own survival. Besides, because of the rising costs, many countries are shifting the burden of payment to the very customers who consume the products and services of higher education. This has resulted in consumers demanding high quality returns for their investments. These trends have necessitated the higher educational institutions to ensure quality of their products and services as a means of survival. The need for TQM in higher education gains importance because it is built on the tradition of a concern for quality. It recognizes the need for continuous development of people, whether students, faculty or administrators. It involves principles applicable to institutional administration, high quality programs, research, teaching and community service. Thus, it provides a bridge between the traditionally separated parts of the system; as a step towards meeting the new challenges and building more effective colleges and universities of the 21st century striving towards excellence and customer satisfaction.

References

Albrecht, K. (1991). Total quality service. *Executive Excellence, 8*(7), 18–19.

Anderson, E. W., & Sullivan, M. W. (1993). The antecedents and consequences of customer satisfaction for firms. *Marketing Science, 12*(1), 125–143.

Armstrong, P. (2000). Never mind the quality, measure the length: Issues for lifelong learning. In R. Edwards, J. Clarke, & N. Miller (Eds.), *Supporting lifelong learning working papers* (pp. 132–146). London: Open University, University of East London.

Barnett, R. (1997). Still breathing: Are universities on their deathbeds? *THES, 3* (May), 10–13.

Bemowski, K. (1991). Restoring the pillars of higher education. *Quality Progress, 24*(10), 37–42.

Bettman, J. R., & Park, C. W. (1980). Effects of prior knowledge and experience and phase of the choice process on consumer decision processes: A protocol analysis. *Journal of Consumer Research, 7*(3), 234–248.

Bleiklie, I., Hostaker, R., & Vabe, A. (2000). *Policy and practice in higher education: Reforming Norwegian universities.* London: Jessica Kinglsley Publishers.

Bonser, C. (1992). Total quality education. *Public Administration Review, 52*(5), 504–512.

Bonstingl, J. J. (1992). *Schools of quality: An introduction to total quality management in education.* Alexandria, VA: Association for Supervision and Curriculum Development.

Brown, D. J., & Koenig, H. F. (1993). Applying total quality management to business education. *Journal of Education for Business, 68*(6), 325–329.

Cannon, J. P., & Sheth, J. N. (1994). Developing curriculum to enhance teaching of relationship marketing. *Journal of Marketing Education,* Summer, 3–14.

Cheng, Y. C., & Tam, M. M. (1997). Multi-models of quality in education. *Quality Assurance in Education, 5,* 22–31.

Cole, R. (1998). Learning from the quality management. *California Management Review, 41,* 43–73.

Corts, T. E. (1992). Customers: You can't do without them. In J. W. Harris & M. Baggett (Eds.), *Quality quest in the Academic process.* Bermingham: Samford University.

Cronin, J. J., Brady, K. M., & Hult, M. T. (2000). Assessing the effects of quality, value, and customer satisfaction on consumer behavior intentions in service environments. *Journal of Retailing, 76*(2), 193–218.

Cronin, J. J., & Taylor, S. A. (1992). Measuring service quality. *Journal of Marketing, 56*(7), 55–68.

Crosby, P. B. (1979). *Quality is free: The art of making quality certain.* New York: McGraw Hill.

Dabholkar, P. A. (1995). Contingency framework for predicting causality between customer satisfaction and service quality. In M. Sujan & F. Kardes (Eds.), *Advances in customer research: Vol. 22* (pp. 101–108).

Dagbladet (1986). (a Norwegian newspaper). 31st August.

Dahlgaard, J. J., Kristensen, K., & Kanji, G. K. (1995). Total quality management and education. *Total Quality Management, 6*(5 & 6), 445–455.

Deming, W. E. (1986). *Out of crisis: Quality, productivity and competitive position.* Cambridge, United Kingdom: Cambridge University Press.

Doherty, G. (1994). Can we have a unified theory of quality? *Higher Education Quarterly, 48* (4), 241–255.

Drucker, P. F. (1997, April 18). The fate of big universities; institutions without political agendas; monkey grooming; risks for poets; the Jewish scholar's responsibility. *The Chronicle of Higher Education,* pp. b7–9.

Eaton, J. S. (2001). Accreditation and quality in the United States: Practice and pressure. In D. Dunkerley & W. S. Wong (Eds.), *Global perspectives on quality in higher education* (pp. 91–105). Aldershot Hants, United Kingdom; Gurlington, VT: Ashgate.

Erwin, T. D., & Knight, P. (1995). A transatlantic view of assessment and quality in higher education. *Quality in Higher Education, 1,* 179–188.

Fields, J. C. (1993). *Total quality for schools: A suggestion for American education.* Milwaukee, WI: ASQC.

Fornell, C. (1992). A national customer satisfaction barometer: The Swedish experience. *Journal of Marketing, 56*(1), 6–21.

Gamage, D. T. (2002). Recent reforms, current issues and policy directions in the Australian and Japanese university systems. *World Studies in Education, 3* (2), 119–136.

Gamage, D. T., & Mininberg, E. (2003). The Australian and American higher education: Key issues of the first decade of the 21st century. *Higher Education, 45*(2), 183–201.

Gamage, D. T., & Ueyama, T. (2001). The American system of higher education: Current issues, challenges and trends. *Studies in International Relations, 21*(4), 267–292.

Gopinathan, S., & Morris, S. (1997). Trends in university reforms in the context of massification. *RIHE International Seminar Reports*, No. 1, pp. 55–71.

Gordon, G. (1993). Quality assurance in higher education: Progress achieved and issues to be addressed. *Quality Assurance in Education, 1*(3), 15–20.

Harvey, L. (1995). Student satisfaction. *Review of Academic Librarianship, 1,* 161–173.

Harvey, L., & Green, D. (1993). Defining quality. *Assessment and Evaluation in Higher Education, 18*(1), 9–34.

Hernes, G. (1986, December 31). Kan man ha ambisjoner I Norge? [Is it possible to be ambitious in Norway?] *Dagbladet* (a Norwegian newspaper).

Hill, F. M. (1995). Managing services quality in higher education: The role of the student as primary consumer. *Quality Assurance in Education, 3*(3), 10–21.

Hudson, P., & Thomas, H. (2003). Quality assurance in higher education: Fit for the new millennium of simply year 2000 complaint? *Higher Education, 45*(3), 375–387.

Kerr, C. (1987). A critical age in the university world: Accumulated heritage versus modern imperatives. *European Journal of Education, 22,* 183–193.

Kotler, P., & Fox, K. (1985). *Strategic marketing for educational institutions.* Englewood Cliffs, NJ: Prentice Hall.

Macfarlane, B., & Lomas, L. (1999). Stakeholder conceptions of quality in single company management education. *Quality Assurance in Education, 7*(2), 77–84.

Mergen, E., Grant, D., & Widrick, M. S., (2000). Quality management applied to higher education. *Total Quality Management, 11*(3), 345–352.

Miller, J. W. (1996). A working definition for total quality management (TQM) researchers. *Journal of Quality Management, 1*(2), 149–159.

Ministry of University Affairs (1998). *The Eighth national Education Development Plan (1997–2001).* Bangkok: Nitikul Publishing.

Morgan, C., & Murgatroyd, S. (1994). *Total quality management in public sector: An international perspective.* Buckingham, United Kingdom: Open University Press.

Muller, D., & Funnell, P. (1992). Initiating change in further and vocational education: The quality approach. *Journal of Further and Higher Education, 16* (1), 41–49.

Newby, P. (1999). Culture and quality in higher education. *Higher Education Policy, 12,* 261–275.

Office of the National Education Commission (2001). *Higher Development Education Plan.* Bangkok: ONEC.

Oliver, R. L. (1980). A cognitive model of the antecedents and consequences of satisfaction decisions. *Journal of Marketing Research, 17*(November), 460–469.

Ouchi, W. (1981).*Theory Z.* Reading, MA: Addison-Wesley.

Owlia, M., & Aspinwall, E. (1996). Quality in higher education: A survey. *Total Quality Management, 7*(2), 161–171.

Peter, M. (1992). Performance indicators in New Zealand higher education: Accountability or control? *Journal of Education Policy, 7*(3), 267–283.

Porter, P. (2000). Globalization and higher education policy. *Educational Theory, 50*(4), 449–465.

Rowley, J. (1997). Beyond service quality dimensions in higher education and towards a service contract. *Quality Assurance in Education, 5*(1), 7–14.

Rust, R. T., & Oliver, R. L. (1994). Service quality: Insights and managerial implications from the frontier. *International Management, 35*(4), 12–18.

Sallis, E. (1993). *Total quality management in education.* Philadelphia, PA: Kogan Page.

Selvaratnam, V. (1994). *Innovations in higher education: Singapore at the competitive edge.* Washington, DC: World Bank.

Seymour, D. T. (1992). *On Q: Causing quality in higher education.* New York: Macmillan.

Shemwell, D. J., Yavas, U., & Bilgin, Z. (1998). Customer-service provider relationships: An empirical test of a model of service quality, satisfaction and relationship oriented outcome. *International Journal of Service Industry Management, 9,* 155–168.

Soutar, G. & McNeil, M. (1996). Measuring service quality in tertiary institution. *Journal of Educational administration, 34*(1), 72–82.

Spreng, R. A., & Mackoy, R. D. (1996). An empirical examination of a model of perceived service quality and satisfaction. *Journal of Retailing, 72,* 201–214.

Suwarnabroma, J. (2004). *Core-criteria for quality assurance: An exploration of students' perceptions of service quality in Thai higher education.* Unpublished doctoral dissertation, University of Newcastle, Australia.

Szymanski, D., & Henard, D. (2001). Customer satisfaction: A meta-analysis of the empirical evidence. *Journal of the Academy of Marketing Science, 29*(1), 16–35.

Tam, M. (1999). Quality assurance policies in higher education in Hong Kong. *Journal of Higher Education Policy and Management, 21*(2), 215–223.

Taylor, A. S., & Baker, L. T. (1994). An assessment of the relationship between service quality and customer satisfaction in the formation of consumers' purchase. *Journal of Retailing, 70*(2), 163–179.

University Grants Committee of Hong Kong. (1996). *Higher education in Hong Kong—A report.* Hong Kong: University Grants Committee.

Vargo, E. (1998). Thailand's economic crisis slows down public and private higher education. *International Higher Education, 18*(Summer), 23–25.

Vazzana, G., Elfrink, J., & Bachmann, P. D. (2000). A longitudinal study of total quality management in business college. *Journal of Education for Business, 76* (2), 69–74.

Vroeijenstijn, A. L. (1995). *Improvement and accountability: Navigating between Scylla and Charybdis.* London: Jessica Kingsley.

Walden, G. (1996). *We should know better: Solving the education crisis.* London: Fourth Estate.

Walton, M. (1986). *The Deming management method.* New York: Corwin Press.

Welsh, F. J., Alexander, S., & Dey, S. (2001). Continuous quality measurement: restructuring assessment for a new technological and organizational environment. *Assessment & Evaluation in Higher Education, 26*(5), 391–401.

Wilkinson, A., & Witcher, B. J. (1991). Fitness for use? Barriers to full TQM in the UK. *Management Decision, 29*(8), 46–51.

Yonezawa, A. (1998). Further privatization in Japanese higher education. *International Higher Education, 13*(Fall), 20–22.

Yonezawa, A. (2002). The quality assurance system and market forces in Japanese higher education. *Higher Education, 43*(2), 127–139.

Yorke, M. (1992). Quality in higher education: A conceptualization and some observations on the implementation of sect oral quality system. *Journal of Higher Education, 16*(2), 90–103.

Internet References

http://www.oer.or.th
http://www.onec.go.th
http://www.siam.th.edu.
http://www.qa.mua.go.th
http://www.auqa.edu.au

6

Developing Higher Degrees in Context and Culture for Globalization

Alan T. LARKIN

—ⱳ—

Abstract

This chapter starts with a discussion of the terms international, internationalization and globalization in relation to post-graduate studies at Australian and western universities. It then makes clear distinctions between the international marketing of educational programmes, learning resources designed for domestic markets and delivery systems and teaching processes designed for a homeland culture and the development of programmes that are designed in a global context. Further, it then discusses what it might mean to design, develop and deliver post-graduate programmes that have global relevance because they are built upon "universals" that apply across national and cultural boundaries and that retain sufficient flexibility to allow different groups of students to explore their interests and needs within their own local context.

International students come not only from different countries but also from different ethnic groups, religious groups and communities that are contained in specific geographical areas. Even different students coming from the same diverse nation such as Indonesia exhibit significant differences in the way that they communicate, form relationships, and they learn. The chapter argues that programmes, learning resources, expected outcomes and teaching methodologies designed for the home students may not be appropriate or relevant to students from other national, cultural or religious backgrounds.

It is argued that, for a post-graduate programme to be sustainable in the global context, it must be designed from the ground up with due regard to the different needs and preferences of all of the participating students no matter from which country or location they may come. The initial influx of international students into graduate programmes in Australia is unlikely to continue unless the international students return to their home country after successfully completing their awards with tales that highlight how well they were included socially and culturally, how well they programmes met their educational needs and preferences. In addition, the transferability and relevance of what they have learnt outside their own country will be the basis of their ultimate recommendations to their employers, their family and friends for their future study plans.

Whilst a number of broad issues are discussed, these take on more significance when the writer refers to many episodes from his own work with international students. He describes a more personal approach to students, to teaching and research, and to forming relationships with students from Australia and from the various countries in the Southeast Asia and Pacific regions.

The chapter includes some insights into the emerging issues, how these might be better addressed and some strategies for those wishing to embark on more global approaches to the provision and delivery of post-graduate programmes for multi-national groups. Whilst there are intentions of improving the lot of international students and ensuring more sustainable programmes as a result, the advantages and improvements to the local students should not be over looked. By adopting a truly global approach, all students including both those from the host country and from other countries will directly benefit at the same time. By creating a truly global approach, all students will benefit in what will inevitably become a "win-win" situation.

Introduction

CThe central focus of this chapter involves the application of the term "globalization" to the provision of coursework or "combined" coursework and research post-graduate awards as they are offered by universities in the so-called developed countries of the world such as Australia. The alternative term of "internationalization" will be distinguished and the implications and ramifications of developing truly "global" approaches to post-graduate education will be introduced and discussed. The author's extensive experience with the coordination, development and delivery of coursework topics and his experiences as a peer of international students when he was himself a mature-age student will be utilized to supplement ideas arising from the literature.

Globalization—Definitions and Key Issues

In 1995, the author was asked to deliver a staff development seminar on globalization in technical education at the Vocational Education Development Centre (VEDC) for Technical Education at Malang, East Java in Indonesia. The pertinent issues raised at the time included the development of high quality products, ensuring reliable supplies available on demand and guaranteeing that supplies would be available in sufficient quantities and at the times and locations that they are required. Each of these factors posed significant challenges for the participants who had, until that time, worked in a government system in which government officials determined production schedules, production volumes and acceptable quality standards. Any move to globalize in the technical field would clearly necessitate attention to new masters—managers involved in exporting, the international clients and those concerned with distribution and supply in other countries.

These observations were strongly reinforced in many discussions about "export quality" and "export incentives" in Australia. Where there was a high export demand on an Australian primary product or manufactured good, the domestic markets would see a shortage of good quality merchandise. This was very apparent at times in the fruit and vegetable markets, fish and lobster markets and in some areas of manufacturing. Such observations may explain why many Australians saw the arrival of international students, in significant numbers, as a threat to access of local young people to higher education. Would these intruders take the university places that our sons and daughters would otherwise get? The truth of the matter, of course, was that the places filled by international students were not the same places that could have been filled by Australian students. Universities were simply supplementing their income, now diminishing as a result of changes in the local political climate, by creating previously unfunded university places. Unfortunately, much of the general public in Australia was not made aware of this and some scepticism prevailed.

Even a short time spent searching the literature, in printed and electronic forms, devoted to the phenomenon of globalization reveals a very diverse range of issues, definitions and wide-ranging discussions. In its early days, globalization was seen to involve quality, matching supply and demand and timely delivery as mentioned earlier. There was little interest or concern about a "bigger picture" view. For example, there seemed to be little or no consideration of impacts on employment figures, ecological issues, social or moral issues or the inter-connectedness of the multitude of marketing, management, development or sales issues when working in the so-called in a "global village."

Knight and de Wit (1997) contribute the following working definition to assist us to clarify the relatedness and contrasts between "internationalization" and "globalization":

> Internationalization of higher education is the process of integrating an international/intercultural dimension into the teaching, research and service functions of the institution. (p. 16)

In 1999, de Wit noted the frequent confusion between international education, which embraces multicultural education, cross-cultural education and study abroad, with internationalization as a set of activities that may in the long term lead to international education.

De Wit (1999, p. 4) provided us with some specific insights into the possible economic rationale for internationalization. He suggested that higher education should be seen much more as a commodity that could be marketed in international market places that should address the needs of a global labour force and one that could significantly increase Australia's export income.

Kezar (2000) identified globalization as one of the significant issues of the time:

> Institutions are forming alliances; others are aggressively seeking new markets in areas that directly compete with institutions that they were never in competition with before. The advent of distance education makes a student a consumer, anywhere in the world. Some institutions are reconsidering notions of cooperative arrangements and are thinking about strategic alliances. (p. 8)

She also poses many pertinent questions and advises her readers that there may well be some significant impacts on the students and their learning, and urges institutions to review their educational alliances.

Fung-Surya (2001) posed the question "Why recruit internationally?" and the answers she arrived at are illuminating:

Colleges and universities recruit international students for two main reasons. First, there are the obvious financial benefits to be gained from enrolling fee-paying international students. More importantly though, is that most institutions try to attract international students to their campuses to foster a diverse student population. This is particularly true for colleges in suburban and rural areas …

A crucial factor in overseas recruitment, which admission personnel should be aware of, is word of mouth. Most international students reported that prior to their applying to a school, they either have relatives staying there or friends currently attending who highly recommend the school to them. Affordable living conditions and a rapidly growing ethnically diverse international community will also attract some applicants. International students also find it appealing and comfortable coming to a city where they can find familiar faces. (p. 2)

Fung-Surya provides considerable insights into the recruitment of and factors influencing the satisfaction of international students studying abroad. She provides a summary of some of the more successful recruiting strategies.

Greenfield and Pringle (2001) share their understanding of the term as follows: Most people see globalization as a process of change, which many have been persuades as natural and inevitable (p. 1). They also advise that it involves breaking down national borders and creating a single "global village."

Greenfield and Pringle (2001), in discussing the meaning of the term, provided the following:

[Globalization is] a rapid increase in international trade and investment in the last 20 years which is breaking down national borders and creating a single global economy—often called the 'global village'. Most people see globalization as a process of change, which many have been persuaded as natural and inevitable. (p. 1)

Pettigrew (2000) made useful contrasts between internationaliza- tion as increased interdependence among societies as nation-states whilst he saw globalization as a more recent phenomenon and as the result of technological advances, trade liberalization and deregulation. He sees a merging of economic spaces and the diminishing influence of political borders.

The internationalization of higher education is the focus of the article written by J. S. Jorgensen (2002). She reported on the numbers of students studying at least one semester outside of their native Denmark. The focus here is on cross-cultural experiences achieved through the movement of students across national boundaries. This writer's interpretation of the term is entirely consistent with the views of Knight and de Wit cited earlier (1997).

Haakenson (1994) identified the trend for curriculum at all levels of education to broaden to include images, issues and information from communities around the world. He noted that media and the entertainment industry have made this trend more apparent and claims that they have contributed to both intercultural understanding and misunderstanding within nations and across the world. It is interesting that this author maintains the interchangeability of the terms global and international education.

In 1999, Tootell (1999) presented a useful overview and chronology of the evolution of the incidence of international student enrolments in Australian universities. In her opening paragraph she said quite frankly:

> International students are an integral component of our higher education system. Historically, Australian universities have viewed international students in an increasingly materialistic manner, following a shift in philosophy from educational "aid" in the 1950s to educational "trade" in the 1970s. A recent development of policy by the Government, and consequently universities, is the policy of internationalization. As universities competitively market courses to this growing group of fee-paying students, questions are emerging regarding the effectiveness and appropriateness of the education offered to them and the scope of their needs. (p. 1)

Later, she quoted Randall (taken from Brown & Dale, 1989), making her meaning even clearer:

> The emphasis has moved from 'aid' and promoting international understanding, whereby selected students from developing countries were provided with opportunities to acquire skills and knowledge, to an emphasis on expanding access and packaging and marketing higher education outside Australia. (Tootell, 1999, p. 2)

At this point, Tootell was flagging up the need for Australian universities to supplement their incomes by moving more explicitly into a client-provider relationship with previously untapped market potential being realized. Now the international activities involve off-shore marketing and the increase in enrolments either on-campus in Australia or in off-shore student cohorts in other countries. Australian universities were selling their domestic products offshore to supplement their diminishing incomes.

Senior staff in universities saw the need to create new units and services to handle the off-shore marketing, the administration of arrangements for international students when they arrived and the handling of things such as international student fees, student visas and medical insurances. These services became part of the university's infrastructure and the era of the International Office had arrived.

Porter and Vidovich (2000) declare that:

> Globalization is a complex concept used with increasing frequency but often with different meaning by different commentators who may be focussing on different dimensions. People throughout the world are experiencing aspects of globalization but the experiences themselves are not all the same for all people. (p. 1)

Taylor, Rizvi, Lingard, and Henry (1997) described globalization as "a set of processes which in various ways—economic, cultural, and political—make supranational connections" (p. 53).

London School of Economics and Political Science, through its Centre for Educational Research provide us with ADMIT which is a valuable synthesis of literature reviews. London School of Economics, in reviewing their position as part of their ADMIT Project for internationalization of higher education, summarized its findings as follows. Firstly, they found that there was no clear agreement on what internationalization meant in the higher education sector. Secondly, the status quo with regard to internationalization was almost entirely based on the mobility of students, particularly under-graduate students, and staff. This might have suggested that internationalization simply meant the export of courses developed for local markets to foreign parts either on-campus (bring the students to us) or off-shore (send our staff there). Further, they found that

> There is little hard evidence on the precise benefits of educating incoming overseas students. However, it is clear that these students, as a group, are of financial importance to the British economy.

A number of non-economic benefits accrue to the staff and students of higher education institutions; these include benchmarking, of standards for quality control purposes; a stimulus to course innovation; cultural and intellectual enrichment; and an environment more conducive to mutual understanding between different ethnic groups. Likewise it is possible to identify several non-economic benefits to the UK. These include promotion of the English language; promotion of British culture; and fostering of understanding between races. (ADMIT, 1999, p. 12)

Various groups, large and small, local and international, have very mixed and often polarized views of globalization. The International Monetary Fund (2000) acknowledged the apparent polarity of views and records some of the perspectives as follows:

Globalization offers extensive opportunities for truly worldwide development but it is not progressing evenly. Some countries are becoming integrated into the global economy more quickly than others. Countries that have been able to integrate are seeing faster growth and reduced poverty. (p. 1)

The on-line report continues with discussion of how the poorest countries can catch up more quickly. It advised that the packaging together of policies, financial and technical assistance and debt relief may be necessary if globalization is to have positive outcomes and that the components of such a package might include:

- macroeconomic stability to create the right conditions for investment and saving;
- outward oriented policies to promote efficiency through increased trade and investment;
- structural reform to encourage domestic competition;
- strong institutions and an effective government to foster good governance;
- education, training, and research and development to promote productivity;
- external debt management to ensure adequate resources for sustainability (International Monetary Fund, 2000, p. 7).

Given that the higher education providers that are delivering education, training and research expertise to students from the developing countries, it may just make sense if those areas were delivered in a context or at least in cognizance of the various components of such packages.

Globalization: Hazards and Responsibilities

Aman (2002) noted that:

> Globalization can, indeed, have very visible, negative effects on communities and individuals' lives. As noted above, some industries may close down and relocate to other jurisdictions or countries. Others may lose market share to global competitors and downsize their workforces considerably. At a minimum, the result for many jurisdictions can be layoffs, fewer jobs, and a lower tax base. (p. 2)

Reflecting on the implications on traditional regulatory systems, Aman (2002) also noted:

> Globalization means that the line that once may have existed between global and domestic economic and political forces, as well as the line traditionally drawn between domestic and international law, is blurry at best and often non-existent. (p. 3)

Mardle (2001) gave us a much broader perspective on globalization:

> Globalization is not a strategy, nor is it a practice or a process. Globalization is a perception, an act of very substantial imagination.
>
> The problem that most of us have is that we identify ourselves with a specific place. That gives us a centre which implies a periphery. There is here, and somewhere else. I call this level playing field thinking. It is two dimensional, bounded in space and time; it has an edge and middle. It is a workable approach for a local business and wholly at odds with any notion of globalization which is 4 dimensional, unbounded in space and time, with no periphery, and no centre. (p. 1)

In the introduction to his address, Mardle warns those of us contemplating entry into the world of global enterprise as follows:

> Globalization is at a turning point. Most of the easy gains have been made and the success stories are being balanced by failures that are exciting criticism and opposition from many quarters. As with any radical revision of human relations, the initial promise was overblown, the downsides minimized and the reality is likely to be more mundane than the prospectus painted. (p. 1)

Mardle introduced his concerns about the sustainability of our planet's ecosystem, the viability of the international economic systems and the quality of our lives should globalization continue the way it has emerged. These should all be sobering thoughts and promote far greater concerns about the impact of opportunistic enterprises in developed countries on the rest of our world. In particular, Mardle questions the viability of globalization in terms of economic and resources world-wide:

> A genuine market is a self-sustaining process in which all the players can create something of value to the others and enough supply competition that no-one has to impoverish themselves to buy the basics of life.
>
> The real challenge of Globalization is to find business models that can continuously and progressively increase the number of potential customers and enrich them enough to become consumers of sustainable goods and services. Which is precisely the opposite of what is happening. (p. 3)

This clearly suggests that globalization must heed the need for larger markets but at the same time strive to achieve self-sustaining processes by which both the client and provider meet their basic needs.

The effects of these changes on higher education are outlined by Porter and Vidovich (2000) who quote Slaughter and Leslie (1997):

> [The] ... worst-case scenario involves less discretionary government funding, institutional destabilization, greater differentiation developing between universities, greater concentration of research funds on commercially exploitable science and technology linked to the needs of industry, academics in fields close to the markets having opportunity to become successful "academic capitalists" and those at a distance from the markets consigned to mass teaching, staff in market driven centres having considerable autonomy and those in non market-driven departments being more tightly controlled, increases in fees/tuition, the employment of part-time and contract staff to save money, and the increased dissatisfaction of the public with the quality of basic undergraduate teaching. (Porter & Vidovich, 2000, p. 13)

The potential long-term side effects could very easily become the main effects of the process of globalization and we are cautioned not to engage in thoughtless battles with our competitors over market share, competitive course fees and staffing strategies to bolster profitability and productivity figures to the detriment of all players.

Globalizations: Lessons We Can Learn From Others

The publications of the YMCA World Index have addressed the emergence of globalization. Khor (2000), Director of Third World Network, has suggested that:

> Globalization as practised today is a kind of apartheid. It is misleading and it skirts the issues to talk only in terms of "sharing better the benefits of globalization" and "helping the marginalized". This presumes that globalization only produces benefits, but some gain more than others. In reality, globalization creates benefits for some, losses for others, and worse, the same process that generates benefits also generates losses. So, part of the benefits of the gainers is at the expense of the losses of the losers. (p. 1)

In the same volume of the World Index, Gomez (2000), Executive Secretary of Africa Alliance of YMCAs, warns readers that:

> It is very dangerous for developing nations to blindly embrace globalization. To equate globalization with a guarantee for economic advancement is indeed a gross over-simplification of realities that surround international trade. Africa today does not have the capacity to enter the global village, as it is still grappling with basic necessities such as road, railways and transport.
>
> To most Africans globalization means nothing but access of products from the developed nations into the developing nations. (p. 3)

This perspective seems to be consistent with the sentiments expressed as film dialogue by Kenneth Branagh as the character Mr. Neville, the Chief Protector of Aboriginal Peoples in Western Australia, in the Philip Noyce movie of the book *Follow the Rabbit-proof Fence* by Doris Pilkington (2002). In justifying the separation of Aboriginal children from their mothers, this Englishman in a position of power in early Australia said:

> … hundreds of half-caste children have been gathered up and brought here to be given the benefit of everything our culture has to offer. For if we are to fit and train such children for the future they cannot be left as they are and in spite of himself the native must be helped. (dialogue from the 2002 film)

These colonialist sentiments are of course now seriously questioned in Australia in the very emotional debates about the so-called "stolen generation" of Aboriginal people taken from their families as young children.

Increasingly, the right and authority of administrators to make life-changing decisions on behalf of the people in their care is challenged and more often than not those challenges are upheld. In the education context, we need to see who makes the decisions about the student's opportunities to learn, the priorities for their preferred learning outcomes and the types of resources and delivery modes available to them. Are we still seeing well-meaning (and ethnocentric) administrators pre-empting decisions by students, possibly of different ethnicity, about their own studies whilst they are driven to economize, rationalize or strive for political correctness?

Khor (2000) reveals his concerns with the following statement:

> Globalization is a process that can be called re-colonization. A new form of colonization is operating. (p. 1)

Globalization in Tertiary Education

Altbach (2002) reviewed several significant articles in the area. In particular, whilst reviewing a 2000 publication of the London-based Council for International Education, he made the following observations:

> In broad terms, globalization refers to trends in higher education that have cross-national implications. These include mass higher education; a global marketplace for students, faculty, and highly education personnel; and the global reach of the new Internet-based technologies, among others. Internationalization refers to the specific policies and initiatives of individual academic institutions, systems, or countries that deal with global trends. Examples of internationalization include policies relating to recruitment of foreign students, collaboration with academic institutions or systems in other countries, and the establishment of branch campuses abroad.
>
> Deep inequalities undergird many of the current trends in globalization and internationalization in higher education and they too need to be understood. A few countries dominate global scientific systems, the new technologies are owned primarily by multinational corporations

or academic institutions in the major Western industrialized nations, and the domination of English creates advantages for the countries that use English as the medium of instruction and research. All this means that the developing countries find themselves dependent on the major academic superpowers. (p. 2)

According to Pratt and Poole (1999), we have seen the emergence from the cocoon of the traditional university, to the global corporate and entrepreneurial university in Australia. With the diminishing tertiary funding for Australian universities, the strategically smart universities are taking up any opportunity to internationalize. However, Pratt and Poole advise:

Yet, in the flourishing of rhetoric and the parallel dash for cash, it appears that something is missing. Analyses of the real impacts of entrepreneurial internationalization are rare, and academics who question the educational compromises sometimes made in the pursuit of entrepreneurial success appear increasingly to be treated as pariahs subject to many of the negative consequences commonly applied to the whistle blowers in times past. (p. 16)

In addition, these writers have provided a must-read overview of the many ways in which the striving by some of Australia's universities to solve their financial problems has impacted on many aspects of their teaching and research programmes, on the stress levels of the academic staff and on the morale of staff involved in off-campus and off-shore delivery of programmes.

In his overview paper on the internationalization of educational programmes at the Royal Melbourne Institute of Technology in Melbourne (RMIT), Adams (1997), who was Dean of International Programmes at the time, identified a number of problems and successes and several lessons to be learned. The commitment of senior staff to internationalization and the existence of appropriate administrative systems are cited as two major factors in success. The development of offshore campuses of the university was acknowledged to be a source of many opportunities for offshore programmes in a significant number of locations. In addition:

The ability of RMIT teaching and administrative staff to be able to operate successfully in a cross-cultural environment is an important part of RMIT's internationalization. In the past, a large number of programmes have been operated for staff, but mainly on an ad hoc basis. From 1997, there will be a much more systematic approach with the development of "course team" based internationalization of curriculum project and a centrally operated training programme for teaching and administrative staff. (p. 10)

Not surprisingly, Collis, Moonen, and Fisser (1997) have seen a potential connection between internationalization and another concept closer to their work in information and communications technologies (ICTs). They then explore the possible relationships between internationalization and "virtual mobility":

> Its [virtual mobility] general characteristics are a university that serves a broader market, that must be more responsive to market demand, that must compete more with others offering similar services, and whose participants are increasingly less defined by physical location. The terms "virtual mobility" and internationalization taken together most frequently suggest a particular scenario: the student can stay at home (or at his home university) and still participate in a course at another university, using some form of communication technology. The student has new international options, without needing (in theory) to spend time and money travelling. (p. 185)

They also point out the obvious considerations for the university. The additional fee-paying students generate additional income whilst there is no need for additional facilities or on-campus resources. The use of ICTs for the provision of "learning at a distance" (external studies) has been an option that many universities have been quick to adopt. In some cases, the same ICTs have been used to deliver courses on-campus to both local and international students. In such cases, the international students are confused about why they have travelled to another country to participate in a programme that they could have just as easily been involves without the cost or time involved in travelling to Australia and without separation from their family for an extended time.

Gray (2002) gives an interesting account of how different groups assess the merits of study abroad for various interest groups. She identifies both the formal planned and the informal aspects of study in a foreign country as having significant benefits. She compared the expectations and overall benefits of short-term travel and longer-term study programmes. Clearly there was considerable merit in the students experiencing, at first hand, the cultural, social and national activities and priorities while they worked in another country or cultural setting. In the author's experience, the most memorable experiences commented upon by his international students are more often than not those best described as extra-curricular, social programme events or cross-cultural activities. These are also the experiences that are taken for granted by locals and by lecturer's who have not travelled themselves or who have not interacted with their international students at a personal level.

The Global Product—Learning From GM

As early as the start of the 1980s, the automotive manufacturing sector set precedents with the creation of the J-car concept that would one day be replicated as globalization advanced into the tertiary education sector. When in 1982 Germany's Opel, the General Motors Corporation in the then West Germany, released its first J-car, it produced one of the very first global products. The car, a small four-cylinder passenger sedan, arose out of extensive market research across many nations and innovative engineering and design. It was successfully marketed and sold throughout at least the western world. In Australia the car was know as the JB Holden Camira. In other countries, the same car was sold as a Vauxhall, an Opel or something else acceptable to the local market. Every subsidiary of GM in the world had one. Three successive models were released at two yearly intervals. In Australia, the Camira was released as the JB, JD and JD in the period from 1982 to 1988. The market research had successfully identified the essential characteristics for a small four-cylinder car in each of the participating countries and the basic car was created. With only very minor changes, the same car was successfully sold in each of the countries with local brand names and local badges. Having changed this concept into realities, the GM organization has continued with a global product concept with the vehicle sold currently in Australia as the Holden Astra and Holden Vectra. With the recent models, only relatively minor modifications were needed in areas such as safety, security and suspension in each of the market places to accommodate local climate, regulations and driving conditions. More than 13 variants of the original J-car were built in North America, Australia, Europe and Asia (Wikipedia, 2006), making it a truly successful global product.

Management and marketing consultants working with companies targeting clients in a global marketplace are constantly balancing the "universal" issues and the "regional" variations. ZS Associates, for example, is an American consultant group which is helping companies to analyse and implement solutions for their clients wishing to address their global marketing issues. They inform their prospective clients that "Global Product Marketing Strategies must simultaneously address universal issues of product/marketing position, resource utilization, competition and best practices, and also the myriad regional variations affecting a products success" (ZS Associates, 2001, p. 2).

Tertiary educators are forming consortia to develop and support such concepts and approaches to global product development and global marketing. The course developed by Oxford University Department of Engineering, Seoul National University School of Mechanical and Aerospace Engineering and the University of Michigan Department of Mechanical Engineering would appear to be a world leader in this field.

Brooks (2001) expresses the fears of many observers concerned about the undermining of national perspectives and traditions with the proliferation of global activities. He explains:

> The general idea is that the whole world is being opened up to world capitalism. All the old barriers are coming down. Capital flows will bring a transfer of technology to the poor countries—which soon will be rich! Extreme versions suggest that all national cultural differences will disappear in a homogenized world of global brands. International capital flows are acting on the world like a giant blender.

According to Martin Khor (2000), Director of Third World Network, "globalisation is a process that can be called re-colonisation" (p. 16).

Appadurai (2001) discussed the social impact of globalization and its likely influences on cultural autonomy and economic survival and more specifically on academic research in related areas. In particular, he argues that:

> Research in the modern, Western sense, is through and through a

collective activity, in which new knowledge emerges from a professionally defined field of prior knowledge and is directed toward evaluation by a specialized, usually technical, body of readers and judges who are the first sieve through which any claim to new knowledge must ideally pass. (p. 13)

The complication he elaborates upon in his article stems from his observation that whilst there is an emerging knowledge of globalization, at the same time knowledge itself is becoming increasingly globalized. This, he suggests, significantly complicates things for those who wish to study regions, there similarities and differences within global contexts. Appadurai (1997, p. 56) explains that there are two approaches to proceeding with the building of a community of genuinely international and democratic researchers. He highlighted the urgent need for western researchers to realize and accept alternative ways of thinking and different perceptions of reality.

Like so many modern-day concepts, globalization has intrigued and captured the interest of large numbers of people. Unfortunately, as has so often been the case, busy people hear the new jargon words and their fertile imagination does the rest. Many people are unable to explore the emerging concepts and the refinements of them because they are unable to access the legitimate literature or to participate in learned discussion about them. The new concepts and the emergence of new authentic terminology needed to adequately elaborate on the new concepts are not available for many of our managers, heads of departments, marketing specialists and budget managers who as a result work with a relatively superficial and more often than not a very naive view of the important new developments. "A little knowledge is very dangerous" has been a widely held truism for many years. Joseph Stiglitz (2002), in his recent book *Globalization and Its Discontents*, discusses frankly the almost catastrophic international results of decision-making and policy formulation by people who are, using his term, "but novices in global economics." This 2001 Nobel Prize in Economics winner, former chairman of the Clinton administration's Council of Economic Advisers and former Chief Economist for the World Bank, clearly explains how "partial truths" and naïve decisions impacted on the economic crises of the SE Asian nations in the 1990s. He provides many cases of where a solution to one nation's problems could either create another problem for the same nation or cause a ripple effect of new problems for neighbouring countries.

Let us, therefore, look closely at the term globalization and its underlying concept and the rhetoric that surrounds the various interpretations and promulgations of it. To what extent, for example, are Stiglitz's assertions in relation to economic aspects of globalization applicable to the educational contexts of globalization? If they are significant, then educators clearly must strive to get a much "bigger picture" view of tertiary education and make far greater efforts to identify and understand the intricacies and inter-relatedness of the many issues and factors involved and pay much more than lip service to the cultural, social and political dimensions of the globalization of tertiary education by so-called developed countries.

Whilst thinking about the language factor in globalization, we might do well to reflect on the words of Vygotsky (1986): "A word without meaning is an empty sound" (p. 212). Although this thought was expressed almost 20 years ago, the thought continues to reappear with authors such as Fu and Townsend (1999, p. 6), Elliott (2000, p. 68), and Orata (1999, p. 582), who used the term "empty verbaliza-tion." To what extent are the discussions and arguments about globalization merely empty verbalizations and not serious considerations of the phenomenon?

Globalization, ICTs and On-Line Learning

Smith (1999) investigated the delivery of an overseas programme that capitalized upon the innovations of on-line teaching and on-line assessments. He cited Cunningham et al. (1998):

> Universities, governments and academics cannot afford to ignore the implications of these developments (multimedia offerings of publishers). A challenge for Australian higher education will be to adapt to a dynamic new environment, where lucrative national and international markets arising from the growing importance of lifelong learning are likely to be contested strongly by traditional universities, new forms of universities, and by non-university providers. (Cunningham et al., 1998, p. 197)

Although many universities in the Western world have furtively grabbed onto ICT for the delivery and management of their graduate programmes, not all of them have seriously estimated and costed the design, development, field testing and implementation of programmes that involve the new technologies. Without a major commitment of both financial and human resources with appropriate knowledge and skills, no university can expect to succeed in the global market place when competing with the larger organizations that have vast financial and other resources at their disposal. With some years of "hands-on" experience in the computer-based training field, the author has seen how futile "half-baked" and poorly planned attempts to utilize computer technology in training and development can be. The novelty value does not prevail.

Earl Mardle (2001) advised that:

> When you become global you say goodbye to nationality and parochialism. There are no foreigners at the global level. Network thinking and action is essential to the sustainability of a globalized economy and the enterprises within it.
>
> The Internet is a very effective model for Globalization. It is the first genuinely global entity that has never been anything else and it has some very powerful paradigms we can use in thinking about Globalization. This is partly because networks have benefits not available to centralized organizations, however widely spread. (p. 11)

It is interesting to note his point that the internet is a useful tool for globalization. Unlike some other authors, Mardle does not equate internet use to globalization but rather sees the potential for them to be related. Clearly, there is more to globalization than simply putting learning materials on the internet. More particularly, globalization involves considerably more effort that the re-packaging of courses designed for local markets into forms that can be economically delivered to international students either locally or off-shore, and possibly utilizing ICTs and modern technologies. Once again, the notion of a globalized product emerges.

Working in increasingly tighter economic climates, the administration of many universities seem to be developing the notion that they can survive without maintaining their capital works and without increasing, even decreasing, numbers of academic staff through the adoption of on-line and internet-based teaching and learning resources and the on-line delivery of their courses. Mason

(1998, p. 15), cited in Rumble (2000, p. 1), referred to what he termed a "sliding scale" of provision of learning at a distance as "from traditional distance education, to international distance education, to on-line courses, to virtual universities and finally edging to globalization."

Rumble's article (2000) continues by addressing what he considers to be the many problems facing providers of international distance learning programmes. He discusses the political, social, financial, operational and technological threats to the success of delivery across national borders, over long distances and into various cultural contexts. He acknowledges that consumerism has come to higher education and highlights the need for high quality products and services that effectively capitalize on new technologies but at the same time:

> The use of new technologies will also favour innovations that create new roles, new social links, and new types of social behaviour within a service context. This is a form of social innovation. (p. 8)

Wilson (2001, p. 1) investigated the cultural considerations that must be made for online instruction and learning. He synthesized the thoughts of numerous other researchers and produced a report that is both informative and challenging. He, for example, cited Allen and Boykin (1992) who described "cultural discontinuities" as

> ... a lack of contextual match between the conditions of learning and a learner's socio-cultural experiences. (Allen & Boykin, 1992, p. 587)

These cultural discontinuities can lead to lack of user-acceptance in global markets.

Wilson (2001) cautions his readers that

> In face-to-face teaching, problems that arise as students construct meaning from the information presented can often be resolved through questions and answers between student and teacher. In print-based and online instruction (especially text-based courses), this feedback loop may not exist and students risk not understanding the information, or constructing a culturally misinformed meaning to it. (p. 1)

Then, in acknowledging the model of Vygotsky and Luria (1994) that defines the essential nature of cultural discontinuities, Wilson (2000) summarized as

Cultural discontinuities occur when psychological structures, elaborately developed to navigate a specific environment, suddenly encounter a different one. The mediating mechanisms can malfunction or break down completely, causing construction of meaning to be blocked or deformed, and attendant learning to be impeded. (p. 2)

In other words, Wilson is another writer who cautions us about the potential for problems when a learning programme developed in one culture for particular groups of students is delivered to students who are immersed in a vastly different culture and with entirely different social, cultural and educational backgrounds.

The author, in his work with post-graduate students in a coursework masters degree, has repeatedly observed many instances where a "cultural discontinuity" has occurred and a student's learning has been curtailed or seriously delayed. For example, many international students are surprised and even shocked by the lack of formalities between post-graduate students and lecturing staff in Australian universities. The frequent social interactions involving academic and their post-graduate students come as a very great surprise. The use of a variety of texts and many references in the preparation of a formal essay or assignment, rather than just the single text written by the lecturer and the lecture notes, takes some time to develop for many students coming from some areas of the Southeast Asian region.

Curriculum, Teaching and Learning and Multi-cultural Groups

Biro, Messnarz, and Davison (2002) investigated the various clusters of characteristics of national cultures as they were developed by Hofstede's seminal work. The clusters were arranged around the four areas of power distance: individualism versus collectivism, and masculinity versus femininity, uncertainty avoidance, and "short-term" versus "long-term" orientation. The authors provide a very comprehensive discussion and interpretation of the significance of each of the four clusters. They, like many other writers in this field, have explored the power distance, often referred to as "PD," characteristic in relation to the transferability of improvement proven in one (Western) culture to another culture. The "individualism versus collectivism" cluster, together with the "uncertainty avoidance" cluster discussed in the management context by Biro et al. (2002), has obvious relevance in education contexts as well. How international students from different cultures respond to different educational processes, participation in a variety of learning activities and assessment tasks will differ from one culture to the next depending on the "openness" or "highly structured" characteristics of their culture.

As early as the mid-1960s, Wheeler acknowledged the cyclic process of curriculum development. He described the on-going process of curriculum development as a wheel of development. The various spokes of the wheel were labelled by Wheeler (1967) as Aims and Objectives, Learning Experiences, Selection of content (subject matter), Integration and Organization of Learning Experiences and Course Content, Selection of Learning Resources and Specification of Learning Assessments. It would seem obvious that, regardless of whether an educational programme is intended for a domestic or a global market, each of the spokes of Wheeler's "wheel" must be addressed.

More recently, educators have attempted to address other aspects of course delivery. They have addressed contextual, environmental and cultural issues that may vary from one location to another and from one ethnic group to another. Clarke and Flaherty (2002), for example, investigated the matching of instructional tools to host-country student preferences. The found that, not too surprisingly, students from the United States, the United Kingdom, and China reacted quite differently to the various instructional activities employed in an MBA delivered in the three countries. It is not unreasonable to expect that students from various nations may respond differently to different teaching techniques, different teaching and learning resources, different student assessment techniques and to different classroom organization and management systems.

Dimmock and Walker (1998) discussed various aspects of power in relationships. They noted that power is distributed differently in different cultures. In those cultures where there is a large discrepancy between the "powers" held by different groups:

> ... in the home, children are education toward obedience to parents, whose authority is rarely questioned; in school, teachers are respected,

learning is conceived as passed on by the wisdom of the teacher, and teacher-centred methods tend to be employed; and in the workplace, hierarchy means existential inequality, subordinates expect to be told what to do, and the ideal boss is a benevolent autocrat or a kind father figure. By contrast, families in small PD societies encourage children to have a will of their own and to treat parents as equals; in school, more student-centred methods are used, teachers enjoy less respect, and learning is viewed as impersonalized truth; and in the workplace, hierarchy means an inequity of roles established for convenience, that subordinates expect to be consulted, and that the ideal boss is a resourceful democrat. Many Asian societies are high PD cultures, whereas many Western societies have low PD values. (p. 13)

Glazer (1999, p. 5) also identified the Confucian origins of this Asian pattern of behaviours. The obedience of subordinates in relation to their elders and superiors, however, was not seen to be as visible in some of the emerging cultures in developing countries. Callicott (2003) makes interesting contrasts between assertive responses and obedience and advised her readers to:

Remember that persons of some cultures are less likely to answer direct questions or provide an accurate self-report. Some cultures would consider humility a more critical value than assertive response, and others might misunderstand the semantics of English. Saudi Arabian students may offer a rote response rather than a (personal) position. (p. 8)

Firoz, Maghrabi, and Kim (2002) provide a concise and useful clarification of culture:

Anthropologists define culture as ways of living specific to any given group, tribe, collection, or nation of peoples. The peculiarities are passed on from one generation to the next. A culture acts out its ways of living in the context of social institutions, which include family, educational, religious, governmental, and business entities. It includes both conscious and unconscious values, ideas, attitudes, and symbols that shape human behaviour. Every culture has its differences from the next.

Further, within countries' cultural differences exist by requiring careful attention by national firms. (p. 2)

This later observation is entirely consistent with the author's observations of students coming from large, widely spread countries such as the Republic of Indonesia. Indonesia consists of a very large number of ethnic groups, many of which are contained in areas geographically bounded such as Acheh and the Batak regions of North Sumatra, Central, East and West Java, Bali, the eastern islands of the country and Jakarta DKI. Each of these Provinces has its own distinctive customs, diet cuisine, local languages, costumes, and even different religious and social norms. In reality, so-called ïinternational studentsî studying in Australian institutions may have very little in common with each other besides the fact that they are not Australian residents and are enrolled in the same academic programmes. In many cases, the diversity of differences is even greater because many students have already studied outside their home country in places like Russia, Germany, French-speaking Canada or elsewhere. In such cases, study patterns in an Australian university come as a third or more different set of experiences.

Resinger and Turner (2002), in their study of cultural differences in tourists in Australia, applied "principal component analysis" to investigate how foreign tourists from five Southeast Asian countries perceived major tourist destinations in Australia. They applied the Hofstede cluster model and found that all of the foreigner's perceptions differed significantly from those of the local tourist providers but were relatively consistent across the treatment groups. The Japanese and Koreans were the groups with perceptions most distinctly different from the local Australians.

The use of computer facilitated learning (CFL) is increasing with many of our tertiary institutions employing them to varying degrees. A number of studies have investigated their uses but the information available at present has been described as "patchy" and "incomplete" by at least one major report. For example, the Department of Education, Science and Training (2002) reported, in its Higher Education Report for the 2000 to 2002 Triennium, on a DETYA commissioned study on computer facilitated learning materials available in the higher education sector. The research team, from RMIT University in Melbourne, surveyed universities and members of the Australian Society for Computers in Learning in Tertiary Education. They found there was a lack of contextual information:

> In particular, information is needed about the educational design of the CFL resources being produced, how educationally effective these resources have been in practice, and reflections on the experience of using the resources in actual teaching situations. (p. 7)

To bring this into a global education perspective, we need to consider some more detailed information about the relevance and suitability of CFL resources for the various ethnic and cultural groups with whom we may wish to work with in various geographical or political districts. At the very least, we may need to provide appropriate orientation and preparation for students meeting new teaching approaches and unfamiliar types of learning resources and assessment practices for the first time. Even if, in the long term, those unfamiliar practices and resources prove to be invaluable for the international students, we should not assume that they will be comfortable with them initially or that they will work effectively for some time. In addition, the challenges we face as providers using unfamiliar techniques and resource types, may be even more critical for those international students who leave their familiar home culture to study a short course of say three, six or even twelve months.

Park (2000), in her article "Learning style preferences of Southeast Asian students," reported on her study of student groups from four Southeast Asian countries and made comparisons with Western students. She noted significant cultural diversities between the various national and ethnic groups of Cambodian, Laos, Hmong and Vietnamese students with regard to their learning style preferences. Her report incorporates reviews of many significant other studies.

Valentine and Speece (2002) investigated the use of "experiential learning" methods in Singapore. He discovered the power distance, "a representation of how readily people accept and expect that power is distributed unequally," can explain why students from a different cultural context might respond differently to teaching strategies such as "experiential learning."

> In some systems, simply getting the right answer by any means is most important, even if the student does not understand why the answer is right. More broadly, communication is not standard across cultures; acceptable ways to interact in any interpersonal context can be quite different. This, acquiring learning in the sense of concept application, problem-solving, and integration of knowledge can be difficult; indeed, even getting the participation upon which experiential learning depends is problematic. (p. 107)

To continue this series of reflections on education in

multicultural contexts, let us look at the role of a "teacher" in relation to their social and cultural context. Solomon (1995) investigated teacher in-service education that addressed issues related to cultural diversity and multicultural classes. He found that many of the participants strongly resisted any attempt to change their somewhat egocentric views about their own culture and the entrance of international students into it. Solomon cited an in-service participant who saw

> ... multicultural and antiracist education as a problem-solving initiative not as an ongoing pedagogical approach for working with cultural diversity. (p. 251)

Sadly, many teachers who are very familiar with working with local students respond in similar ways. Their thinking reflects an "assimilationist" approach of "How can we get the new foreign students to adapt and adopt our ways of thinking, doing and behaving? " They fail to perceive the enormous potential teaching resource that comes when international students enter their classroom. Solomon concluded that education faculties are in the best position to make necessary changes. Solomon (1995) advised that

> ... teacher educators must be progressive and equity conscious, able to move professional development for multicultural and antiracist education well beyond a set of discrete utilitarian prescriptions. They must be willing to do more than merely tinker at the fringes of institutional structures and leave unaltered the main fabric of systems that continue to reproduce themselves. Instead, schools need faculty who will encourage teachers' introspection and self-examination to uncover how their own socialization has influenced their beliefs and assumptions about diverse groups in society. This is a crucial starting point in the preparation of teachers for culturally diverse schools.
>
> Readiness for this task must come from in-service education that provides a clear rationale for culturally diverse schooling and makes linkages with teachers' civil responsibility, moral accountability, enhanced political sensibility, and critical participation embedded within a commitment to work equitably with the challenges of diversity. (p. 256)

The Australian Vice-Chancellors' Committee in 1990 published the *Code of Ethics* and standards for the provision of courses for international students to protect both the students and the institutions themselves. In Section 9, now available online (Australian

Vice-Chancellors' Committee, 2001), states that each university must:

> ... adopt consistent and caring procedures in the recruitment, reception, education and welfare of international students, ... ensure that all staff involved with international students ... are competent to deal with [their] special circumstances, [and]

> ... develop training programs, including cross-cultural programs, appropriate to the different levels of involvement and responsibility among staff. (p. 11)

Clearly, the most senior staff of Australian universities have committed to providing courses in contextually relevant, culturally appropriate and sensitive ways and to employ staff with the necessary insights and personal characteristics to achieve that end. It is clear, from direct observation and from reading recent literature, that there are individual academic and general staff members who become very close to their international students and who are highly committed to recognizing and embracing cultural, religious, value and prior experience differences and to capitalize on the priceless resources—the students with vastly different experiences and knowledge—brought together in their post-graduate classes. The question that must be asked, then, is what are the middle and upper-middle managers doing to realize the expectations of their Vice-Chancellors and to support their academic staff working with increasing numbers of international students? Are Faculty Heads, Deans of School and Heads of Unit providing real and necessary support for teaching staff, supervisors and the resources, human, physical and financial, that are required to deliver effective programmes and an effective level of support for their international students? Or, are they more concerned with on-going marketing for prospective students and using the income from full tuition fees to supplement other activities? Whilst this is a critical question, it is not appropriate to pursue it in this paper.

Reflections on Personal Experiences

For more than 12 years, the author has worked very closely with international students from some 25 countries and many more geographical regions and ethnic sub-cultures. In addition, he has worked in various locations in the East Asian cultures in various conferences, seminars and developmental projects. He has taken a very keen interest in the experiences of international students, particularly those from eastern Asia, whilst they have studied in one or other of the Western countries of the world. Most particularly, he has investigated the experiences of students enrolled at his workplace, Flinders University, in Adelaide, South Australia. As Director of Studies for the highly successful, in terms of content and outcomes and the number of international students participating, the Master of Educational Management he has taken a keen interest in the study programme, social programme, cultural experiences and family welfare for some hundreds of post-graduate students over a period of some twelve years or more. Some examples of student comments he has gathered in various informal discussions, in class seminars and discussion activities, through written assignments and student research projects are paraphrased below:

- What we really value here is your ability to balance theory with specific examples based on your experience in Australia and in our countries. Few of our lecturers in our own country are able to share this practical dimension.
- I am very surprised that you are not only willing to have your students have an opinion or perspective other than your own; you seem to positively encourage them to do so.
- Whilst, at first, I found it somewhat confusing to decide what my assignment would be about, I really appreciate the opportunities that you provide for us to explore things that we are interested in and which we can utilize on our return to our own country.
- You know, whilst I am in Australia, I think of your as my father. Is that OK?
- I do not need to explain to you; you have lived and worked in my country and in our government bureaucracy so you already know and understand.
- I came to see you yesterday and I came back again but you seemed to be very busy so I did not like to interrupt you.
- I really like the (management) ideas that I have learned working in the programme here, but I am worried about whether or not I can use them back in my office when I return.

- I really need to undertake my research in the area of (…) because my Director has already told me what he wants me to investigate and he is eagerly waiting my report.
- I was very anxious about presenting my first seminar in class. However, my friends back in the office will be impressed if I am more confident sharing my new knowledge with my friends there.
- Back in my home country, I am a very small "potato." I am not sure whether or not I will be able to really utilize all of the great strategies and techniques that I have developed here in this course.
- I have worked on some large projects and my experiences are very similar to the ones you have talked about. I can see that what you are suggesting is very helpful for me and I will share them with my friends at my office.
- Back in my country, we had to read the textbook written by our lecturer and use the information in it together with his lecture material to write our assignments. Here we need to use a variety of textbooks, the lecturer's notes and our own thinking as well when we write our assignments.
- In my country, it is not possible for me to criticize anyone or their ideas but here I am often required to compare different viewpoints, criticize and assess the merits of the work from different authors and actually decide which is the best reference to use in my assignments and research papers. It seems very strange here.
- My father is critically ill and I am sending money home to help with the medical expenses. I should be there as I am the eldest son and my family really needs me there.
- I feel very sad because every time I ring my family back home I miss my young son again very much. I want to go home in the Christmas holidays to be with my family. I know that it will be very hard to come back for next year.
- Some of my friends back at the office are very keen to come to Australia and to join this programme. Please give me some information to send to them.
- Thank you for suggesting that I bring my family to meet one of the student counselors. I am sorry, bit I am not comfortable talking to someone who I do not know about my situation.

And, actually, I do not feel confident talking with a female about such things.

- At first I found it very confusing that you did not direct me to specific knowledge that you wanted me to learn. Now I realize that the processes of deciding what to learn and how to explore my own interpretations and meanings are what are important for us all. The outcomes for each of us may be different but right for us.

These comments provide considerable insights into the underlying differences in values, expectations and previous experiences that pervade our work with students who come from cultures vastly different from our own. Even though Australian universities do have International Offices, Student Counsellors, Student Support Units created to support, encourage and assist our new international students from several different nations, have we created bureaucratic systems based on Western values and rationalized in accordance with prevailing economies or have we addressed the prevailing values, beliefs and expectations of the people for whom the assistance is provided? These are questions that are easy to pose but maybe difficult to answer honestly and the consequences of our answers may costly and time consuming.

Some Emerging Issues?

It seems, therefore, that whilst a lot of time and energy has been devoted to clearer definitions for the terms and better distinctions between "globalization," "internationalization" and "international education," very little time has been spent on exploring what they mean in the practical context of higher education. These seem to be the real issues:

- Globalization can be much more than a set of rhetoric and the basis of opportunistic ventures to bolster up dwindling enrolments and reductions in traditional funding for Western universities.
- Globalization can give rise to new generations of thinking, new infrastructures and new educational perspectives that spawn exciting new opportunities for local and international

students using new learning resources, new technologies and new approaches to tertiary education.

- By developing new programmes, new approaches and new resources, a university can create enormous new opportunities for increased enrolments, to create increased local and international interest in their programmes and to be seen as contributing something very significant in global terms. The GM J-car has been proof of the benefits of this "global perspective" approach and what is more important the long-term sustainability of a more "global" approach.

- Taking up these opportunities will require more than simply marketing traditional programmes and more efficient utilization of existing unmodified resources and current staff attitudes, existing infrastructures and professional practices.

- To simply place traditional course materials "on-line" and offer existing courses by "distance" or "correspondence" modes will not succeed, in the short or long term, as "globalized" neither will they lead to sustainable programmes.

- The uses of information and communications technologies and on-line or web-based and the materials and processes will not overcome the problems inherent in the traditional approaches used to develop, deliver and evaluate programmes designed for local or domestic markets.

- The personal traits and professional capabilities of teaching staff, together with their insights into and interests in working with people from other cultures may be the most critical factors in the success or otherwise of more global approaches to higher education.

- A lecturer's depth of understanding and willingness to learn about the cross-cultural issues involved when students come from one culture to study in a significantly different culture and the how they can be identified, responded to and capitalized upon are essential prerequisites for success with multicultural groups of international students from different nations and cultures.

- Western teaching methods, approaches to learning and teaching, teaching aids and learning resources, and approaches to student assessment and evaluation may need to be sensitively introduced to students who are not already familiar with them because they come from a culture that does not employ them or changed.

What Should Happen Next?

- A university wanting to globalize should aggressively rethink its current priorities and continuing practices with regard to provision of courses and topics for international students and embrace a "global product" concept in the design, development and delivery of their programmes.
- New global courses (processes and products) should be designed and developed from the ground up. The results will reflect universal needs, as the GM J-car project did, based on extensive market research across the various cultures and client groups, and embrace those approaches, strategies and emphases that will reinforce the recognition of international "universals" and at the same time recognize local and regional context, culture, condition and prevailing environments.
- A globalized university will need to realize that both international and local (Australian) course participants will benefit from the broader perspective, beyond local domestic issues, provided with a "global" product in what become "win-win" situations.
- The appropriateness and suitability of all aspects of the curriculum (design, expected outcomes, learning resources, organization, staff characteristics, assessment methods, learning models, teaching and learning processes, communications and relationships) should recognize and embrace the multicultural and ethnic diversities of all participating groups, including locals.
- Due consideration should be given to how the participants may be able to capitalize on their new global perspectives and apply their new knowledge and skills on their return to their home country and in their home workplace environment and organizational (corporate) sub-culture. To do these, they will need insights and skills to adopt, adapt and to re-package their new knowledge and skills in culturally sensitive and acceptable forms.

How Might This Be Achieved?

It seems that the real challenges for universities in developed countries should globalize in the following ways:

- Design awards and topics with a foundation based on global issues which embrace cultural, contextual, and political circumstances and the prevailing conditions for students from various nations and cultures.
- In addition to the "universals," incorporate opportunities for students to choose their preferred options and to negotiate those aspects of the course that best address their specific "regional" needs.
- Develop pedagogies and approaches to learning that encourage course participants (the clients) to identify and explore their own general and specific needs within their own local culture, working environment and the local contexts and condition of their staff and employer organizations.
- Develop learning resources that are conducive to the new global thinking and that will facilitate the development of global context and universal theories that can be customized for local regional applications.
- Provide Human Resource Development activities for academic and general staff that will develop greater sensitivities and insights into the needs and priorities of course participants coming from cultures other than their own.
- Develop ICT applications that are appropriate and timely for the new global approaches being implemented for each and every context of national, political and ethnic group likely to participate in a programme.
- Create a working climate and university culture that facilitates effective working relationships between academic staff, general staff and international and local participants in culturally inclusive ways.
- Clarify who the real client is as far as the university is concerned. Is it the student in the school or the funding organization in the context of the university's infrastructure?

Reflecting on Stiglitz's (2002) concerns about the tendency for bureaucrats to over-simplify very complex situations, the current situation in Australian universities requires urgent action. In particular, the various cohorts of staff, academic teaching and research staff, general and administrative staff, staff who travel prospecting in markets overseas for new students in different locations and those who develop and coordinate academic programmes all need to come together to share their perspectives on globalized courses. Success in a truly global context will require far greater depth of understanding of all of the issues and a shared and coherent "vision" and agreed "mission" across the various areas of a university.

Some Observations Related to International Students

Those of us who have worked extensively with international students both abroad and in our home countries have undoubtedly noticed the frequent and profound mismatch of culturally defined expectations. For example, Indonesian students of Javanese background are particularly polite and accommodating; they avoid conflict situations and are very agreeable participants in university life. When they are introduced to some of the Western management models, strategies and techniques, they are particularly uncomfortable, often exhibiting their "obedient culture," with the often very assertive or even aggressive approaches implicit to the Western work culture. Add to this the gender-based differences in worker rights and the relatively low status of junior staff in some developing countries, the notion of "managing up" can be quite offensive and particularly alien to these people. The frequent lack of questioning and high regard and respect for older and more senior managers in high status positions, particularly if they are male, in some cultures can pre-empt the implementation of models of democratic decision-making and many contemporary management tools and strategies such as participation models in management and decision-making.

In one situation, an international student, when faced with the task of defining the "problem underlying the research" for their dissertation, became particularly distressed and was unable to focus on their investigations. Some discussion over several occasions revealed that the cultural sensitivity which revolved around acknowledgement that a "problem" existed and that that should be addressed in the ensuing research was the key impediment. Once this was identified, the student's supervisor was able to reframe the task as the identification of a "situation" or an "issue" that "can be improved" to be the basis of the proposed research. In a similar way, the notion of "less advantaged people" existing within a developing country seemed rather quaint for Westerners who are much more familiar with notions of "disadvantaged groups" of people.

Students come from some Eastern cultures with the expectation that they must not challenge their teacher, supervisor or manager. As a result, they continue to accept, without challenge everything that they read or hear in their classes and research. When these students are asked to write a formal essay or report they tend to provide a carefully worded summary that explicitly or implicitly accepts the views being expounded by each and every author. For these people, the requirement for them to provide a critical analysis and identify consistent and contrasting points of view is quite an unnatural experience.

Immediate consequences of these observations arise when an international student is asked to investigate a diverse range of ideas and viewpoints and to construct an "argumentative" style essay or written report. It is often necessary for a university to provide formal training in the need and techniques of constructing a written argument and techniques of critical thinking for students from many Southeast Asian cultures. The same student will very likely be required to undertake studies in a topic such as "critical thinking" or "critical reasoning" as a prerequisite to further progress with their studies at a university in a western culture. This means that the underlying culture, values and social norms of a student from one region or district may impact on what is taught, how it is taught and how they are assessed in relation to some topics in the curriculum. Observations such as these remind us of the complexities of planning an academic programme based on a global perspective.

Globalization in Tertiary Education

The literature portrays many and varied interpretations of globalization and internationalization. Even in the area of tertiary education, the term has a variety of definitions and implementations.

The main perspectives relate to one or more of these:

- international marketing of courses developed for domestic (local) markets;
- increase in market share by larger institutions wishing to increase their productivity and income by increasing the loci of their operations to include more countries;
- global economy and the operations of large multi-national organizations;
- global economy and the financial networks of the world;
- conservation and ecological issues for a sustainable global environment—greenhouse gases, ozone layers, unusual weather pattern effects;
- implementation of electronic course delivery systems utilizing technologies including on-line, world-wide web (internet) and multi-media techniques; the so-called "flexible delivery" generation;
- implementation of e-school and e-learning; and
- international studies; studies of cross-cultural and similar programmes.

These approaches can best be described as strategic marketing and sales, corporate opportunism and internationalization of products and services developed in one culture and offered to other cultural groups in the interests of profit and efficiencies in large organizations.

The Global Education Product

It is clear from reflections on the literature and the survey reported in this paper that for tertiary courses to be truly global, they must:

- be designed and developed from the outset for a global context and produced with due recognition of cultural, ethnic and environmental factors and the needs of the course participants (adult learning);
- be packaged and delivered in ways that embrace the cultural, ethnic and environmental factors;
- design assignments and student assessments in a way that can reflect the priorities and characteristics of the course participants;
- employ learning and teaching models that are culturally and

ethnically inclusive for the various individuals and client groups participating;

- utilize learning resources and information sources that embrace the diversity of needs by the various client groups; and
- be evaluated and quality assured in ways that are sensitive to the cultural and ethnic characteristics of all client groups.

Characteristics of a Globalized Tertiary Coursework Programme

The creation of a truly global coursework programme should be based on:

- foci that embrace truly global issues often thought of a "universals" that transcend national, cultural, ethnic and aesthetic boundaries;
- flexibility through negotiable and customizable implementations of topics and content that adapt to the specific needs and priorities of various client groups;
- delivery (teaching) in a climate and working environment consistent with those of the work culture of the participants (clients); and
- achievement/progress of participants assessed by means and with priorities negotiated by the individual student participant and the lecturer.

Several members of the academic staff working with international students in the School of Education at Flinders University have approached their teaching in various innovative ways. Consideration of the literature sampled in this paper, and other resources not reported upon here, has enabled the author to clarify and understand an evolutionary process in which we are moving from a traditional university model to one which is more responsive to the student client. If present indications are accurate, some Flinders University staff members are moving, perhaps intuitively, towards a truly global product in at least one programme area. In the Master of Educational Management (MEM), a 2-year programme involving a combination of coursework and a research project has been evolving for more than 15 years. It has come from a solid foundation of theory-based and rigorous argumentative style involving critical analysis and formal written assignments to a broader-based approach. The teaching of several of the topics has evolved from a very "lecturer dominated" model to one in which students are considered to be active participants working in a supportive and democratic learning environment. In the new environment, the participating students are much more likely to:

- negotiate the topics (subjects) they take in their study programme;
- determine to some degree at least the emphasis and focus of their learning;
- set the approach and context (political, social, ethnic, national, environmental) of what they are studying;
- choose whether they undertake a small, medium or large research component;
- select their preferred choice of assessment tasks from a number of options (essay, discussion paper, position paper, seminar paper, annotated bibliography, formal written report, professional development package) offered in a topic;
- determine the form of outcome that they develop (written paper, simulation package, presentation package such as Microsoft PowerPoint, internet [web] site or web pages, oral presentation) to communicate the extent of their learning;
- select the learning resources they use to achieve their learning outcomes; and
- negotiate attendance patterns (weekly classes, compact courses, weekend conference seminar programme, and sandwich course) and schedule for assignment submissions.

To explain the evolution of how some specific topics are delivered, some discussion of several on-going topics follows:

In a topic such as **Managing Human Resources,** the participants have traditionally been offered a predetermined selection of assessment tasks. The subject matter is assessed with formal written essays and papers on topics pre-determined by the lecturer or programme deliverer or coordinator. The resources used in this traditional model are typically and predominantly derived from Anglo-Celtic and Western perspectives, and revolve around Australia as being "one country, one culture."

A variation of this is prescriptive ethnocentric approach can be found in **Project Management in Professional Settings.** In this topic, participants are introduced to a core of universal concepts and terminology applied to project management in various human services including human resource management, educational projects, and school-based management. Each individual participant, or small group of students, on the basis of written guidelines provided, defines the tasks that are used for their assessment. There is considerable flexibility and choice for each student with format ranging from essay, position or discussion paper, annotated bibliography, formal report, detailed project brief and seminar paper. Clear guidelines and assessment criteria are provided at the beginning of the topic and these are discussed and interpreted from time to time through the duration of the topic.

Representing an even later stage in the evolution, the topic **Current Issues in Education (Educational Administration)** has encouraged (even required) the students to negotiate most aspects of how the topic is assessed. In 2002, each participant has been required to identify those issues that are of current interest or likely to emerge in the foreseeable future for them within their home culture, climate and working environment.

To create a clear understanding of how the participants can proceed, the lecturer sets the scene by working with some global issues with the class group. Seminars and workshops demonstrate and model the techniques, strategies and approaches that could be used by the participants in their own explorations of their own chosen issues. The students can elect to work alone on their own issues or they can work on a common or shared interest or need in a small or medium-size group. The students negotiate assessments individually or in their small or medium-size group. The assessment tasks are designed to achieve an optimization for the explorations of the investigations of participant-selected issues and to maximize the transferability (portability) of their newly acquired concept. Malcolm Knowles's "adult learning" principles are utilized where the participants have every opportunity to capitalize on their individual prior experiences and to tap into those vast ranges of experiences and knowledge drawn together when a class group is brought together.

The approach used in the **Current Issues in Education (Educational Administration)** topic is clearly one of Problem-Based

Learning (PBL). The students are encouraged to identify an issue as the basis of a problem encountered in their working life or perhaps an issue that may present as a problem to their work friends in the future. Rather than giving the course content to the students, the lecturer works as a facilitator and encourages each student to investigate those areas of immediate or future importance to them. In this way, each student work on topics of their choosing and in ways in which they felt comfortable. The group, as a whole, is presented with a variety of strategies, models of working and examples of investigations as "works in progress" and they experience the satisfaction of resolving the issue and reaching and acceptable outcomes.

Conclusion

It is clear that the structure of the Master of Educational Management in the School of Education at Flinders University is evolving from a very traditional teacher-directed and academic didactic methodology to one that embraces a more participative model that empowers students, both individually and in groups, by providing a clear understanding of learner-centred (client-centred) approaches that encourage democratic decision-making and full participation in a dynamic learning-teaching process. The process has been described as a model of problem-based learning (PBL).

Whilst experiencing approaches such as these to post-graduate study in at least one post-graduate combined "coursework and research" award, international students have many opportunities to negotiate, with their lecturer and their fellow students, "how they are learning," "what they are learning," and even "when they are learning." Little of this can occur, of course, unless the lecturer is highly skilled in the role as a "facilitator of learning" and has a considerable store of personal resources and adequate supply of educational resources that will allow this process to develop. What are the prerequisite and desirable professional and personal characteristics for a lecturer who wants to work in these ways with their students? This chapter will not adequately address these but acknowledges that there are likely to be numerous fundamental characteristics involved. The teaching and learning process is a dynamic situation and the lecturer will need to be very adaptable, have a broad knowledge base and be highly skilled with a vast range of pedagogies and approaches to teaching including the use of "problem-based learning," problem-solving and guided discovery methodologies. Only when the lecturer is highly skilled, insightful and very responsive to the emerging issues and personal traits of his students with the students be able to negotiate how their learning is achieved, what is learned and how their achievements are assessed and the focus or approach that they use within specific topics. This very limited discussion cannot explore the minute details and critical issues involved and further investigation and discussion is certainly warranted.

With the evolution of this approach to the development, delivery and assessment within topics and for whole educational programmes, comes great potential for true globalization of the content, teaching/learning approaches utilized and the ways in which academic staff and their students relate to one another.

The critical factors in the on-going success or failure of this emerging globalization process and the accumulation of successful outcomes are:

- support from senior staff in the university that encourages and recognizes the achievements as they occur;
- recognition of the demands on personal resources of the lecturing staff attempting to work in these ways;
- accounting for workload implications of this kind of work when staffing is calculated and staff are assigned professional duties;
- willingness of academic staff to move from a power position of being an all-knowing expert in a narrow field of expertise of their choice to a more level playing field where the interests and needs of students, local or overseas, are identified acknowledged and supported (teacher as facilitator rather than expert);
- recognition of the need for new patterns of academic work that include close working relationships with international post-graduate students and significant amounts of time devoted to individual students and small groups in workload calculations, human resource allocations and financial and resource implications of the new ways of working;

- ensuring that academic and administrative staff make the necessary efforts to develop greater insights into cultural, ethnic, national, political and sociological influences that arise for their student participants in their various home countries and sub-cultures; and
- ensuring that academic and administrative staff identify and address the many challenges faced by students residing far from home and away from family, friends and familiar support structures, and working in a culture vastly different from their own.

It is unlikely that additional resources, whether they are human, physical or financial, will be committed to such developments unless the senior decision-makers and budget managers come to understand the enormous potential for far greater international student participation.

Appadurai's (2001) discussion of what he calls "weak internationalisation" and "strong internationalisation" is quite pertinent at this point. The former he defined as "essentially a superficial engagement with the issues'' whilst "strong internationalisation" is "a deeper more sophisticated and genuine desire to explore what it means to become internationalised" (p. 16).

Clearly, "weak internationalisation" refers to a rather superficial approach and one that promotes courses essentially those developed for local markets and delivered to international students and sometimes in foreign locations. The creation of facilities and support services to cater for an anticipated influx of international students simply does not equate to the globalization of programmes in a university. Sanderson (2002, p. 7) is working in this area and we should eagerly anticipate the outcomes for his doctorate research at Flinders University.

The added richness to local and international student programmes needs to be documented and the benefits to the students and their employers must be better understood. The point to be made is that some investment in effective globalization of programmes, models of teaching and the learning resources available for staff and students and the various supporting infrastructures (counselling, writing and language skills, peer and cross-cultural activities) can be handsomely rewarded with greater participation rates by students from both local and international sources.

This might suggest that planning, both strategic and operational, is needed to alert university staff in all areas of administration, academia and support services to the enormous potential for improvement in work achievements, job satisfaction and enhanced budget considerations. In other words, the conservative budgeting and cost reduction strategies that are arising as the only possible responses perceived in the financially strapped economy of universities need to be reviewed and more informed and enlightened, even visionary, investments in real globalization must be initiated.

References

Adams, T. (1997). *The internationalization of the Royal Melbourne Institute of Technology (RMIT): A case study, Dean of International Programs*. Retrieved October 20, 2004, from RMIT, Faculty of Education Language and Community Services website: http://www.homepages.eu.rmit.edu.au/mlaidler/dean/tony.html

ADMIT. (2001). *Higher education admissions and student mobility within the EU* (Centre for Educational Research, Clare Market Papers No. 18) [Electronic version]. Retrieved October 20, 2004, from http://www.lse.ac.uk/collections/CER/pdf/cmp18.pdf

Allen, B., & Boykin, A. (1992). African-American children and the educational process: Alleviating cultural discontinuity through perspective pedagogy. *School Psychology Review, 21*(4), 586–596.

Altbach, P. G. (2002). *Perspectives on international higher education change*. New Rochelle, NY: Heldref Publications.

Aman, A. C. (2002). A global perspective on current regulatory reforms: Rejection, relocation, or reinvention? *Indiana Journal of Legal Studies, 2*, 429.

Appadurai, A. (1997). The research ethic and the spirit of internationalism. *Social Science Research Council, 51*(4), 55–60.

Appadurai, A. (2001). Grassroots globalization and the research imagination. In A. Appadurai (Ed.), *Globalization* (pp. 1–21). Durham, NC: Duke University Press.

Australian Vice-Chancellors' Committee. (2001). *Code of practice in the provision of education to international students by Australian universities*. Retrieved October 20, 2004, from http://www.avcc.edu.au/news/public%5Fstatements/publications/code.htm

Biro, M., Messnarz, R., & Davison, A. G. (2002). The Impact of national cultural factors on the effectiveness of process improvement methods: The third dimension. *Software Quality Professional, 4*(4), 34–41.

Brooks, M. (2001). What is globalisation? Retrieved October 20, 2004, from http://www.marxist.com/Economy/what_is_globalisation_mb.html

Brown, R. K., & Dale, E. C. (1989). (Eds.). *Overseas students: Educational opportunity and challenge.* Curtin, Australia: The Australian College of Education.

Callicott, K. J. (2003). Culturally sensitive collaboration within person-centred planning. *Focus on Autism and other Developmental Disabilities, 18,*(1), 60–69.

Clarke, I., & Flaherty, T. B. (2002). Teaching internationally: Matching part-time MBA instructional tools to host country student preferences. *Journal of Marketing Education, 35*(2), 233–242.

Collis, B., Moonen, J., & Fisser, P. (1997). *A categorization of opportunities for the internationalisation of higher education in the European university.* In Kvetn K. Hlavicka (Ed.), *Role of Universities in the Future Information Society* (pp. 183–186). Prague: Czech Technical University, Publishing House.

Cunningham, S. S., Tapsall, S., Ryan, Y., Stedman, L. Bagdon, K., & Flew, T. (1998). *New media and borderless education: A review of the convergence between global media networks and higher education provision.* Canberra: Commonwealth of Australia.

Department of Education, Science and Training. (2002). *Higher education report for the 2000 to 2002 triennium.* Canberra: Commonwealth Government.

de Wit, H. (1999). *Rationales for internationalization of higher education.* Retrieved October 20, 2004, and June 12, 2006, from the Polytechnic Institute of Viseu website: http://www.ipv.pt/millenium/wit11.htm

Dimmock, C., & Walker, A. (1998). Comparative educational administration: Developing a cross-cultural concept framework. *Educational Administration Quarterly, 34*(4), 13.

Elliott, M. (2000). The risk of losing something big. *Newsweek, 134*(24), 68–71.

Firoz, N. M., Maghrabi, A. S., & Kim, K. H. (2002). Think globally manage culturally. *International Journal of Commerce & Management, 12*(3/4), 32–51.

Fu, D., & Townsend, J. S. (1999). Serious learning: Language lost. *Language Arts, 76*(5), 404–414.

Fung-Surya, K. (2001). Opening minds to the world: An Asian perspective. *Journal of College Admission, 171*(7), 1–2.

Glazer, N. (1999). Two cheers for Asian values. *The National Interest, 57,* 27–32.

Gomez, J. (2000). A new form of oppression. In "What is Globalization," *YMCA World Index, No. 3.* Retrieved October 20, 2004, from the World Alliance of YMCAs website: http://www.ymca.int/publications/YMCA world/ Sept2000/3_2000 global.htm

Gray, K. S. (2002). Assessing study abroad's effect on an international mission. *Change, 34*(3), 44–51.

Greenfield, G., & Pringle, T. (2001). What is globalization? *Asian Labour Update, 41.* Retrieved October 20, 2004, from http://www.amrc.org.hk /4101.html

Haakenson, P. (1994). Recent trends in global/international education. ERIC Digest. Educational Resources Information Centre (ERIC) ED373021.

International Monetary Fund. (2000). *Globalization: Threat or opportunity?* Retrieved October 20, 2004 and June 12, 2006, from the International Monetary Fund website: http://www.imf.org/external/np/exr/ib/2000/041200.htm#II

Jorgensen, J. S. (2002). Internationalization of higher education in northern light. *Journal of Faculty of Humanities.* Denmark: Aalborg University.

Kezar, A. J. (2000). *International higher education: ERIC trends (1999–2000).* In International Higher Education, Educational Resources Information Centre (ERIC) Clearing House on Higher Education (ED 446648). Retrieved October 20, 2004, from http://www.eriche.org

Khor, M. (2000). A new form of colonialism? *YMCA World Index, No. 3.* Retrieved October 20, 2004, from the World Alliance of YMCAs website: http://www.ymca.int/Publications/YMCA World/Sept2000/3_2000global.htm

Knight, J., & de Wit, H. (1997). Internationalization of higher education in Asia Pacific countries. In European Association for International Education (EAIE), p. 8. Amsterdam.

Mardle, E. (2001). Globalization and the level playing field: Reconciling the geometry. *The Ethical Spectacle, 7*(7). Retrieved June 12, 2006, from http://www.spectacle.org/0701/globalisation.html

Mason, R. (1998). *Globalising education: Trends and applications.* London: Routledge.

Orata, P. T. (1999). The problem professor of education. *The Journal of Higher Education, 70*(5), 589–598.

Park, C. C. (2000). Learning style preferences of Southeast Asian students. *Urban Education, 35*(3), 245–268.

Pettigrew, P. (2000). Seattle—globalization vs. internationalization: A collision between two worlds. *Vital Speeches of the Day, 66*(22), 610–616.

Pilkington, D. (2002). *Follow the rabbit proof fence.* Brisbane, Australia: University of Queensland.

Porter, P., & Vidovich, L. (2000). Globalization and higher education policy. *Educational Theory, 50*(4), 449–465.

Pratt, G., & Poole, D. (1999). Global corporations "R" us? The impacts of globalization on Australian universities. *Australian Universities' Review, 42*(2), 5–64.

Resinger, Y., & Turner, L. W. (2002). Cultural differences between Asian tourist markets and Australian hosts, part 1. *Journal of Travel Research, 40*(3), 295–315.

Rumble, G. (2000). The globalization of open and flexible learning:

Considerations for planners and managers. *On-Line Journal of Distance Learning Administration, 3*(3). Retrieved August 7, 2005, from http://www.westga.edu~distance/ojdla/fall/rumble33.html

Sanderson, G. (2002, December). *Living with the other: Non-Western international students at Flinders University.* Paper presented at "Internationalising Education in the Asia-Pacific Region: Critical Reflections, Critical Times," annual conference of the Australian and New Zealand Comparative and International Education Society, University of Armidale, New South Wales, Australia.

Slaughter, S., & Leslie, L. (1997). *Academic capitalism: Politics, policies, and the entrepreneurial university.* Baltimore: Johns Hopkins University Press.

Smith, M. (1999). On-line delivery of an overseas program: Turning virtual teaching into a learning reality (School of Commerce Research Paper Series No. 99(6)). Adelaide, Australia: Flinders University.

Solomon, R. P. (1995). Beyond prescriptive pedagogy: Teacher inservice education for cultural diversity. *Journal of Teacher Education, 46*(4), 251–258.

Stiglitz, J. E. (2002). *Globalization and its discontents.* New York: W. W. Norton.

Taylor, S., Rizvi, F., R., Lingard, B., & Henry, M. (1997). *Education policy and the politics of change.* London: Routledge.

Tootell, K. (1999, November). *International students in Australia: What do we know of the quality of their education?* Paper presented at the Australian Association for Research in Education (AARE) Conference, Melbourne. Retrieved October 20, 2004, from the Australian Association for Research in Education website: http://www.aare.edu.au/99pap/too99642.htm

Valentine, D., & Speece, M. (2002). Experiential learning methods in Asian cultures: A Singapore case study. *Business Communication Quarterly, 65*(3), 106–122.

Vygotsky, L. (1986). *Thought and language.* Cambridge, MA: The MIT Press.

Vygotsky, L. S., & Luria, A. R. (1994). Tool and symbol in child development. In R. van der Veer & J. Valsiner (Eds.), *The Vygotsky Reader* (pp. 99–174). Cambridge, MA: Blackwell Publishers.

Wheeler, D. K. (1967). *Curriculum process.* London: University of London Press.

Wikipedia. (2006). GM J platform. Retrieved June 12, 2006, from: http://en.wikipedia.org/wiki/GM-J-platform

Wilson, M. S. (2001). Cultural considerations in online instruction and learning. *Distance Education, 22*(1), 52–64.

ZS Associates. (2001). Global product marketing strategy. Retrieved July 20, 2005, from http://www.zsassociates.com/expertise/issue/global.htmlw

7

Community Colleges in a Global Society: Is There One Best Governance Model?

Cheryl D. LOVELL & Catherine TROUTH

—m—

Abstract

Community colleges are becoming an increasingly important aspect to any country's higher education system. Specifically in the United States, the Community College System has evolved in the last century from one institution in 1901 to over a thousand institutions today. There is a well-documented history, but little is known about how statewide governance systems shape or influence community colleges. Few discussions have examined statewide patterns and far fewer have examined community college governance systems. The statewide system design of higher education and its relationship to the structure of the State Government is also critical to examine. Since many countries are modeling their community colleges after the United States, it makes sense to identify and to discuss the various aspects to community college governance found in the United States to see if there is any relevance to the rest of the world. Thus the purposes of this paper are to describe what other countries are doing with respect to community colleges; to provide a brief overview of the United States post-secondary system; to define different types of governance taxonomies that exist in the United States today and to determine the strengths and weaknesses of each model; and to propose questions that other post-secondary leaders should consider when determining the type of governance system that would be best for their post-secondary community.

Introduction

The community college system in the United States has evolved in the last century from one institution in Illinois in 1901 to over a thousand institutions (Tollefson, 2000). This remarkable past has been documented and chronicled from those within and outside of the community college movement (Brint & Karabel, 1989; Cohen & Brawer, 1996; Cohen, Brawer, & Associates, 1994; Goodchild & Wechsler, 1997; Ratcliff, Schwarz, & Ebbers, 1994). Even with this well-documented history, little is known about how statewide governance systems shape or influence community colleges in the United States and the extent to which they are effective. To date, few discussions, outside of Lovell and Trouth (2002) and Richardson, Bracco, Callan, and Finney (1999), have examined statewide patterns and far fewer have examined the factors that influence the governance mechanisms for community colleges. The statewide system design of higher education and its relationship to the structure of the state government is critical because a flawed or inadequate structure nets limited successes even when strong and effective leaders are present (Richardson et al., 1999).

The issue of how to construct a community college governance system is critical for higher education policy makers around the world. The primary role of this paper is to review the different types of community college governance models in the United States and to make observations about these models hoping to determine, if possible, if there is one best model. This is preceded by a short discussion of how different countries are adapting the U.S. model to their own systems. Readers should note that a related paper that focuses on the governance models as well as issues of effectiveness that affect community college governance only in the United States is also available (Lovell & Trouth, 2004).

Comparisons of any type often over generalize observations and stereotypes, hence the authors admit that comparing the educational systems of other countries to that of the United States is a tremendous undertaking that could lead to inaccurate assumptions or conclusions. The authors caution that what has worked in the United States is not necessarily appropriate for another country without consideration of their own history, culture, educational goals, and government system.

Adapting U.S. Community College Models Around the Globe

Many countries have adopted or are considering adopting the community college model to their own needs (Raby & Tarrow, 1996). Adopting a foreign model is problematic for some of these countries because of the globalization issues introduced by such an adoption. As Altbach (2002) points out:

> Deep inequalities undergird many of the current trends in globalization.... A few countries dominate global scientific systems, the new technologies are owned primarily by multinational corporations or academic institutions in the major Western industrialized nations, and the domination of English creates advantages for the countries that use English as the medium of instruction and research. All this means that the developing countries find themselves dependent on the major academic superpowers. (pp. 29–30)

South Africa has considered establishing community colleges because the local and inclusive nature of community colleges could aid in redressing the wrongs of apartheid. However, îSouth Africans have been opposed to any attempt to import foreign models, but have opted instead for a process that would lead to development of a South African Community College modelî (Zuma, 1996, p. 322). Latin American nations have had varying success with 2-year institutions, and some are turning to American community college models for help. However, the intent is to learn from the U.S. community colleges, not imitate them (de Moura Castro, Bernasconi, & Verdisco, 2001).

For countries adapting the U.S. model, some aspects of community colleges in the U.S. system may transfer well, while others may not transfer. For example, while Egypt has successful 2-year vocational institutions, the concept of local control in governance common in U.S. community college systems would not translate well in that society. The deans of the institutions are appointed by the national minister of higher education. Local councils are in place to implement national educational policies and administer the institution rather than to establish their own policies (Elmallah, Gezi, & Soliman, 1996).

Jordan has also adopted community colleges into a system controlled at the national level rather than the local level. In 1998, all community colleges were put under the control of one university (Reiter, 2002). This is a different adaptation of governance than in U.S. community colleges, where community colleges are normally free-standing institutions separate from the 4-year university sector. Israel's regional colleges have a governance system that falls between the U.S. and Jordanian system. The colleges are governed locally for adult education programmes but their academic tracks are governed by the 4-year universities (Iram, 1996). In Vietnam, the universities are also involved with the community colleges. To ensure articulation from the community colleges to the universities, the universities monitor academic programmes delivered at the colleges and also monitor entrance exams taken at the colleges for transfer to the university (Do & Ngo, 2002).

Japan has also adapted the community college model to its own needs. In the U.S. model, private 4-year institutions have mostly disappeared in favour of public institutions (June, 2003). In Japan, most 2-year junior colleges are private. These private institutions are structured in a similar fashion to 4-year institutions and educate most of the women in higher education. However, several partnerships with American community colleges have established community colleges with an American structure. These institutions have not been as successful in graduating students (Yamano & Hawkins, 1996). Aruba has recently decided to merge four independent technical colleges into one community college based on the American model. They face the task of merging four governance structures into one new governance structure. Trinidad and Tobago faces a similar task as the nation merges seven technical institutions on Trinidad into one community college (Wright, 2000).

Two interesting proposals exist internationally to adapt the community college concept to the level of a continent. In Europe, the Association for Community Colleges (ACC) is working to establish European community colleges. These colleges would be based in a locality and reflect the local culture but be open enrollment for all Europeans and offer courses with a common European theme (see ACC web site, http://www.acc.eu.org/). There is also a proposal to create an African Virtual Community College (AVCC). Once again, there would be local online campuses in each country, but Pan African themes would be emphasized in the curriculum (Darkwa & Eskow, 2000). Governance would rest both with the local colleges and with coordinating councils consisting of representatives from each participating country. The governance issues would be similar to local community colleges having local control but oversight from a state or national government.

A Brief Overview of the U.S. Post-secondary System

As far as post-secondary (or tertiary) options for continuing education, the United States offers students options for attendance at a community college, vocational and technical institutions, baccalaureate granting universities, then graduate or professional schools. The United States has had a longstanding policy effort to provide access and opportunity at the tertiary level. The goal of making post-secondary education available to the masses is embedded in federal policies through federal student financial aid of grants and loans. Over the last few decades, more reliance has been on loans than grants. Regardless of federal funding support levels, it has become "expected" that participation in postsecondary education in the United States is an entitlement. State policies also have supported post-secondary education opportunities through additional state student financial aid as well as direct financial support to the public institutions in the state.

The community colleges are typically funded on a local city or county level in addition to receiving state and federal funding as described above. The community colleges in the United States have become broad based institutions offering vocational and occupational education yet also provide the foundational years (i.e., 2 years of general education) required for the completion of a baccalaureate college degree. These institutions are also known as "open access" institutions where admission is not competitive. Students may enter a community college for vocational interests or general higher education interest. Assessments are administered to ensure adequate placement in appropriate coursework.

Because of multiple streams of revenue, decision making at the post-secondary level is complex with many stakeholders in the decision making process. It is necessary to understand the nuances of governance in the United States to understand better how governance in the community college system works.

Definitions and Taxonomies of Governance Systems in the United States

Governance is a key term that needs to be defined to better understand how community colleges in the United States make decisions. Governance is the decision-making authority for an organization that is typically exercised by boards. For community colleges in the United States, governing boards typically appoint the chief executive of the institution or system, establish policies and approve transactions related to faculty and personnel, ensure fiscal integrity, and perform other management functions (Education Commission of the States, 1997). Although governing boards have control over their institutions, in practice they attempt to balance their authority with some level of institutional autonomy (Berdahl & McConnell, 1999).

Historically, boards have been categorized as consolidated governance systems, segmental systems, and campus-level boards (Education Commission of the States, 1997; Kerr & Gade, 1989). In a system with consolidated governing boards, one board governs all public institutions within a state, or one board governs all baccalaureate campuses with different arrangements for community institutions. A segmental system is characterized as having separate boards for different types of institutions. Under a segmental system, all types of institutions, including research universities, comprehensive colleges, and community colleges may have separate boards. An institution-level board is an autonomous board with authority over a single institution, even if the institution itself has multiple campuses.

Another key term is statewide coordination. Statewide coordination is necessary to ensure that post-secondary systems work collectively towards the state interest (Education Commission of the States, 1997). Statewide coordination comprises the formal mechanisms that states use to organize higher education in a united manner. Coordinating boards tend to have the functional responsibility for statewide planning and policy leadership; policy analysis and problem resolution; defining the mission for each postsecondary institution in the state; academic program review and approval; budget development, development of funding formulae, and resource allocation; providing financial aid to students;

information, assessment, and accountability systems; licensing and oversight; implementing statewide projects and initiatives; and quality assurance (McGuinness, 1997).

These definitions will guide our discussion about the common classification systems of statewide governance. The five taxonomies, we have identified, include two that describe statewide governance for all public higher education institutions, and three that describe governance taxonomies specifically for community colleges.

In the first taxonomy, developed by McGuinness and ECS, states are formally divided into three types of decision-making structures: governing board states, coordinating board states, and planning/ service agency states (Education Commission of the States, 1997; McGuinness, 2002). Consolidated governing board states assign coordinating responsibilities to a board that also has primary responsibilities to govern the institutions under its jurisdiction. There are 21 states classified in this taxonomy as governing board states. Coordinating board states have boards that function as coordinating agencies between the state government and the governing boards of the institutions as governance is decentralized in these states. There are 25 coordinating board states. Finally, planning/service agency states have no statutory entity with coordinating authority, but may have an entity to ensure good communication among the institutions or sectors in post-secondary education. There are four planning/service agency states.

The second statewide governance taxonomy is based on a recent study that classifies states in terms of federal systems, unified systems, and segmented systems (Richardson et al., 1999). A federal system, according to Richardson et al. (1999), organizes institutions under a range of governing boards that are required to work directly with a statewide coordinating board. In this system, the coordinating board has authority from the legislature to represent the public interest in areas such as budgeting, program planning and approval, articulation, and information collection and reporting. This system is termed a federal system because it reflects the influences of federalism (a federation of entities) such as the one described in the U.S. Constitution.

A unified system places all institutions under a single governing board that works directly with the governor and legislature in budgeting, programme planning and approval, articulation, and information collection and reporting. A segmented system has two or more governing boards that supervise single institutions or groupings of institutions. In a segmented system there is no single statewide agency with statutory authority in the areas of budgeting, programme planning and approval, articulation, and information collection and reporting.

Part of the problem with these two statewide taxonomies is that they do not take into consideration the context of the complex structures found in many states, such as multi-campus systems, single board institutions, vocational and technical institutions, and most importantly, community college governance systems. To reflect the specifics of community college coordination and governance, three additional taxonomies are examined.

In the third taxonomy, developed by ECS in 1997, the states are classified according to the type of board that has primary responsibilities for community colleges. This effort is an important contribution to the literature as it was the first attempt to provide a descriptive view of current statewide structures of community college governance and coordination.

When analyzing this taxonomy together with the first ECS taxonomy of statewide governance, certain observations come to mind. For example, if the state is a governing board state, community colleges governance tends to be placed under a consolidated governing board with both 2-year and 4-year institutions. For community colleges in states that use a coordinating board system, community college governance tends to be in the hands of local boards.

In the fourth taxonomy, Tollefson (1996, 1999) sorts states into five types of state-level coordination and governance with each state classified according to which type of state board has responsibility for community colleges. In the first classification, the State Board of Education is responsible for community colleges along with the K-12 system. These boards usually have minimal control over the community colleges and often the community college local boards remain autonomous to control their own institution(s). In the second classification, responsibility for community colleges resides in a State Higher Education Board or Commission. These boards generally have authority to approve programmes and recommend appropriations priorities. The states in this classification typically also have local governing boards for community colleges. In Tollefson's third classification, Statewide Community College Coordinating Boards exercise responsibility for community colleges. These boards have moderate control, particularly in financial and academic operations. In the fourth classification, there is a State Community College Governing Board with direct control over the community college operations. In Tollefson's final classification, a State Board of Regents is responsible for community colleges. These boards typically govern both community colleges and state universities.

Though similar to the first taxonomy by ECS it is useful in highlighting the level of state control involved in delegating responsibility for community colleges to one type of board as opposed to another type. As noted within Tollefson's (2000) taxonomy, the states are more evenly distributed across the five classifications. Most community college governance systems were classified as having State Higher Education Board or Commissions ($n=12$), the second highest number of states were classified as having Statewide Community College Coordinating Boards ($n=11$), and the third highest number of states classified as having a State Board of Regents ($n=10$).

A fifth taxonomy of community college systems structures was suggested by Richardson and de los Santos (2001). This taxonomy posits seven categories for describing the array of statewide governance systems in place today for community colleges. The authors build on the three categories noted above about statewide governance structures (Richardson et al., 1999). The seven categories in this fifth taxonomy include Federal/Federal States, Federal/Unified States, Federal/Segmented States, Unified States, Segmented/Federal States, Segmented/Unified States, and Segmented/Segmented States (Richardson & de los Santos, 2001).

Richardson and de los Santos (2001) provide a conceptual overview of statewide structures for all higher education and specifically for community colleges. Their typology reveals that almost half of the states ($n=23$) have community colleges and technical institutes governed by a single statewide board to which all higher education institutions report. Fifteen of these states have the community colleges as part of a consolidated system that includes some of the baccalaureate institutions. Eleven states have coordinating boards that focus solely on community colleges.

The first category is the Federal/Federal States category. Two states, Illinois and Washington, are included in this category. According to Richardson and de los Santos (2001), these states "have a coordinating board for all higher education, a separated statewide coordinating structure for community colleges, and local governing boards" (p. 45). The second is Federal/Unified States with 7 states under this category including the states of Alabama, Colorado, Connecticut, Kentucky, Massachusetts, Tennessee, and Virginia. These states have "a statewide coordinating board for all higher education and a single statewide governing board for community colleges and technical institutes" (p. 46). The Federal/Segmented States is the largest category with 11 states including Arkansas, Indiana, Louisiana, Maryland, Missouri, Nebraska, New Jersey, Ohio, Oklahoma, South Carolina, and Texas. These states have "a statewide board that coordinates all higher education and more than one community college or technical institute with its own governance arrangements" (p. 47). The Unified States category includes 9 states: Alaska, Hawaii, Idaho, Montana, Nevada, North Dakota, Rhode Island, South Dakota, and Utah. These states have "a single board that governs all degree-granting institutions of higher education" (p. 47). However, it should be noted that South Dakota does not have any community colleges, but the state does have 2-year technical colleges.

The Segmented/Federal States category represents the second largest group of 10 states. These states are Arizona, California, Florida, Georgia, Kansas, Mississippi, New York (SUNY), North Carolina, Wisconsin, and Wyoming. These 10 states "have two or more governing boards for higher education along with a coordinating or governing board for community or technical colleges" (p. 48). The Segmented/Unified States category includes 7 states: Delaware, Maine, Minnesota, New Hampshire, New York (CUNY), Vermont, and West Virginia. These states "have two or more statewide governing boards for higher education, one of which has responsibility for community colleges or technical institutions" (p. 50). Finally, the Segmented/Segmented States category has 5 states, including Iowa, Michigan, New Mexico, Oregon, and Pennsylvania. These states "have two or more governing boards for higher education, local governing boards for community colleges, and no statewide agency with effective coordinating or governing responsibilities for community colleges and technical institutions" (p. 50). In summary, the five taxonomies presented in this paper include two taxonomies that address U.S. statewide governance models: (1) McGuiness as noted in Education Commission of the States (1997), and (2) Richardson et al. (1999); and three models that address the specific decision-making models for community colleges: (3) Education Commission of the States (1997), (4) Tollefson (1999), and (5) Richardson & de los Santos (2001).

Is There One Best Model?

The question now becomes, is there one best model that most adequately describes the U.S. governance systems for community colleges in the United States? A simple question to ask but a very complex one to answer. The direct and immediate answer is no. No one model is best as each of the taxonomies has unique features that are useful to understand community college governance. However, while the last typology is meant to explain state structures in a simple model, there are also some problems. As with any model meant to simplify a complex subject, not all categories are distinct or clearly defined. For example, not all states fit neatly into one category. Richardson and de los Santos (2001) admit to making a number of "judgment calls" in placing states that exhibited characteristics of more than one category. Also, the designated names for the categories do not give a good sense of the governance arrangement implied by the category without explanation. For instance, in this taxonomy, a federal system is a state structure, which is confusing to readers who may associate the term with national-level governance rather than with the concept of "federalism." Thus, it could be difficult for some readers to grasp the concept of a federal/federal system that only applies at the state level. In addition, since the terms federal, segmented, and unified were developed to identify separate types of systems (Richardson et al., 1999), combining them into categories in this matrix (i.e., federal/segmented, segmented/unified) further confuses whatever distinction is being made between the systems.

On the other hand, one of the strengths of the Richardson and de los Santos (2001) taxonomy is that it ties together community college systems that have similar issues in governance. For instance, federal/federal systems of community college governance may not be cost-effective structures. On the other hand, federal/segmented systems show a tendency towards lack of coordination as too little oversight is provided and the system becomes more segmented. The Richardson and de los Santos taxonomy is an important step in understanding why it is necessary to gain better knowledge of how different statewide community college governance systems work. By understanding governance and coordination systems, leaders can predict the strengths and weaknesses of the systems in meeting future challenges. States with underdeveloped, inefficient systems will have difficulty in responding to challenges in a relevant and efficient manner (Richardson & de los Santos, 2001, p. 53).

The last three taxonomies examined, those that speak directly about community colleges, shed light on the complex relationships states have developed with community colleges. Part of the explanation for these complex patterns is found in the history of the development of community colleges. Community colleges have been seen, at various times in their development, as an extension of high school and therefore part of secondary education; as the first 2 years of a college system; and as a unique educational enterprise separate from both secondary and higher education (Diener, 1994). As the interpretation of the purposes of the community college changed, governance and coordination patterns also changed, reflecting the move towards placing community colleges firmly in the postsecondary community (Tollefson & Fountain, 1994).

Considerations for Other Countries

As global populations increase and as the number of tertiary institutions made available to its people increase, governance issues may rise. Several considerations come to mind. For example, how will the community colleges govern themselves? How do the programme offerings of these universities coordinate with the rest of the higher education system? Is there some level of state decision making (or governance) that would better coordinate the different universities and institutions? Equally important is to consider what level of control should the institution have and what level of control should remain at the central (or provincial) level. This question is critical for both institutional administrators of the community colleges and for government leaders to consider. It is possible with more local control to have a more dynamic institution with accommodations to the local populations. Local control would not have to mean no central control. Some decisions could be made at the local, institutional level why others could be at the provincial level. This flexibility might allow the community colleges to flourish and have more adaptability to the changing economic conditions of the country. Since a country's educational system is so integrally linked to improving economic aspects of the country, a community college system that allows institutions to be led by local administrators who would be able to make decisions that affect the institution's direction at the local level might allow for innovations in curriculum and programme offerings. Finally, a suggestion for local control does not mean governance is totally in the hands of the local campus. As in the United States, a blended system of institutional decision making with state decision making is the most common governance model. Shared governance is very common and might be worth considering.

References

Altbach, P. G. (2002). Perspectives on international higher education. *Change, 34* (3), 29–31.

Berdahl, R. O., & McConnell, T. R. (1999). Autonomy and accountability: Who controls academe? In P. G. Altbach, R. O. Berdahl, & P. J. Gumport (Eds.), *American higher education in the twenty-first century: Social, political, and economic challenges* (pp. 70–88). Baltimore: Johns Hopkins University.

Brint, S., & Karabel, J. (1989). *The diverted dream: Community colleges and the promise of educational opportunity in America, 1900–1985*. New York: Oxford University Press.

Cohen, A., & Brawer, F. (1996). *The American community college* (3rd ed.). San Francisco: Jossey Bass.

Cohen, A., Brawer, F., & Associates. (1994). *Managing community colleges*. San Francisco: Jossey Bass.

Darkwa, O. K., & Eskow, S. (2000). Creating and African virtual community college: Issues and challenges. *First Monday*, 5(11). Retrieved September 15, 2003, from http://www.firstmonday.dk/issues5_11/darkwa/

de Moura Castro, C., Bernasconi, A., & Verdisco, A. (2001). *Community colleges: Is there anything in them for Latin America?* Washington, DC: Inter-American Development Bank.

Diener, T. (1994). Growth of an American invention: From junior to community college. In J. L. Ratcliff (Ed.), *Community Colleges* (2nd ed., pp. 3–12). Needham Heights, MA: Simon and Schuster.

Do, K. B., & Ngo, D. T. (2002). *University and community college articulation for engineering and science education in Vietnam.* Retrieved September 10, 2003, from http://daihoc.tripod.com/199805-asee.html

Education Commission of the States (1997). *State postsecondary structures sourcebook: State coordinating and governing boards.* Denver, CO: Education Commission of the States.

Elmallah, A. A., Gezi, K., & Soliman, H. A. H. (1996). Egyptian community colleges: A case study. In R. L. Raby and N. Tarrow (Eds.), *Dimensions of the community college: International, intercultural, and multicultural perspectives* (pp. 273–290). New York: Garland Publishing.

Goodchild, L., & Wechsler, H. (1997). *The history of higher education.* Needham Heights, MA: Simon and Schuster.

Iram, Y. (1996). Michlalot Ezoriyot—Regional colleges in Israel: Challenges, promises, and prospects of an alternative model in higher education. In R. L. Raby & N. Tarrow (Eds.), *Dimensions of the community college: International, intercultural, and multicultural perspectives* (pp. 291–302). New York: Garland Publishing.

June, A. W. (2003). Where have all the private 2-year colleges gone? *The Chronicle of Higher Education, 50*(3), A23–25.

Kerr, C., & Gade, M. (1989). *The guardians: Boards of Trustees of American colleges and universities: What they do and how well they do it.* Washington, DC: Association of Governing Boards of Universities and Colleges.

Lovell, C. D., & Trouth, C. (2002). State governance patterns for community colleges. *New directions for community colleges, 117,* 91–100.

Lovell, C. D., & Trouth, C. (2004). Statewide community college governance structures: Factors that influence and issues that test effectiveness. *Handbook of Theory and Practice,* XIX, 133–174.

McGuinness, A. (1997). The function and evolution of state coordination and governance in postsecondary education. In Education Commission of the States (Ed.), *State Postsecondary Structures Sourcebook: State Coordinating and Governing Boards* (pp. 1–48). Denver, CO: Education Commission of the States.

McGuinness, A. (2002). *Models of postsecondary education coordination and governance in the states.* Denver, CO: Education Commission of the States.

Raby, R. L., & Tarrow, N. (Eds.). (1996). *Dimensions of the community college: International, intercultural, and multicultural perspectives.* New York: Garland Publishing.

Ratcliff, J., Schwarz, S., & Ebbers, L. (1994). *Community colleges.* Needham Heights, MA: Simon and Schuster.

Reiter, Y. (2002). Higher education and sociopolitical transformation in Jordan. *British Journal of Middle Eastern Studies, 29*(2), 137–164.

Richardson, R. C., Bracco, K. R., Callan, P. M., & Finney, J. E. (1999). *Designing state higher education systems for a new century.* Phoenix, AZ: Oryx Press.

Richardson, R., & de los Santos, G. (2001). Statewide governance structures and two-year colleges. In B. K. Townsend & S. B. Twombly (Eds.), *Community colleges: Policy in the future context* (pp. 39–56). Westport, CT: Ablex Publishing.

Tollefson, T. A. (1996). *Emerging patterns in state level community college governance: A status report.* (ERIC Document Reproduction Service No. ED 437 076)

Tollefson, T. A. (1999). Mission, governance, funding and accountability trends in state systems of community colleges. In T. A. Tollefson, R. L. Garrett, W. G. Ingram, & Associates (Eds.), *Fifty state systems of community colleges: Mission, governance, funding and accountability* (pp. 23–32). Johnson City, TN: Overmountain Press.

Tollefson, T. A. (April, 2000). Martorana's legacy: Research on state systems of community colleges. Paper presented at the annual meeting of the Council for the Study of Community Colleges, Washington, DC. (ERIC Document Reproduction Service No. ED 443 461)

Tollefson, T. A., & Fountain, B. E. (1994). *A quarter century of change in state-level coordinating structures for community colleges,* in J. L. Ratcliff (Ed.), *Community Colleges* (2nd ed., pp. 105–108). Needham Heights, MA: Simon and Schuster.

Wright, S. W. (2000). Community colleges catching on around the globe. *Community College Week, 12*(20), 6–8.

Yamano, T., & Hawkins, J. N. (1996). Assessing the relevance of American community college models in Japan. In R. L. Raby & N. Tarrow (Eds.), *Dimensions of the community college: International, intercultural, and multicultural perspectives* (pp. 259–272). New York: Garland Publishing.

Zuma, M. S. (1996). A review of community college development in South Africa. In R. L. Raby & N. Tarrow (Eds.), *Dimensions of the community college: International, intercultural, and multicultural perspectives* (pp. 303–325). New York: Garland Publishing.

8

The Formation and Transformation of the Teaching Profession in the Global Era

Brian Caldwell

—∿—

Abstract

Any consideration of change and reform on a global scale in education must include an exploration of the role of the teacher and address issues such as the preparation and ongoing development of the profession. This chapter draws on a presentation to a regional conference of the International Baccalaureate Organization (IBO) to examine the possibilities. It is appropriate to do so because the International Baccalaureate (IB) is one of a very small number of programmes that can claim to be international in orientation and global in delivery. Initially designed for students at the senior levels of secondary education, there are now rapidly growing numbers of schools offering studies in the early and middle years. The chapter is framed by work undertaken by Cheng in Hong Kong and the scenarios developed by the Organization for Economic Cooperation and Development (OECD) in its Schooling for Tomorrow project. Cheng calls for teachers and teaching that are individualized, localized and globalized, describing this as the "new triplization paradigm," compared to the traditional "site-bound paradigm" of the profession. The OECD scenarios are broadly classified as status quo, re-schooling and de-schooling. The role of teachers in the preferred re-schooling scenarios differs in important ways from the role in the status quo scenarios.

This chapter is based on an invited keynote address at the 18th Annual Regional Conference of the International Baccalaureate Organization, Asia-Pacific Region, Singapore, March 21–23, 2003.

The chapter challenges current approaches to teacher education that are mainly based in undergraduate programmes for students who have recently completed secondary schooling or are "end-on" diplomas following an undergraduate degree. The notion of teacher formation rather than teacher education is canvassed, suggesting the need for prior experience in the workforce before preparing for teaching. Traditional programmes of professional development with occasional in-service is deemed to be inadequate. Schools and school systems should develop a capacity for knowledge management that is as deep and rich for the education profession as it is for the medical profession. The case is made for abandonment of much of the existing approaches to preparation and professional development.

Introduction

Recent work by the OECD (2001) on the future of education suggests that the most likely and the most preferred scenarios may result in the transformation of schools on a dramatic scale in the early years of the 21st century. Transformation means change that is significant, systematic and sustained. Transformation of schools means that the school of the future will look quite unlike the school of the present; it also means the transformation of work for those engaged in the core business of learning and teaching. Expressed simply, the transformation of schools is the transformation of the teaching profession. If the profession is transformed then the way in which the professional is formed will be transformed.

Planning for change of this magnitude is of profound importance to those with an interest in the International Baccalaureate (IB): for those who work in schools that offer it; for those who lead the endeavour at the local, national, regional and global levels; and for those with a role in the formation of professionals engaged in the enterprise. In many ways, all of these people are well placed for success in the transformation, because the IB, by its very nature, has characteristics of the transformation in its vision and in the programmes it delivers.

I will address the following topics in this chapter. My starting point is the priority being given in a number of nations to a review of teaching and teacher education. I will then address the issue of the transformation of schools, drawing on two perspectives, one from Cheng's work (2001), the other from the OECD. The heart of the chapter is a reflection on teacher formation, going beyond both teacher training and teacher education. A central theme in the transformation of the teaching profession is that of knowledge management and I will propose a leading role for the International Baccalaureate Organization (IBO) and IB schools. I will conclude with a challenge and an opportunity as I describe the terrain for transformation, suggesting that a golden era lies ahead for the IB if this opportunity is seized.

The Future of Teaching and Teacher Education

Matters related to the formation and transformation of the teaching profession have been on the agenda of policy-makers in many nations. In Australia, for example, one of nation's most distinguished educators Kwong Lee Dow has been commissioned by the Minister for Education, Science and Training (DEST) to conduct a Review of Teaching and Teacher Education. An interim report was released in February 2003 (Committee for the Review of Teaching and Teacher Education, 2003). The terms of reference, like those for similar reviews in other nations, mean a starting point in problems in the present, with recommendations for their resolution in the short- to medium-term. For Australia, these relate to problems of supply and demand of teachers, especially in the areas of science, mathematics and information technology; and to the development of a capacity for innovation.

Reviews of this kind are necessary. They should, at the same time, include the kind of perspective I described at the outset, namely, using a scenario approach to describe likely and preferred futures, and work back to the present, which becomes a starting point for making choices for policies that will help ensure success in the transformation of schools in the 21st century. It is the intention of the Australian review to do just that, for it will produce by mid 2003 an action plan that will consider "the current situation and future scenarios" (Committee for the Review of Teaching and Teacher Education, 2003, p. 57).

The Transformation of Schools

It is worthwhile to examine some of these perspectives in more detail.

I have selected two. One draws from the work of a distinguished scholar, Cheng Yin Cheong, Director of the Centre for Research and International Collaboration at The Hong Kong Institute of Education. The other is the six scenarios developed by the OECD, referred to in my opening remarks.

The Globalization, Localization and Individualization Paradigm

Cheng proposes that every enterprise in education, including schools, school systems, universities and others with a role in the formation and transformation of the profession, need a new paradigm or framework to shape their operations. There are three dimensions in this paradigm: globalization, localization and individualization. He has coined the concept of triplization to give it coherence. The case for triplization is based on different kinds of intelligence that are necessary in the 21st century. These are learning intelligence, technological intelligence, economic intelligence, social intelligence, political intelligence, and cultural intelligence. He describes these as "contextualized multiple intelligences" (CMI). He refers to a "CMI education" and contends that "the development of students' CMI is the basic condition for the development of individuals, institutions, communities, societies, and international communities in the complex local and global contexts" (Cheng, 2001, p. 39).

It is readily apparent that schools offering the IB are providing a large measure of CMI education and that the concept of triplization is inherent in the vision and programme of the IBO. This is a remarkable achievement considering that the Diploma Programme for the final 2 years of secondary education had its first full year of operation in 1970.

Cheng illustrates the paradigm shift in teaching by contrasting the new triplization paradigm with the traditional site-based paradigm, as illustrated in Table 8.1.

Six Scenarios for the Future of Schools

While it is common to refer to a school as an IB school, in most instances the programme is nested in a large school that offers a

Table 8.1. Illustrating the Paradigm Shift in Teaching

New triplization paradigm	Traditional site-bound paradigm
Individual teacher and teaching	*Reproduced teacher and teaching*
• Teacher is the facilitator to support students' learning • Multiple intelligence teacher • Individualized teaching style • Teaching is to arouse curiosity • Teaching is a process to initiate, facilitate, and sustain students' self-learning and self-actualization • Sharing joy with students • Teaching is a life-long learning process	• Teacher is the centre of education • Partially competent teacher • Standard teaching style • Teaching is to transfer knowledge • Teaching is a disciplinary, delivering, training, and socializing process • Achieving standards in examinations • Teaching is a transfer and application process
Localized and globalized teacher and teaching	*School-bounded teacher and teaching*
• Multiple local and global sources of teaching and knowledge • Networked teaching • World-class teaching • Unlimited opportunities for teaching • Teacher with local and international outlook • As a world class and networked teacher	• Teacher as the sole source of teaching and knowledge • Separated teaching • Site-bounded teaching • Limited opportunities for teaching • Teacher with only school experiences • As a school-bounded and separated teacher

Source: Cheng (2001), p. 52.

relatively conventional programme. It is in this respect that the scenarios generated by the OECD are worth closer examination.

The OECD undertook an analysis of the internal and external environment for schools in 2000. A conference on "Schooling for Tomorrow" in Rotterdam in November 2000 led to the presentation in April 2001 to OECD Ministers of Education of a set of six scenarios (OECD, 2001). The scan of the external environment considered childhood, generational issues and the ageing society; gender and family; knowledge, technology and work; lifestyles, consumption and inequality; and geo-political dimensions—local, national and international. The internal environment was analysed in terms of existing robust school systems; trends in the development of schools as learning organizations; issues related to evaluation, assessment and certification; and teachers and teacher policies. The six scenarios described the possible strategic directions for schools over the next 10–15 years, with two considered an extension of the status quo, two involving the "re-schooling" of society, and two resulting in "de-schooling."

The following is a brief account of the major features of each of the six OECD scenarios, including a description of the likely characteristics of the teaching profession.

Two Scenarios Extending the Status Quo

Scenario 1: Robust bureaucratic school systems. This scenario is characterized by strong bureaucracies and robust institutions; vested interests resisting fundamental change; and continuing problems of school image and resourcing (OECD, 2001, p. 79). Characteristics of the teaching force are:

- highly distinct teaching corps, sometimes with civil service status. Strong unions and associations in many countries and centralized industrial relations;
- professional status and rewards problematic in most countries. "Craft" models of professionalism remain strong; and
- growing attention to professional development [INSET], and efforts to retain teachers. This is partly in the face of major teacher supply problems, exacerbated by ageing.

Scenario 2: Extending the market model. This is characterized by widespread dissatisfaction leading to a re-shaping of public funding and school systems; rapid growth of demand-driven "market currencies," indicators and accreditation; and greater diversity of providers and professionals, along with greater inequality (OECD, 2001, p. 82). Characteristics of the teaching force are:

- less distinct teaching force, a wide range of new professionals with diverse profiles—public, private; full-time, part-time. Potential quality issues;

- the new "teaching professionals" in ready supply in areas of residential desirability and/or learning market opportunity. Otherwise, problems of shortages and pace of market adjustment;
- flourishing training and accreditation for professionals to operate in the learning market; and
- transition problems until new markets become embedded.

Two "Re-schooling" Scenarios

Scenario 3: Schools as social core centres. This is characterized by high levels of public trust and funding; schools as centres of community and social capital formation; and greater organizational and professional diversity as well as greater social equity (OECD, 2001, p. 85). Characteristics of the teaching force are:

- a core of high-status teaching professionals, but not necessarily in lifetime careers;
- more varied contractual arrangements and conditions, but significant increases of rewards for all;
- a prominent role for other professionals, community actors, parents, and so forth; and
- more complex combinations of teaching with other community responsibilities.

Scenario 4: Schools as focused learning organizations. This is characterized by high levels of public trust and funding; schools and teachers networking widely in learning organizations; and strong quality and equity features (OECD, 2001, p. 89). Characteristics of the teaching force are:

- a high status teaching corps, enjoying good rewards and conditions;
- somewhat fewer in lifetime careers, with greater mobility in and out of teaching and other professions;
- more varied contractual arrangements but good rewards for all;
- major increases in staffing levels, allowing greater innovation in teaching and learning, professional development, and research; and

- networking the norm among teachers, and between them and other sources of expertise.

Two "De-schooling" Scenarios

Scenario 5: Learner networks and the network society. This is characterized by widespread dissatisfaction with and rejection of organized school systems; non-formal learning using ICT potential that reflects the "network society"; and organization around communities of interest with potentially serious equity problems (OECD, 2001, p. 91). Characteristics of the teaching force are:

- demarcation between teacher and student, parent and teacher, education and community, blur and break down. Networks bring different clusters together according to perceived needs; and
- new learning professionals emerge, employed especially by the major players in the network market. These operate via surgeries, various forms of "helpline" and home visits.

Scenario 6: Teacher exodus—The "meltdown" scenario. This is an extension of the status quo in some settings, characterized by severe teacher shortages that do not respond to policy action; retrenchment, conflict, and falling standards leading to areas of "meltdown"; with a crisis spurring widespread innovation with a future still uncertain (OECD, 2001, p. 94). Characteristics of the teaching force are:

- teacher rewards increase as part of measures to tackle shortages;
- conditions of teaching worsen as numbers fall, with problems acute in worst-affected areas, exacerbating the sense of crisis;
- strenuous efforts made to bring trained—especially retired— teachers back into schools. Often only disappointing results, particularly where school politics are very conflictual and in areas of severe shortage;
- In some countries, the distinctiveness of the teaching corps and role of unions/associations increase in proportion to their relative scarcity. In others, established conventions, contractual arrangements, and career structures are rapidly eroded;

- as schools shorten teaching time, many posts created for semi-professional "child-minding." The market in home tuition flourishes, possibly with government subsidies to lower-income households.

The OECD exercise is a significant one and deserves serious attention by all with an interest and stake in the future of schooling. The report cited in this paper and more recent developments warrant careful reading. Like all scenarios, they reflect just some of the possibilities and generate considerable passion in discussion and debate. The "re-schooling" scenarios clearly captured the imagination of participants in the process, being deemed both likely and desirable, and Hutmacher's (2001) description is cited in detail:

> At around 80 percent support, they clearly represent the "dream" schooling scenarios for those questioned. What do these visions convey? Briefly put, schools would remain in the public sector, operating in a largely consensus-based environment where funding is guaranteed, but where central government and education departments would play a different role. In contrast to the situation at present, they would be able to provide everyone with better access to knowledge as a public good but confine themselves to setting educational goals for schools through strategic medium-term targets and a general frame of reference and guidance. While education would be increasingly individualized, schools would keep the key collective function of providing a place of social integration at the local level. The acquisition of knowledge and skills by all would be of central concern but socialization—passing on the values of community, democracy and solidarity—would be just as important. Reducing the social inequalities of education would be permanent goals of systems and individual schools. (p. 238)

Formation of the Teaching Profession

How are people prepared for work in schools? Traditionally, this has been viewed as teacher training, and most nations have had institutions generally known as teacher training colleges. More recently, especially when teacher training colleges were incorporated in programmes of universities, it has been more common to refer to teacher education rather than teacher training. For most people who have entered the profession, they have done so after completing a programme of up to 4 years' duration immediately after graduating from a high school. Programmes have generally been full-time and of two kinds, either a concurrent sequence of studies in one or more discipline areas and studies in education, with periods of practicum or school experience, or they have been a 1-year end-on programme of education studies after a 3- or 4-year degree in another field. Those who did so were embarking on what they and others considered to be a lifelong career in teaching. There may be periodic professional development or higher degree studies.

There is evidence, as in the Australian review, that this pattern is breaking down. The average age of entry to preparation programmes is higher, and an increasing number are turning to teaching after a career of varying length in another field. More students study part-time rather than full-time. Those who have followed the traditional route are more likely to leave the profession after less than 10 years of service. Several nations are experiencing a shortage of people who are willing to enter the profession, although the shortage tends to be in particular disciplines and in schools in particular usually difficult-to-staff locations.

The new pattern is usually seen as an aberration and measures are proposed and enacted in an effort to return to the traditional. Such efforts are, however, more consistent with less desirable scenarios in the set of six provided in the OECD project, especially Scenario 1 ("robust bureaucratic systems"), Scenario 2 ("extending the market model") and Scenario 6 ("teacher exodus—the 'meltdown scenario"). Indeed, many of the characteristics of the apparent aberration are characteristics of likely and preferred scenarios. Consider, for example, the characteristics of teachers for Scenario 4 ("schools as focused learning organizations"):

- a high status teaching corps, enjoying good rewards and conditions;
- somewhat fewer in lifetime careers, with greater mobility in and out of teaching and other professions;
- more varied contractual arrangements but good rewards for all;
- major increases in staffing levels, allowing greater innovation in teaching and learning, professional development, and research; and
- networking the norm among teachers, and between them and other sources of expertise.

Teachers with these characteristics would also be better equipped to work in the triplized paradigm proposed by Cheng described earlier, with its focus on globalization, localization and individualization in addressing the CMI of learning intelligence, technological intelligence, economic intelligence, social intelligence, political intelligence, and cultural intelligence. A teacher entering the profession after, say 4 years of university education, is less likely to have these capacities than one who enters the profession after a career in another field and a richer range of life experiences.

Central issues for the IBO and IB schools are the expectations you set for those commencing a career in your institutions and whether there should be special programmes of one kind or another in preparing for or enhancing that career. Regional Director Helen Drennen made clear that teacher education was a priority for the IBO. Reflection on the matter in the light of the needs for transformation in schooling in the 21st century is of paramount importance.

It is helpful, however, to move beyond teacher training and teacher education to consider whether the notion of teacher formation might be more applicable in times of transformation. Formation is a term that has often been applied in some vocations. In religious circles, for example, it has been common to refer formation in the priesthood. Formation suggests that the process is a lengthy one, beginning with early socialization in the family and in school, extended through higher education, and enhanced through the wider development that comes from contact with others, including peers, partners and mentors, and a range of life experiences, including travel or work in another field. The broader the education and the richer the range of life experiences, the more likely the person entering the profession is to have the Contextualized Multiple Intelligences described by Cheng, be equipped to work in one of the preferred OECD scenarios and, it might be surmised, to serve in an IB school.

The implications for programmes in initial teacher education are significant and warrant brief mention. Cheng contrasts the aims and curriculum for a triplized (globalized, localized and individualized) programme with those of a traditional programme:

Shift in the aims of teacher education:

> Traditionally, teacher education often aims to equip teachers with the necessary competence to deliver knowledge and skills to students such that students can survive in a local community or can meet the manpower needs of a society in the economic and social developments. But in the triplization paradigm, the aims of the new teacher education should be developing teachers into triplized [globalized, localized, individualized] life long learning teachers with CMI—[Contextualized Multiple Intelligences] ... (Cheng, 2001, p. 54)

Shift in curriculum of teacher education:

> In the traditional paradigm, the focus of curriculum is on the content and delivery of subject knowledge. The structure of a curriculum is mainly based on the structure of subject knowledge and the needs for same standard contents and same arrangements for the same subject teacher group. Therefore, the curriculum is often linear, step by step, and subject dependent. Whether the teacher education curriculum is globalized (or world-class), localized or individualized is not the concern. In contrast, the new paradigm puts the focus of curriculum design on teachers' multiple intelligences and ability to enhance triplization in (or of) their own teaching and learning, students' learning and development, and schools' development. Therefore, the design and structure of new teacher education are based on the characteristics of CMI development, aiming at creating and materializing opportunities for the development of teachers' learning and teaching through individualization, localization, and globalization. The curriculum structure is often hybrid, integrative, and interactive with the support of IT, networking, local and global exposure, and virtual reality. (Cheng, 2001, p. 54)

It is clear that formal programmes of teacher education must be transformed if schools are to be transformed. There are likely to be six scenarios for the future of teacher education that match the six scenarios for the future of schools. The IBO and the leaders of IB schools can contribute to the design of the new paradigm in teacher education as surely as its graduates are needed for the IB school. Projections for the rapid growth of the IB, especially in the primary and middle years, suggest that there is some urgency in such a partnership.

Knowledge Management and the Transformation of the Teaching Profession

The successful transformation of schools calls for a "new professionalism" in which teachers' work is increasingly research-based, outcomes-oriented, data-driven, and team-focused at the same time as it is globalized, localized and individualized, with lifelong professional learning the norm for teachers as it is for medical specialists.

This suggests that the capacity of a successful school will be determined as much by its intellectual assets or its intellectual capital as much as its financial and physical capital. Thomas A. Stewart has energized the recent interest in intellectual capital. Stewart (2002, p. 11) describes intellectual assets as simply "talent, skills, know-how, know-what, and relationships—and machines and networks that embody them—that can be used to create wealth" or, in our terms, "to ensure learning." Intellectual assets are intangible assets that are comprised of human capital (the knowledge and skills of students and staff), structural capital (patents, processes, databases, networks) and customer capital (relationships with customers and suppliers) (adapted from Stewart, 2002, p. 13). This raises an issue for the IBO and IB schools of what account is taken of the intellectual assets of the organization, and what strategies are in place or are planned to enhance them. One of these strategies is knowledge management.

Knowledge management includes knowledge creation, dissemination and utilization for the purposes of improved learning and teaching and to guide decision-making and priority setting in every domain of professional practice. According to Bukowitz and Williams (1999), "knowledge management is the process by which the organization generates wealth from its intellectual or knowledge-based assets" (p. 2). In the case of school education, "knowledge management is the process by which a school achieves the highest levels of student learning that are possible from its intellectual or knowledge-based assets" (p. 2). Successful knowledge management is consistent with the image of "the intelligent school" (MacGilchrist, Myers, & Reed, 1997) and the data–information–knowledge–action–wisdom sequence (Bahra, 2001, p. 155) illustrated below:

Data are collected, stored and processed to create
↓
Information that is reflected on to produce
↓
Knowledge that is the basis for
↓
Action
↓
Reflection on which may lead to *wisdom.*

Knowledge management calls for a school to develop a deep capacity among its entire staff to be at the forefront of knowledge and skill in learning and teaching and the support of learning and teaching. This is more than occasional in-service training or professional development. This is a systematic, continuous and purposeful approach that starts with knowing what people know, don't know and ought to know. It assumes a "new professionalism," as already described, and includes a range of functions such as selection, placement, development, appraisal, reward, succession planning, contracting of services and ensuring that every aspect of the workplace is conducive to efficient, effective and satisfying work. Illustrations of practices that may be found in a coherent and comprehensive approach to knowledge management at the school level are included in a self-assessment instrument (see Appendix). The following is a sample of the kinds of questions that are posed:

- Intranet: Do you use technologies across the school to assist the knowledge sharing process?
- Search engine: Have you created a substantial, systematic and sustained capacity for acquiring and sharing knowledge?
- Knowledge coordinators: Are their individuals with responsibility for coordinating knowledge within a department or unit within the school?
- Staff election: Is a capacity to create and share knowledge a criterion in the selection of staff?
- Competencies: Do you ensure that knowledge-sharing competencies are part of training and development initiatives?
- Metrics: Do you measure the impact of knowledge sharing in different areas of the school?

The IBO and IB schools are well placed to develop a capacity for knowledge management, given that the Theory of Knowledge lies at the heart of the model for the Diploma Programme. It should also lie at the heart of teacher education but more particularly at the graduate or post-graduate level, and especially for leaders and managers.

The Terrain for Transformation

Transformation of the profession undoubtedly calls for innovation. However, if we are not to have an over-worked profession, a capacity for systematic innovation must be balanced by a capacity for systematic abandonment. Drucker (1999) calls for "organized abandonment" for products, services, markets or processes:

- which were designed in the past and which were highly successful, even to the present, but which would not be designed in the same way if we were starting afresh today, knowing the terrain ahead;
- which are currently successful, and likely to remain so, but only up to, say, five years — in other words, they have a limited "shelf life"; or
- which may continue to succeed, but which through budget commitments, are inhibiting more promising approaches that will ensure success well into the future.

Each of these criteria presents a challenge for the IBO and IB schools. Experience suggests it is a difficult task in each instance. Best practice in abandonment is as worthy a subject for research as best practice in innovation. It is likely that the rest of the educational world will wish to learn more about the IB because of your clear mission, engaging vision and the curriculum and pedagogical framework that is, at the same time, highly focused and conducive to continuous adaptation. It is an excellent framework for balancing innovation and abandonment.

In conclusion, one might ask if it really is possible to transform the teaching profession along the lines I have proposed. Writing in *Creating the Future School*, eminent Australian educator Hedley Beare (2001) concluded an uplifting chapter about teachers for the school of the future with these words:

This terrain is *not* for the immature, the shallow, the unworthy, the unformed, or the uninformed, and society needs to be very careful about what people it commissions for this task. (p. 185)

References

Bahra, N. (2001). *Competitive knowledge management.* Basingstoke, United Kingdom: Palgrave.

Beare, H. (2001). *Creating the future school.* London: Routledge Falmer Press.

Bukowitz, W. R., & Williams, R. L. (1999). *The knowledge management fieldbook.* London: Financial Times Prentice Hall.

Cheng, Y. C. (2001). New education and new teacher education: A paradigm shift for the future. In Y. C. Cheng, K. W. Chow, & K. T. Tsui (Eds.), *New teacher education for the future* (pp. 33–68). Hong Kong: The Hong Kong Institute of Education; Dordrecht: Kluwer Academic Publishers.

Committee for the Review of Teaching and Teacher Education. (2003). *Review of teaching and teacher education* (Interim Report: Attracting and Retaining Teachers of Science, Technology and Mathematics). Canberra: Commonwealth of Australia.

Drucker, P. F. (1999). *Leadership challenges for the 21st century.* Oxford, United Kingdom: Butterworth Heinemann.

Hutmacher, W. (2001). Visions of decision-makers and educators for the future of schools: Reaction to the OECD scenarios. In OECD (Ed.), *What schools for the future?* (pp. 231–242). Paris: OECD.

MacGilchrist, B., Myers, K., & Reed, J. (1997). *The intelligent school.* London: Paul Chapman.

OECD. (2001). Scenarios for the future of schooling. In OECD (Ed.), *What schools for the future?* (pp. 77–98). Paris: OECD.

Stewart, T. A. (2002). *The wealth of knowledge: Intellectual capital and the twenty-first century organization.* London: Nicholas Brealey.

Appendix
KNOWLEDGE MANAGEMENT
A SELF-ASSESSMENT INSTRUMENT

The following are illustrative items, adapted for schools, drawn from a self-assessment instrument developed by Rajan et al. (1999), *Good practices in knowledge creation and exchange* (Tunbridge Wells, United Kingdom: Create), as reproduced in Bahra (2001), pp. 110–114. Among 38 items, 12 are included in the following excerpts, each concerned with a knowledge culture that fosters a systematic approach.

Your response

> Relevance: how relevant are the identified elements to the current circumstances of your school? Score 1 for low, 2 for medium, 3 for high.
> Implementation: to what extent is each of these elements currently being implemented in your school? Score 1 for low, 2 for medium, 3 for high.

Section A: Knowledge Culture—Systems

Process	(A) Relevance 1 or 2 or 3	(B) Implementation 1 or 2 or 3	(B – A) Difference (+) (–)
Item 1 Competitor benchmarking: Identifying and implementing best practices by competitors			
Item 2 Groupware / intranet: Using technologies across the school to assist the knowledge sharing process			
Item 3 Search engine: Creating a substantial, systematic and sustained capacity for acquiring and sharing knowledge			

Item 4 Knowledge coordinators: Giving individuals the responsibility for coordinating knowledge within a department or unit within the school			
Item 5 Staff selection criteria: Ensuring that new staff are able to subscribe to the values conducive to knowledge sharing			
Item 6 Competencies: Ensuring that knowledge-sharing competencies are part of training and developmental initiatives			
Item 7 Contractual obligations: Getting senior management to actively endorse knowledge management			
Item 8 Virtual teams: Bringing together teachers and other professionals from different departments or units and in different locations via video conferencing to offer different approaches to learning and teaching			
Item 9 Communities of practice: Promoting self-organized groups where teachers and other professionals exchange ideas and thoughts on common issues, practices, problems and possibilities in the workplace			
Item 10 Team-based rewards: Recognizing and rewarding teamwork			
Item 11 Metrics: Measuring the impact of knowledge sharing in different areas of the school			
Item 12 Balanced scorecard: Ensuring that the impact of knowledge management is assessed in terms of learning and other outcomes			

9

Internationalizing Teacher Subjectivities: English Language Teachers, Post-colonial Contexts and Global Educational Markets

Dianne BLOOMFIELD & Cathryn McCONAGHY

—ɯ—

Abstract

Australian-based teacher education programmes need to respond to the increasing globalization of teaching as a profession. Australian graduate teachers are being actively recruited to sites such as Hong Kong where there appears to be strong employment opportunities for native English-speaking teachers. Student teachers are increasingly seeking teaching experiences in overseas settings and perceive this as a means of preparing themselves for future employment outside Australia. The University of New England has developed a programme in partnership with The Chinese University of Hong Kong in which a group of Australian teacher education students are placed for their final practicum in Hong Kong schools to teach within the English curriculum area. Such professional experience involves students in complex inter-cultural work and thus they need to be assisted to develop a critically reflective capacity as they journey through a field of contested discourses and teaching identities.

The place of such programmes in assisting student teachers to develop more internationalized professional identities is examined through their on-going reflective writing. This data is considered with respect to the broader discourses associated with trans-national teacher education and in particular those underpinning programmes such as the Hong Kong Native-Speaking English Teacher (NET) employment scheme.

Globalizing Teacher Subjectivities

A major outcome of economic globalization and the attendant flow of people and ideas across the world is a reduction in the defining power of nation states (Appadurai, 1997). As boundaries, national and otherwise, that have traditionally defined identity and culture break down, spaces are emerging for new cultural forms and identities. One such identity construct emerging from the globalization of education is that of the "internationalized teacher." With the increasing interest shown by Australian teachers in teaching in other countries, teacher education programmes that seek to respond with integrity to such expanding international employment opportunities need to consider what might be the preferred shape of such an "internationalized teacher identity" for their students, and further, what are the appropriate responses in terms of teacher education curriculum and pedagogy in shaping teacher subjectivities. In many Australian universities, one response has been the development of international practicum programmes within teacher education, allowing student teachers to undertake professional experience within overseas schools (Hill, Thomas, & Cote, 1997).

A recent project, in which student teachers from an Australian regional university were placed in English language programmes in a number of Hong Kong schools, provides an opportunity to consider more closely the complex interplay of subjectivity, context, culture, desire, economy and discourse that merge within the dynamics of globalizing teacher subjectivities. This particular professional experience programme is also of interest in that it has arisen in Hong Kong at a time when pressures for educational reforms are occurring against broader social and cultural questions concerning language, in particular, the place of Cantonese, Putonghua and English, in Hong Kong society. One response to the heightened attention to language in the new Special Administrative Region is government support for native English-speaking teachers contributing to the English language teaching programmes in both primary and secondary schools. In what could be termed an arrangement of mutual benefit, an international teaching experience for Australian student teachers in Hong Kong was exchanged for native English language knowledge and ESL (English as a Second Language) teaching methodology. Hence, through this programme, schooling reform in Hong Kong becomes structurally linked to Australian teacher education.

Behind this interplay of multiple desires and expectations set within complex structural relationships, there is a broader issue of the native English-speaking teacher as a commodity within the global educational market, albeit a very privileged commodity. As with any commodity relationship, questions concerning the relative value of the exchange components are of particular interest: The Australian student teacher as native English speaker offers a valued skill in the Hong Kong context; Hong Kong schools offer the Australian student teacher as learner/neophyte valuable professional experience; local English language teachers contribute as experts in Hong Kong curriculum and pedagogy; the Australian student teacher provides support to Hong Kong leaders in current English language teaching reforms; and local English language teachers with non-native English speakers' oral skills offer a cultural and language bridge between the local students and the Australian student teacher. From the perspective of the universities involved in this project, there is a multiple interplay of interests, responsibilities and accountabilities to be navigated: quality assurance (QA) responsibilities for the delivery of quality educational programmes, in this case in unfamiliar off-shore settings; accountability requirements to produce tangible/ measurable outcomes for government grant bodies; the desire to provide a research-base to teacher education practice; and strategic imperatives for international collaboration and partnerships. Within such a context, it becomes necessary for the interested players to read these contested interests and complex cultural politics and to consider the power relations at work in each stage of the programme development. This paper documents some of these readings made more difficult by the dynamics of post-colonial educational reforms in two countries at empire's end, both set within rapidly globalizing educational markets.

Critical Contextual Readings and Teacher Internationalization

It is in such a context that this paper examines the issues arising from an Australian student teacher placement programme as English teachers in Hong Kong schools. In particular, it seeks to identify the dominant discourses around the teaching of English language within the Hong Kong educational context and the Native-Speaking English Teachers (NET) scheme. Through examining data collected during the Australian-based preparatory workshops for student teachers and throughout their English teaching placements in Hong Kong schools, the paper determines the extent to which this web of socio-political and historical factors influences the student's experiences, and indeed, the extent to which the contexts can be "read" by them. This links to the guiding principle of our teacher education programme which posits that in order for student teachers to contribute productively to English language learning in Hong Kong schools, they need to be equipped not only with broad inter-cultural knowledge, but also with the skills to "read" and navigate through the landscape of discursive fields and contested cultural politics that inform this teaching context. It is through the work of critical contextual readings that "internationalized teacher subjectivities" begin to form.

Of course, this is difficult work for many student teachers, particularly as they are faced with the challenges of learning the basic skills of the craft. Our contention, however, is that all teachers require an ability to read complex contexts; that all teaching is situated in a cultural politics and contested discursive terrain. Indeed, the Australian schooling context is also characterized by rapidly changing dynamics and global impacts. Thus the Hong Kong practicum placement emerges as an interesting site for us to evaluate the extent to which our teacher education programmes equip student teachers to do this contextual reading. Further, we are interested in the appropriateness of our student teacher responses to these readings. Following Britzman (1998), we are aware that these responses emerge as student teachers navigate both the internal conflicts taking place in the intimate spaces of the teaching self, and the external conflicts experienced by the social or socializing teaching self. We explore these processes in the formation of internationalized teacher subjectivity through the traces of the conscious and unconscious journeys found in student texts, reflective journals and through our conversations with the students. Before considering an analysis of these traces we need to further establish something of the richness and challenges of the social contexts in which their journeys took place.

The Hong Kong NET Practicum in 2002

The project came to fruition as a collaborative venture between the Faculty of Education, The Chinese University of Hong Kong (CUHK) and an Australian university, the University of New England, Armidale (UNE). Funding was obtained through the Hong Kong government's Quality Education Fund for the project titled "Enhancing English Proficiency through School-Based Learning." The project arose from evidence that the NET scheme in its present form was somewhat problematic and required reforms. The focus of reforms related to the selection of suitable teachers, induction and support for NETs and some evidence that there was a high rate of withdrawal of NETs from the scheme. The *South China Morning Post* reported that "100 replacement English teachers [would be] needed to be imported under the Native English Teachers (NET) scheme when contracts of 300 teachers expire in August. Education officials conceded some overseas teachers could not adapt to the local teaching environment" (Ng, 2002, p. 4). Following the placement of 8 Canadian student teachers early in 2002, a group of 11 UNE student teachers in the final stages of their teacher education awards with majors in ESL, English or Languages other than English, were selected to undertake an additional practicum experience in Hong Kong schools for an 8-week period late in that year. Travel and living costs were funded through the grant, with the academic support and assessment of the student teachers' practice being the responsibility of UNE. The major aims of the project were:

- to provide selected Hong Kong schools with additional teaching support for the English language programme and in particular the teaching of oral English,
- to provide a group of student teachers with an introduction to working as a NET in Hong Kong,
- to provide a "pool" of potential NET recruits who could be expected in future to take up NET positions in a more informed way, and
- to provide research opportunities for both universities with respect to issues of inter-cultural teaching practice and placements.

Significantly the programme was contributing to the growing market of NETs throughout the world.

The Native English Language Teacher as Global Commodity

Graduating teachers around the world are increasingly moving into an employment scene in which teacher supply is not meeting demand. Trends in Australia, the United States and the United Kingdom are indicative of an aging population of teachers, increasingly early rates of retirement and, at a government level, insufficient planning and funding for teacher education. Indeed, this situation is currently being reviewed by the Australian government. Lam (2001) also notes similar trends taking place in Hong Kong. At UNE, graduating students are now lured by competitive offers of employment from Departments of Education in many Australian states, by educational agencies from the United Kingdom, and by stories of job opportunities in most developed countries. UNE students are indicating that they are less constrained by allegiances to local contexts or employment providers. There is a sense of student teachers "shopping around" and seeing their lives in terms of diverse professional possibilities and lifestyle choices. Communication and technology developments are also contributing strongly to this globalization of education. Student teachers access overseas teaching possibilities through websites, communicate across the world by email and download curriculum materials and job advertisements from the Web. Though the commitment may be hesitant, there appears to be an increasing desire on the part of student teachers to experiment or "flirt" with international teaching identities. One of the challenges of our teacher education programme was to open up possibilities for our graduates whilst also giving them some sense of their own privilege and the responsibilities of this privilege in the international English teacher market.

The place of English language teaching in this globalizing educational market is complex. In many Asian countries with emerging or established capitalist economies, the place of English as the world's dominant language of commerce and trade has seen native English language competence being increasingly sought by countries. Mainland China and Malaysia are interesting examples. Hong Kong, whilst having a long history of English language study within its school curriculum, appears to be in a period of reaffirming the significance of English as a curriculum area at all levels within its education system. However, in spite of an increase in the numbers of graduates undertaking post-graduate teaching qualifications for a surplus teaching workforce, there remains a shortage of qualified English language teachers in Hong Kong (Taylor, 2002, p. 5). Additionally, there is increasing concern expressed about the quality of English language teaching being delivered by local teachers. The increase in schemes employing native English teachers is indicative of their growth as a valued commodity on the world educational market. Linked to the new demand for English teachers is the formation of post-colonial states in the former British colonies.

Post-colonial Hong Kong

Hong Kong has often been characterized as a bridge between East and West, geographically, culturally and in terms of identity and language. Kwok-kan Tam (2002) extends this metaphor in stating that "since the 1970s Hong Kong has become more and more a bridge that not only crosses but gathers" (p. 112). Here he not only adds complexity to the too simplified East/West binary, but also alludes to the trend towards Hong Kong being seen at all levels as a place not just of transition or margin but increasingly of "home." Timothy Weiss (2002, p. 133) aligns himself with Abbas' ambivalence concerning the usefulness of the "East/West" binary as a descriptor for Hong Kong, in stating binaries "tend to stabilise a shifting terrain." Abbas (1997) states: "Of all the binarisms that keep things in place, perhaps the most pernicious in the Hong Kong context is that of East and West ... this is not to say there are no differences, but that the differences are not stable; they migrate, they metastasise" (p. 117). Captured here is not just a picture of diversity; it is also one of fluidity and evolution, applicable to considerations not just of culture but also of identity. Another binary that carries a similar potential to convey too strong a sense of stabilization is that of "colonial/post-colonial." After 1997, Hong Kong has undeniably moved beyond many of the defining constraints of British colonial rule. However "post-coloniality" as a defining condition brings its own new configurations of power-knowledge relations. In many ways Hong Kong is not decolonized and, in fact since 1997, can be seen as once more "colonized" in terms of its relationship with Mainland China. Additionally, together with signalling significant political and economic shifts, the term "post-coloniality" also signals important shifts in identity and social relations of power (Crowley & McConaghy, 1998).

Thus Hong Kong provides an interesting site for an analysis of the struggle for local identities in a period of political transition (Fung, 2001). It is a good example of the significance of attending to the local during periods of rapid globalization. Hong Kong has been also described as a site in which the uneasy coexistence of localism (a complex mix of nationalism and traditionalism) and globalism (urbanization and modernism) is evident (E. Cheung, 2001, p. 571). Social analysts have been interested in considering what new socio-spatial orientations the handover of Hong Kong from the British to the People's Republic of China in July 1997 gave rise to. The term "Heunggongyan" (Hong Kong people) signifies a distinctive identity of which local residents are proud, an identity described as cosmopolitan and modern (Fung, 2001, p. 595). In contrast, the "mainlanders" historically were referred to as "a backward people." However, July 1997 signalled the need for Hong Kong people to re-consider their relationship with mainlanders and to re-define the boundaries of their distinctive identity. Renegotiating the spatial distance between the national and the local, resisting having the local subsumed within the (new) national, became an imperative. What emerged was that Hong Kong people are ambivalently positioned in social terms as both Chinese and non-Chinese. Kwok-kan Tam (2002) sees Hong Kong as a "place where people continually search for and forge new identities." Additionally he links this fluidity of identity not only to "a high degree of adaptability of Hong Kong people, but also [to] the lack of stability in Hong Kong's cultural and language policy" (p. 124). It is within this context of emergent post-colonial Hong Kong subjectivities that we explore the tensions surrounding Hong Kong educational reforms and English Language teaching.

Education in Post-colonial Hong Kong

Hayhoe (2002) describes current reforms to Hong Kong education as including the following: a stronger emphasis on learning to learn; the integration of key learning areas in the curriculum; the improvement of young people's skills in communication, problem solving and analytical thinking; and the development of the capacity to make intelligent use of information technology. However, perhaps the most significant reforms currently taking place in Hong Kong, for the purposes of Australian teacher education, are the reforms to language teaching.

Whilst there are many complex and competing forces at play around Hong Kong's approach to language and its place in the education system, there are also signs that the government is seeking to stabilize its approach in terms of the development of several policies that are strongly influencing the place of English language teaching within the Hong Kong schools' curriculum. Some of the elements in this history are condensed in the sections that follow.

English and the Post-colonial Curriculum

Prior to the handover to Chinese sovereignty in 1997, English was the official language in Hong Kong. There was a privileged status associated with English medium schools (EMI), and many schools used a mixed medium approach in implementing the largely British derived curriculum. This privileged status for English is still evident in parents seeking EMI schools for their children's education, in perceptions of recruitment preference in employment, and in terms of the high priority given to the English language curriculum by the Hong Kong Department of Education. Lam (2001) observes:

> English as a dominant language has through the past century of conscientious nurture become the language of the elite and the powerful and has penetrated into the minds of the public, rendering change of status unattainable despite radical political changes in Hong Kong. (p. 93)

The events of 1997 brought a reversal of English being accorded dominant linguistic status at an official level. The elevation of Cantonese and Putonghua introduced a move towards "bi-literacy/ tri-lingual" approaches. While the bi-lingual nature of communication (English and Cantonese) in the now Special Administrative Region of China ("one country, two systems") is not new, "the reversal of dominant linguistic status (between these languages) has created much political, social and psychological dissonance" (Lam, 2001, p. 91).

Despite what could be seen as a diminishing of official language status since 1997, it would appear that English language proficiency has been linked to the broader issue of whole school reform. Lam (2001) cites the Chief Executive's Policy Address of 1997 as "underscor[ing] the message that English Language proficiency was a crucial factor accounting for the success or failure for the whole school reform" (p. 94). With the re-categorizing of schools in 1998 by medium of instruction, more rigorous guidelines were developed with a significant reduction of EMI schools and the remaining majority designated as Chinese medium schools. Lam further claims:

> It is upon the basis of greater language proficiency that the government hopes to have a more reliable criterion in restructuring two distinct streams of schools by medium of instruction. In this fashion the nurturing of the elite can be accomplished without sacrificing the egalitarian principle of educating the mass. (p. 101)

As part of the reform agenda, the government instituted a Language Proficiency Assessment for Teachers (English Language) "to determine a teacher candidate's ability for the effective teaching of English in primary and secondary school classrooms in Hong Kong" (Government of the Hong Kong Special Administrative Region, 2000, p. 1). This criterion-referenced assessment includes Reading, Writing, Listening, Speaking and Classroom Language Assessment and is compulsory with exemption only for those teachers with an English major degree. This policy change was met with a degree of unprecedented industrial unrest within the teaching profession, involving petitions, rallies, advertisements in the media, protest marches and moves to boycott the proficiency tests (Lam, 2002). Whilst the government appeared to step back in an attempt to de-escalate political unrest in the teaching profession, the on-going linkage of professional assessment, and in particular with respect to English teaching proficiency, to a reform agenda remains a defining point in Hong Kong education.

Lam (2001, p. 98) relates the "language issue" not only to the government's reform agenda for education but also to a perception on the part of teachers that it was representative of a new climate involving "an unwanted infringement on the professional integrity of the teaching profession," and that teachers were in fact being marginalised in the reform movement. The "language issue" focussed attention on an underlying insecurity around the threat of strong government intervention against rising aspirations from teachers for greater professional autonomy.

Despite the perceived threat to teacher autonomy signalled by the English Language Proficiency test, Kwok-kan Tam (2002) cites the new English syllabus documents for primary and secondary schools as one piece of evidence that "the Hong Kong people have emerged collectively and suddenly as a subject with a new identity of their own" (p. 12). The undoubted enthusiasm of this statement appears to arise from the context specific approach of these new syllabuses being seen to signal a move away from reliance on British-based curriculum and pedagogy. In these documents he reads a significant shift from a "direct method, based on British sources to the ESL and communicative approach, in which the description of local life becomes the source material of the English syllabus" (Tam, 2002, p. 122). The Introduction to the *Syllabuses for Secondary Schools: English Language 1999* signals the philosophical underpinnings of this new approach to the English language curriculum as well as its alignment with the larger curriculum reform agenda:

> In addition to education in the mother tongue and the opportunities for learning and experiencing that language offers, every student in Hong Kong is offered the right to a second language which provides further opportunities for extending knowledge and experience. Such extension of knowledge and experience is even more important for the twenty first century, with the advancements in information technology bringing about not only rapid socio-economic changes and demands, but also turning the world into a global village. The development of personality, values and abilities in preparation for adult life must be compatible with these changes. Analytical, critical and independent thinking, problem-solving strategies, including creativity, social competence and cultural awareness are of vital importance to our students. (p. 1)

The rhetoric concerning the place of language learning within a context of globalization and socio-economic change is undeniable here. English language acquisition is presented as extending not only students' knowledge but also life experience options. It is further linked not only to "creativity, social competence and cultural awareness" but also to such cognitive and behavioural approaches as "analytical, critical and independent thinking, [and] problem solving strategies." This is the language of curriculum and pedagogical reform calling for changed identities for both students and teachers in Hong Kong schools. Within this rhetoric, language learning is positioned in terms of developing a communicative tool that will equip individuals for a place in a new world. Such documents appear within a climate of increasing debate in Hong Kong regarding not only the place of languages within the curriculum but also of broader questions concerning the quality of teaching and learning of language within the education system. There is a concern that as Cantonese has become the major medium of instruction in Hong Kong schools, the standard of English has dropped and with it Hong Kong's assured status as an international city. In a *South China Morning Post* article in which the English proficiency of Hong Kong graduates was unfavourably compared to the improving proficiency of those from Mainland China, it is claimed "a deteriorating competitiveness in English has become a cause for alarm among companies operating in the SAR." The answer to this problem, the article claimed, was to push for "language to become our competitive advantage," requiring Hong Kong people to become not just bilingual but trilingual (Rousseau, p. 18).

In recent years there has been increasing dissatisfaction with the influence exerted on schools' curriculum and pedagogy by the public examinations system in Hong Kong. Despite recommendations such as that of introducing School-based Assessment components, as exists elsewhere throughout the world and in many Australian states (D. Cheung, 2001), the examination system continues to exert a powerful influence throughout both primary and secondary schools. Consequently, curriculum documents such as the Syllabuses for English Language do not appear to exert as strong an influence on what is taught in schools and how it is taught as do the form and content of the examinations. Whilst the rhetoric of such documents may signal reform, their power continues to be diluted within an exam-centric system.

Arising also from the first policy address of the new HKSAR government, was the recommendation to initiate a NET programme, which aimed to place at least one native English-speaking teacher in every Hong Kong secondary school. By the end of 2000, 441 secondary teachers were working as NETs in Hong Kong schools. In 2000–2001, the scheme has been extended to include primary schools. Fanny Law, the Director of Education, wrote in May 2000:

"As well as helping to enhance the English language proficiency of individual students, NETs are a source of inspiration in the on-going instructional review of teaching in our classrooms" (Education Department of the Government of Hong Kong Special Administrative Region, 2000, p. 1). More recently, Chris Wardlaw, Senior Assistant Director of Education, in giving support to the extension of the scheme to primary schools, described NETs as "levers of change": "NETs aren't just teachers. They are here to support local English teachers and English language development" ("Primary NET scheme," p. 4). Encapsulated within these statements is the source of much of the tension that has surrounded this scheme since its inception. The government clearly has a dual agenda concerning the NET scheme, that of English language contribution within schools and that of contributing to their broader educational reform aspirations. It would appear that the scheme has been undermined to some extent by lack of clear articulation of its perceived purpose and in some cases to resistance to the broader reform agenda and the place of NETs within this. It is within such a context of tensions around NET-driven reforms that our student teachers took up their NET practicum places.

Native English Teachers in Contested Terrains

A report arising from an evaluation of the NET scheme commissioned by the Standing Committee on Language Education and Research (SCOLAR) and carried out by a Hong Kong Institute of Education group chaired by Dr. Peter Storey was released by the government in February 2002. In a research period covering November 1998 to 2000, it appears to capture well both the contribution of the NET programme to English language teaching in Hong Kong and the challenges it raises. To structure its extensive qualitative and quantitative data collection and analysis, the report used the following objectives of the scheme, stated as aiming to:

[E]nable native-speaking English teachers to enhance the teaching of English by:

- acting as English language resource persons in the schools;
- assisting in school-based teacher development; and
- helping to foster an enabling environment for students to speak English

and practise their oral skills. (Standing Committee on Language and Research, 2001, p. 6)

The report found that across the 40 schools surveyed, NET teachers have been acting as "English-language resource persons" as intended. They have helped schools to create materials for language learning as well as introducing teaching innovations. However, amongst the constraints identified with respect to this aspect of their role is a lack of collaboration between NETs and local teachers, arising from not only workload pressures but also from a perceived lack of a "sharing culture." The entrenched practices and expectations largely associated with the exam-oriented system are seen as limiting the extent to which "real innovation is possible." The report quotes one NET respondent: "NETs are caught in a predicament between the expectations of the Education Department for NETs to act as change agents and the resistance of local staff who cling to traditional practices" (Standing Committee on Language and Research, 2001, p. 211). Whilst NET teachers themselves saw their potential impact as positive, local teachers saw it as limited considering their ratio of staffing was generally one NET to 1,000 students. Additionally, the NET work was seen by some principals, local teachers, parents and students as incorporating more "fun and games," and as largely peripheral to learning for examinations.

In terms of the third objective, that of creating an "enabling environment for students to speak English and practice oral skills," data from the Hong Kong Attainment Tests was examined in an attempt to gauge the effect of the NET on learning outcomes. Whilst there were definite indications of improvement in oral and listening scores due to the presence of a NET, it appeared that lower ability and younger students benefited most if the NET co-taught with a local teacher. Attitudinal data strongly indicated that students developed more positive attitudes to both English language and the learning associated with it when they had exposure to NET teaching. Building on the assumption that "greater exposure to and understanding of the culture of the language has resulted in enhanced attitudes," the report advocates a NET role as that of a "cultural ambassador":

> The role of the NET in secondary schools should be reconceptualized to that of a resident English ambassador. The role of the ambassador has

distinct connotations in terms of cultural representation and good-will mission to promote a synergetic relationship between the language and culture the ambassador represents and the language and culture of the local teachers and students. (Standing Committee on Language and Research, 2001, p. 244)

Additionally the NET, rather than being used as a teacher of oral English, is recommended to act as a school-based resource person promoting English language learning and teaching in that particular school. Such work would involve: building up resources, "cultivating an English-speaking culture inside and outside the classroom through close collaboration with other teachers" (Standing Committee on Language and Research, 2001, p. 244), organizing cultural activities, and supporting local English teachers in everyday classroom teaching through collaborative teaching programmes. In younger classes and those with lower ability students a more collaborative teaching approach in conjunction with local teachers is seen in particular as being more effective. Additionally, the report recommends the NETs take a "pro-active role in organising ELT-related experience sharing, workshops or seminars with local English teachers," to be conducted in "an atmosphere of two-way interaction" (Standing Committee on Language and Research, 2001, p. 244).

With respect to the local English teacher and their role in complementing the work of the NET, the report recommends this role needs to be more closely defined, so that a collaborative approach can be taken in which English is being used for genuine communication:

> A whole school approach should be adopted to instil in students the message that learning a language involves more than learning the grammar and vocabulary, but the acquisition of the manner of speaking and behaving, and that the latter can be better acquired through interactive experience in using the language for meaningful communica- tion. (Standing Committee on Language and Research, 2001, p. 246)

The challenges around the roles of the NET as cultural ambassadorship, collaborative teacher and school resource arise within a context influenced by Hong Kong's move from the influences of British colonialism to a form of post-coloniality with increasing alignment to Mainland China. Against this backdrop, the issue of language has been centrally positioned. At a more micro scale, school education is under increasing pressure as a site of reform, not only of curriculum and pedagogy, but also of teacher and student identity. The "good" English language teacher in Hong Kong appears to be one who not only conforms to an examination system, but also includes in their teaching more innovative, interactive, context specific, needs-based approaches, including working collaboratively with NET and other teachers. These changes remain in tension with many more traditional philosophies and values. Although the Hong Kong education is a system in which change is evident, and the NET scheme is evidence of this, significant areas of resistance to such changes are also evident. Within this context local and traditional educational approaches and values are in tension with those of the NETs, whose backgrounds are in many cases significantly different both professionally and culturally. Jackie Wenner (2000), an Australian NET, after a year and a half of teaching experience in Hong Kong describes the post-colonial language context of Hong Kong education as a volatile situation for overseas teachers employed in the NET Scheme. From her own experience she observed that many local teachers were antagonistic towards the scheme, feeling that they themselves were "well able to meet the needs of local students and that the NETs were being given preferential employment conditions" (p. 2).

In addition, Wenner (2000) writes, NETs tended to have different expectations of teaching and learning than their local counterparts, assuming greater teacher autonomy, active and interactive approaches to learning, needs-based rather than syllabus-driven content, and assumptions around the need to make the curriculum relevant. Their own teacher education experiences tend to emphasize their roles as change agents, the importance of research and experimentation and regular critical reflection. Although the Hong Kong Education Department viewed the NETs as part of the schooling reform process, and indeed, their "new" pedagogies were "officially" welcomed, this was not the case within the staff of local schools where there was "a less collaborative framework." "Everyone is too busy with marking, setting tests and getting students through an enormous quantity of exercises and tasks," Wenner continues, resulting in considerable unease over the imported pedagogies and approaches to curriculum. As Wenner (2000) writes of her own experience: "While my colleagues have been appreciative of my expertise as a native speaker, and interested in my ideas about teaching, there is no space in their working lives for them to seriously consider integrating such ideas into their own teaching." In addition to an awareness of the marginality of their approaches, the NETs experience considerable discipline problems in their classes, unexpected considering the commonly espoused rhetoric about the obedient Chinese student. This, and the mono-cultural nature of Hong Kong education, meant that many conflicts have occurred in the implementation of the scheme and there is "considerable public discontent." Wenner's view, whilst providing an interesting account based on personal experience, does not reflect the experiences of the Hong Kong teachers.

Wenner (2000) observes that the approach to English teaching in Hong Kong schools tends to mirror approaches to other subject areas such as Biology or Mathematics. That is, English is taught in order to be examined. This contrasts with language teaching and learning approaches that consider the significance of communicative competence as the main aim. English language teaching, she claims, is crammed with content, speedily presented and tested. There is little long-term retention beyond the examination performance. Rather than encouraging language learners to take risks, which is commonly thought to be a necessary skill for language learning, Wenner argues that in Hong Kong "fear of failure is a significant tool in the teacher's student management repertoire and tests seem to be designed so that some students will always fail." Further, she argues, language teaching pedagogies in Hong Kong assume passivity rather than active engagement.

What appears from the local literature on language learning in Hong Kong is that, despite attempts to introduce reforms that incorporate global developments in language learning, the structures and cultures of schooling seem to present obstacles to engagement with these innovations. As Wenner (2000) concludes:

> The reform process underway here in Hong Kong is very much driven from the top down. Government officials and Education Department officers are enthusiastic ambassadors for change, but in the classrooms and staffrooms the same commitment for reform isn't as evident. There has already been a lot of work done on shifting approaches to teaching and learning, and the Education Department has produced resource books and curriculum documents advocating much of what many NET

teachers would like to be implementing, but these documents seem to have lain, largely ignored in the staff rooms of Hong Kong schools. Implementing change here in Hong Kong will be an enormously challenging and demanding task. (p. 8)

In summary, it is possible to list some of the discourses that operate to inform the more traditional or Confucian educational approaches in Hong Kong as follows: teaching as prescriptive, exam-centred, knowledge transmission; English language teaching as about teacher-centred transmission of a body of knowledge; English as the language of colonial legacy; English as the conduit to privilege, university access and employment advantage; pedagogy as prescriptive, hierarchical, teacher-centred; and the NET teacher as a privileged interloper, threat to local values, jobs, and discipline.

Discourses significant around the more reform-oriented post-colonial approach include: teaching as facilitative, knowledge constructing, interactive; language teaching as about interactively developing communicative competence; pedagogy as arising from within context, flexible, autonomous, productive; English as the language of the global market; NET teacher as pedagogical reformer within the Hong Kong education system; NET teacher as valued bearer of valued English language skills, innovative curriculum and pedagogy; and NET teacher as a teacher of English language competence, especially oral skills.

It is in this contested educational context that NET teachers have been working since 1998 and it is also this context that forms the backdrop to the CUHK/UNE international professional experience project. Rather than the NET teacher, in most cases an experienced practitioner from countries such as Australia, Canada and the United Kingdom, these "apprentice" NETs come to Hong Kong as beginner teachers, attempting to make the transition from university to the work-place.

International Professional Experience as a Transitional Space

The practicum or professional experience is commonly a space beset by challenge, tensions and contestation. Student teachers move across the boundaries between the university and school sites, traversing what is seen by many as a theory/practice divide. Within schools as neophytes, they occupy marginal positions, on the boundaries of the profession. They are under pressure to demonstrate to the profession and the university the professional knowledge and skills needed to move from the margins to more central positions within the profession. Practicum then is commonly experienced by student teachers as a place where not only must learning about teaching practice occur, but where understanding of power relationships and hierarchies, knowledge and meanings intersect with emerging professional identities. At its best, it is a place in which neophyte student teachers are supportively mentored by the profession; where possibilities for experimentation and flirtation with ideas, practices and teaching identities are possible; where speaking from the position of the beginning teacher can be played with and professional "voice" developed. It is a place where learning about the need to conform and follow prescriptive teaching identity constructs exists side by side with desires for experimentation and in some cases resistance. However, what counts as the "good teacher" and the "good student" is a product of place, time, politics, culture and history. Similarly, what counts as quality in terms of curriculum and pedagogy is culturally and politically situated, bound by the specifics of time and context. What is privileged in terms of knowledge and meaning arises from and at the same time determines the discourses of education and teaching and beginning teacher transitions across networks of shifting power relationships. Thus it is in Hong Kong as it is in Australia.

When student teachers are placed in an international setting for practicum, additional layers of complexity are laid down. There are different cultural, historical and political intersections around power, knowledge and subjectivity to be encountered. The challenge for universities supporting their student teachers within such international programmes is thus to develop in them the capacities to be able to "read" each new terrain and to be able to navigate them competently and knowledgably. Further, as we explained to students during their preparation workshops, our aim was to prepare them sufficiently to encounter challenges "without falling over." That is, we had a duty of care in ensuring that the Hong Kong practicum was for them a positive experience at the same time as ensuring that their contribution to the programme was professionally valuable.

Student Teacher Preparation Workshops: Post-colonial Teacher Education

UNE has participated in an offshore professional experience programme in Wuxi, China each year since 1998. Experience with student groups participating in this programme has reinforced the belief that comprehensive preparation of students and accompanying staff is an important component to the success of any international programme.

Thus a series of three 2-day Preparation Workshops were held at UNE prior to the group's departure for Hong Kong. The workshops aimed at forming a cohesive and supportive group as well as introducing them to a range of relevant knowledge and skills. These included an introduction to Cantonese language, spoken and written, a brief history of Hong Kong, issues in Hong Kong education, ESL methodologies and resource preparation, and strategies in intercultural oral communication. As a departure from an approach that mainly focuses on increasing each student's cultural knowledge bank and ESL teaching competence, the workshops also aimed to provide students with a skills base from which to analyse complex cultural and social phenomena whilst in Hong Kong. This included theories of culture, culturalism and cultural difference, post-colonial studies in education, critical discourse analysis and critical incident analysis. Thus included in this preparatory work for students was the development of their capacity to discern their own positioning with respect to the competing and complex discourses that inform this context.

Structure of the Student Teacher Placement Programme in Hong Kong

During 2002, a range of Hong Kong primary and secondary schools were surveyed by CUHK to indicate interest in accepting a UNE student teacher. Schools selected were asked to appoint a mentor teacher and to provide teaching experiences in the English language programme appropriate to NET teaching, but at a level suited to a student teacher at the point of graduation. Not only did the student teachers enter the programme from a variety of backgrounds in terms of university studies and life experiences, they also were placed in a variety of school settings in Hong Kong. Of particular interest was the issue of differences in the teaching experiences the schools chose to allocate to the student teachers. In both primary and secondary, some schools chose to concentrate their experience in one grade level only. At the other extreme some students taught only one lesson from over a cycle to a range of classes. Most students were involved in the English speaking and listening programme within their placement school, though those teaching individual classes for several lessons each cycle were expected to also teach grammar. All students were involved in extra-curricular English related activities, such as English corner, English society, conversation groups, and verse speaking training. Additionally student teachers were encouraged to informally mix with students in recess breaks and to engage them in conversation as much as possible. Students generally were placed with the English teachers in the staffroom and in most cases the English panel chair was the designated mentor teacher. In all but one school a NET teacher was also on staff, providing varying levels of support.

Student Teacher Journeys: Early Perceptions

During the 6 days of Preparation Workshops at UNE, the students were asked to share their thoughts and feelings through question-naires and focus group discussions. Additionally they completed one short piece of reflective writing in the week following the last workshop. One student described her participation in the workshops as "a journey from pre-workshop expectation to post-workshop enthusiasm." She continues:

> Initially I thought my biggest concern would be financial and family issues. Following the workshops I feel my predominant concerns revolve around issues of intercultural communication and creating/obtaining appropriate material resources to facilitate the types of lessons I hope to give…. The most important things I took away from the workshop were the realization that a smile and a nod do not infer understanding and that my idealism needs to be tempered with reality (in theory I would love to have fully interactive communication lessons but I need to be prepared for any eventuality and to be aware of limitations). Student 1 (S1)

This comment encapsulates several of the issues seen as significant to members of the group prior to their departure. These issues can be summarized into the following three areas:

Stepping Into the "Unknown"

S11: "I am excited but apprehensive, happy but nervous, confident but insecure."

S2: "I think it will be a shock to the system! ... The unknown is also an issue for me as we really are stepping out into an unknown."

S4: "The prospect of becoming part of a minority; culturally, linguistically, ideologically and so on, presents a number of prospective issues and situations to be encountered and handled in the setting in which we will be living."

An Expectation of Cultural Difference

S2: "I think it would be pretty easy for spoken words (and even physical actions) to be taken the wrong way and so I think this is a key issue that I will need to look out for."

S9: "Australian society is very different and we are accustomed to discussing ideas and mounting a case for your opinion. The concept of 'face' (in Hong Kong?) is very important and we will need to be aware of this in order not to upset our teacher or the school community by being insensitive to this issue."

S6: "You need to be aware that even though the people you are teaching do not speak English as their first language, they are not deaf or stupid."

S4: "Of definite concern is the language barrier. As non-speakers of the local dialect, or even national language, we will be placed on the outer in linguistic terms.... Having lived in a foreign country I have experienced the isolation associated with this situation and can appreciate the potential for English speakers to feel marginalized.... Added to this is the potential for us as native-speaking English language teachers to be regarded as modern-day missionaries by members of the community. They may view us as intent on corrupting and dissolving one of the dwindling bastions of the culture of the Hong Kong people, that of their language."

The Need for Differences in Approaches to Teaching, Curriculum and Pedagogy

S9: "It is no use if we embark on the prac with a concrete notion of how and what we are going to teach."

S3: "It must be very difficult (for local teachers) to step down from the authoritative teacher role, and to hand one's class to foreigners, regardless of how capable, compliant, well intentioned or invited they may be."

S4: "I hope to make it clear to my supervising teacher/staff that I am open to criticism but will more than likely be using quite different teaching methods to them. I hope to be able to devise a blend of established and individual teaching practices as a compromise."

S6: "You need to be flexible and adaptable in your teaching to cope with differences."

The Hong Kong Teaching Experience

The UNE coordinator of the programme accompanied the group to Hong Kong and spent the first 3 weeks visiting the group in their placement schools and at their accommodation on the campus at CUHK. She undertook a liaison role between the students and the CUHK programme coordinators, clarifying, mediating, and communicating. During this time, the UNE coordinator kept a journal in an attempt to record the impressions and thoughts of the group during these first few weeks. Additionally at the mid point of the practicum student teachers completed a reflective writing assignment. In week eight, the last week of the programme, the UNE coordinator returned to Hong Kong to assess and report on the students and to collect data from the student group through focus group work and final reflective writing assignments. Observations, comments and reactions to the early weeks can be grouped into the same three issue areas identified in the Preparation Workshops and thus provides a comparison to the perceptions held by student teachers prior to commencing their Hong Kong teaching placement.

Stepping Into the "Unknown"

Comfort zone issues. These not unexpectedly arose soon after arrival. Despite the high quality of the accommodation, early days brought forth issues of access to showers, computers, washing machines and the library. As CUHK graciously accommodated these demands, the students' sense of security seemed to rise.

Workload and energy. Students quickly became exhausted. This arose not only from workload expectations in the schools but also early mornings for travel, long journeys to school for some and an expectation to remain at school until early evening, often involved in extra-curricular activities. S11 commented that the teachers work ìsooo!î hard, at their desks from early morning until late. He was advised to bring food to school to save time. Student teachers in Australia are commonly exhausted during practicum, however these students were very surprised at the expectations under which Hong Kong teachers worked.

Relationship issues. The 10 students who had participated in all the Preparation Workshops seemed to form quite a cohesive group, which after 3 weeks in Hong Kong seemed to have a quality of mutual support and genuine friendship. The group appeared to offer an important sounding board, a source of teaching ideas and resources, shared domestic support and company, as well as significant overall support to the well-being of its members.

Despite some emergent tensions, stepping into "the unknown" appeared to create a strong desire to belong to the security of the group. For S6, when this support was threatened she moved to isolate the threat to ensure her own security. Such behaviour attests to the strong emotional work involved for students and perhaps NET teachers dealing with new cultural challenges.

Issues Around Inter-cultural Communication

At the midpoint of the practicum students were asked to select a critical incident that highlighted for them issues of inter-cultural significance and to identify any changes in their personal and professional understanding arising from the incident and their reflection upon it. An analysis of the students' reflective writing in response to this task indicates a diversity of critical incidents and responses and these have been summarized in a table (see Appendix). Students' "reading" of what for them were critical incidents reveal that most students were working with a pleasing depth of contextual understanding and sensitivity within what was experienced as challenging environments. The majority of students, when presented with a situation requiring inter-cultural sensitivity, chose a response of what could be termed "strategic accommodation," indicative of a level of political and cultural astuteness. In fewer cases a response of "refusal" or resistance occurred, but examination of the reflections in these situations indicated student teachers not so much showing a lack of capacity to "read" the context as of choosing to resist being "disciplined" to the position of student teacher.

It is of interest that the critical incidents chosen for analysis by most students, involved situations in which their capacity to "read" and respond required a level of inter-personal competence that was significantly heightened by the challenge of cross cultural complexity. Such complex inter-cultural work provides justification for the University's decision to prepare student teachers for this international experience not only in terms of their teaching competence but also in terms of their capacity to understand and respond to the social and political inter-cultural challenges. The common choice of "strategic accommodation" by the student teachers faced with a critical incident could be sees as indicative of student teachers operating with appropriately developed political and cultural sensitivity.

The situations summarized indicate the significance and complexity of the power/knowledge intersections around this programme. While the student group had, on one hand, a lower status as student teachers, they also secured status from their native English language competence. At times incidents arose that proved more complex for students to "read" and caused some confusion to them. Student S4 was advised she would not be able to observe lower ability classes in her primary school as teachers were both embarrassed about their level of English and also about the pupils' behaviour. She was also advised she must report to the principal any child who cries in class, as this is conveyed also to the parents. Another student teacher (S7) described being introduced to the whole school on his first day, "feeling like Chairman Mao," tripping when descending from the stage, and from then on causing laughter whenever he entered a classroom. S11 was asked whether he was a Christian by his mentor and then told that the school "was very pro China."

Differences in Approaches to Teaching, Curriculum and Pedagogy

Observations of local teaching practice. Some students were given little opportunity to observe local English teachers and were expected to teach without classroom support from the first day. Others were given little opportunity to teach in the first few weeks due to the closeness of examinations and the English staff wanting to use all available time for preparation. Some comments from students were indicative of their own perceptions of "correct" educational practices being challenged. S1, who on noting the number of red crosses for correction in books said, "that will be hard to deal with." This same student expressed surprise at the focus on the higher achieving students and that it was these students alone who were given additional work. Another student reported over-hearing a local English language teacher say to a class, "If you don't know 110%, don't speak." As this student teacher was struggling to encourage participation in English discussion in her classes, she found such an approach at odds with her aspirations for a communicative approach to language teaching.

Examinations and assessment. All students commented on the strength of the examination system in driving the curriculum. This appeared to have a strong bearing on the classes and activities they were assigned. One mentor teacher in explaining the significance of the Examination and Assessment Authority relative to the Department of Education and the Curriculum Development Institute highlighted the importance of the examination preparation document to schools compared to the new curriculum documents in English. In stressing the importance of exams in the curriculum, she indicated that her student teacher would not be able to contribute directly to the exam preparation and so it was "OK for him to have fun activities." Comments such as this imply a marginal status for the work of NET teachers, and a challenge for teachers aiming to include a more interactive, communicative approach to their language teaching. Linked to an exam focus appeared to be the strong reliance on developed texts as the basis for curriculum design. Several students expressed frustration that they were expected to teach within the confines of the text, despite believing they could develop more appropriate and engaging resources. One student with particularly challenging secondary Form One classes had to teach English tongue twisters, such as "Peter Pecker ..." to all his classes in this form, despite it emerging as largely an impossible activity. This student teacher expressed disappointment at the didactic, disciplinarian approach he was needing to take in his teaching which he attributed to the established mores around student discipline and the fact his assigned Form One classes had a low level of English competence. The mentor teacher of this student teacher perceived the UNE student's role as "getting past a perception of lack of relevance of English by students." The UNE student was frustrated with attempting to meet this aim within the confines of prescribed activities. Most students commented on the challenge of eliciting interaction and conversation in the classroom. However, observation in the first few weeks indicated that for most this aspect of their practice was improving and that despite some constraints with resources and designated programmes, the students were employing some innovative ideas that were proving effective in their teaching.

The End of the Hong Kong Journey?

The Quality Education Fund project that supported the student teacher placements in Hong Kong schools was evaluated and a final report, based largely on quantitative survey data, was prepared by the project coordinator Professor Y. L. Jack Lam (Lam, 2003). This evaluation draws on surveys that were designed to tap the perceptions of three groups: the student teachers, both Australian and Canadian, the school students they taught and the mentor teachers assigned to them within each school. Student teachers were asked to indicate on a 1 to 5 scale their assessment of their teaching expectations, professional competence, relationships with the placement school and mentor teachers as well as feelings about teaching in Hong Kong in general and in the future. In all 27 items surveyed students teachers' responses scored well above the mean, within a range of 3.2 to 4.7 indicating the group perceived the experience as valuable professionally and personally. The three areas that scored the lowest across all student teachers in the project are revealing. Firstly, data indicated there was a degree of doubt amongst the student teacher group as to whether their students were understanding what they were aiming to teach. However, responses from the students themselves indicated levels of perceived comprehension well above the scale mean. A second area of concern was the student teachers' perceptions of their students' involvement in classroom learning. "Conditioned by more active learners in Canada and Australia, Hong Kong students seem more lay-back and passive" (Lam, 2003, p. 3). However again the student survey indicated a perception that the students themselves saw their participation in the learning process as high. A third area of concern to the student teachers was related to the low level of support provided by the schools where they had been assigned. This finding aligns with some of the critical incident analysis reflective writing completed by the student teachers in which uncertainty or strain within the student teacher/mentor teacher relationship was revealed. Both sources of data suggest that apart from communication challenges at both an institutional and an inter-personal level, the students' capacity to navigate the complex spaces and relationships within their teaching experience calls on a significant degree inter-cultural understanding and competence.

A second source of data from the Lam report concerned the school student's perceptions of the UNE and Canadian student teachers' professional competence as well as their own participation and perceived attainment of learning outcomes. Scores across all indicators of between 3.54 and 4.11 reinforced data above from the student teachers and indicated that their "impact on the classrooms that they had been assigned to teach was way above average" (Lam, 2003, p. 2). Data from the mentor teachers involved in the programme also indicated high levels of satisfaction with the contribution these student teachers made to their classes and schools. Scores ranged from 3.5 to 4.75. The small sample size in this study (11 Australian students) does not support definitive conclusions being drawn. However it is of interest for example that whilst these student teachers were rated very highly for "encouraging student participation" (4.45), their lowest score awarded by their mentors was in response to the question, "Does he/she manage the class well?" (3.68). What needs further exploration here are perceptions as to what constitutes a "well managed" classroom in the educational contexts of Australia and Hong Kong, and further what is "good" teaching and who is the "good" teacher!

The report concludes:

It seems obvious that without much speculation, most of the student teachers from Canada and Australia were pleased to note that they enjoyed their professional experiences, teaching in Hong Kong. The cooperating teachers too note that these international scholars had made a substantial contribution to the schools involved in the project. No wonder, many principals called to express their appreciation and wondered if the project would be able to continue. (Lam, 2003, p. 9)

Internationalizing Teachers: Successes and Resistances

Our analysis of the successes or otherwise of our preparation of Australian student teachers following an 8-week teaching experience in Hong Kong schools can be tentative at best. Rather than success or failure, however, we are interested in the quality of their learning journeys. Our post-colonial ethic also requires us to attend to the experiences of our host institutions and schools. We observe desires, fears, tensions and ambivalences in all concerned. Although the host school principals were very supportive and welcoming, the local mentor teachers and other English language staff in some cases were more ambivalent around the presence of our student teacher's novice/expert presence. Our student teachers have shown both mature abilities to read complex situations well and to respond appropriately. At the same time, others have taken more rebellious positions in asserting their rights to "be Australian," knowing their full value in a demand-driven global educational market. Complex plays of manners, both good and bad, avoidances, friendships, senses of belonging and fear of estrangement have been observed. Our desire was for our students to be able to critically read complex contexts and respond appropriately. Whilst this hasn't always been the case, nonetheless each of the student teachers was developing their own sense of a teaching self, finding their own way with, or in spite of, our support. This then is the journey of becoming an internationalized teacher in a complex global environment, a deeply personal journey in which good preparation and support cannot guarantee predictable outcomes. Nor can they necessarily produce our ideal of the good teacher. This is perhaps a good thing.

References

Abbas, A. (1997). *Hong Kong and the politics of disappearance.* Minneapolis, MN: University of Minnesota Press.

Appadurai, A. (1997). *Modernity at large: Cultural dimensions of globalisation.* Minneapolis, MN: University of Minnesota Press.

Britzman, D. (1998). *Lost subjects, contested objects.* Albany, NY: SUNY Press.

Cheung, D. (2001). Concerns of teachers about school-based assessment. *Education Journal, 29,* 105–123.

Cheung, E. (2001). The Hi/stories of Hong Kong. *Cultural Studies, 15*(3), 564–590.

Crowley, V., & McConaghy, C. (1998). Postcolonialism, feminism and pedagogies. *Discourse, Studies in the Cultural Politics of Education, 19*(3), 269–274.

Curriculum Development Council. (1999). *Syllabuses for secondary schools: English language. Secondary 1–5.* Hong Kong: The Education Department.

Education Department of the Government of Hong Kong Special Administrative Region. (2000). *NET-Working: Examples of good professional practice within the NET Scheme.* Hong Kong: Printing Department.

Fung, A. (2001). What makes the local? A brief consideration of the rejuvenation of Hong Kong identity. *Cultural Studies, 15*(3), 591–601.

Government of Hong Kong Special Administrative Region. (2000). *Syllabus specifications for the Language Proficiency Assessment for Teachers (English language).* Hong Kong: Printing Department.

Hayhoe, R. (2002). Teacher education and the University: A comparative analysis with implications for Hong Kong. *Teaching Education, 13*(1), 5–23.

Hill, B., Thomas, N., & Cote, J. (Eds.). (1997). *Into Asia: Australian teaching practicums in Asia.* Carlton, Australia: Asia Education Foundation.

Lam, Y. L. J. (2001). Language proficiency controversy: Touching on the very core of school reforms in Hong Kong. *Canadian and International Education, 30*(2), 89–108.

Lam, Y.-L. J. (2003). *Final report on "Enhancing English Proficiency Through School-Based Learning"* (Tech. Rep. No. EMB/QEF/2000/0037). Hong Kong: The Chinese University of Hong Kong.

Ng, K.-C. (2002, January 22). One in three NET recruits to quit. *South China Morning Post,* p. 4.

Primary NET scheme woos sceptics in debut week. (2002, September 7). *South China Morning Post,* p. 4.

Rousseau, L. W. (2002, October 24). Why we should have three official languages. *South China Morning Post,* p. 18.

Standing Committee on Language Education and Research (SCOLAR). (2001). *Monitoring & evaluation of Native-speaking English Teacher Scheme (MNETS).* Hong Kong: Hong Kong Institute of Education.

Tam, K.-K. (2002). Post-coloniality, localism and the English language in Hong Kong. In K.-K. Tam, W. Dissanayake, & T. S.-H. Yip (Eds.), *Sights of contestation: Localism, globalism and cultural production in Asia and the Pacific* (pp. 111–130). Hong Kong: The Chinese University Press.

Taylor, M. (2002, November 5). Would-be teachers go back to school. *South China Morning Post*, p. 5.

Weiss, T. (2002). Hybridity and the transcultural imaginary in identity construction. In K.-K. Tam, W. Dissanayake, & and T. S.-H. Yip (Eds.), *Sights of contestation: Localism, globalism and cultural production in Asia and the Pacific* (pp. 131–154). Hong Kong: The Chinese University Press.

Wenner, J. (2000). Reflections of a "NET" in Hong Kong. *International Education,* 4(3). Retrieved September 30, 2001, from http://www.canberra.edu.au/education/crie/ieej_home.html.

Appendix: An Analysis of the Students' Reflective Writing in Response to the Task Indicates a Diversity of Critical Incidents

	SCHOOL (level; location)	CRITICAL INCIDENT	STUDENT TEACHER RESPONSE	APPARENT OUTCOME
S1	Primary; Shatin	Initial avoidance of professional and personal contact by the English panel chair observed by the student teacher	S1 confused, speculation as to possibility of her "threatening" him in terms of her English competence. The student teacher persisted in attempting contact and was able to demonstrate her confidence and competence to the panel chair over time. STRATEGIC ACCOMMODATION	Panel chair after watching S1 teach in week 3 became enthusiastic and communicative, ultimately inviting the student teacher to address his staff on cooperative learning techniques
S2	Primary; Ma On Shan	In teaching the concept "long/short," S2 aimed to use her students' personal photos and refer to their hair length. The student was directed to teach the concept as in the text only using vocabulary related to "mice and rabbits."	S2 frustrated at the limited way she would be able to "teach using my own ideas because they will not fit the mould." Realization that much teaching is text and examination driven. STRATEGIC ACCOMMODATION	Resignation, "this type of incident will occur again and again (and) I will find it very difficult to stick to the content books only."
S3	Primary; Tai Po	Student teacher allocated very little teaching. Reasons given: preparation for examinations, broken placement due to sickness, mentor teacher stress leaving "no time to look after you at the moment."	Loss of confidence in her teaching capacity, feeling it was because she was an "older" woman, feeling she was not "taken very seriously." Accepted minimal practicum without questioning her mentor. CONFORMITY	Student: finally unsure about her capacity to teach off-shore. School: Operated on the assumption that because the student teacher was mature-age, she would be undertaking a "non-vocational experience."

	SCHOOL (level; location)	CRITICAL INCIDENT	STUDENT TEACHER RESPONSE	APPARENT OUTCOME
S4	Primary; Tai Po	S4 experienced difficulty in gaining support for her request to observe lessons given by experienced English teachers at her school.	Uncertainty, acquiescence at first, then despite difficulty, S4 repeated requests including writing to individual teachers. Feeling she was a possible "threat" to local teachers. REFUSAL	Interpreted the reluctance of local teachers to be observed was an "issue of saving face which was not to be ignored." Perceived the need to "compromise and adapt behaviour."
S5	Secondary; Fanling	Student teacher's difficulty in implementing his preferred communicative language teaching approaches combined with dealing with low levels of motivation in classes.	Moderated expectations and gained success in lessons which involved topics related more closely to his students' own lives. STRATEGIC ACCOMMODATION	Student teacher able to combine his own aspirations for teaching within the requirements and constraints of his teaching context.
S6	Secondary; Tsing Yi	Student teacher placed in a school with a conservative (on Australian standards) dress code. She was reprimanded about her standard of dress in not wearing a skirt, sleeved blouse and closed shoes.	Student resisted the request from both the school and UNE for her to moderate her dress—feeling that this would mean a loss of her own culture: "It is expected of us that we respect the culture we will be living in and I totally agree with that, but the culture we are living in cannot deprive us of our own culture." REFUSAL	Student refused to compromise her stand, continued to assert her right to dress as she chose. School apparently chose not to insist on her conforming to their dress code.
S7	Secondary; Tsz Wan Shan	Student teacher challenged in "reading" students' responses to him as a teacher, e.g., causing laughter when entering classes, and	Sought guidance from mentor teacher and NET and was told, "as a Westerner you are expected to be different." Interpreted that his	Appeared able to combine a fair degree of informal socializing with an effective teaching role.

	SCHOOL (level; location)	CRITICAL INCIDENT	STUDENT TEACHER RESPONSE	APPARENT OUTCOME
		uncertainty about appropriate boundaries between the personal and professional, e.g., eating lunch with student groups.	role in the school allowed him to have a more "informal relationship with students." STRATEGIC ACCOMMODATION	
S8	Secondary; Shamshuipo	S8 experienced difficulty with behaviour management in some classes.	Told class she would request the principal to give her only classes who "really wanted to learn." S8 reprimanded by mentor teacher and told "it was the responsibility of the teacher to make all students learn." S8 continued with her own approach. REFUSAL	According to the student teacher, her approach improved the students' behaviour in her lessons.
S9	Secondary; Kwun Ton	Mentor teacher's request that S9 not socialize with members of the English staff other than himself led to the student teacher feeling caught within complex staff politics.	Student on assessing the groups within the staff chose to socialize with all English staff which gained the disapproval of the mentor teacher. REFUSAL	By not aligning herself exclusively with her mentor teacher the student was seen as not highly suited to NET teaching and received an unenthusiastic mentor teacher report.
S10	Secondary; Homantin	Large class sizes and the difficulty of implementing cooperative learning approaches.	Observation that local teachers concentrate only on students who want to learn. STRATEGIC ACCOMMODATION	Designing lessons with a range of activities to keep students involved, realization of need to adapt her aspirations.
S11	Secondary; Tai Hang Tung	Student teacher wishing to be encouraging of his students' efforts in English became aware that marking comments written by	Moderated his marking approach: "I simply identified a balance between what I thought was appropriate and what their usual teacher would do." He also	"I now understand and appreciate the value of good conversation and the importance of open lines of communication."

SCHOOL (level; location)	CRITICAL INCIDENT	STUDENT TEACHER RESPONSE	APPARENT OUTCOME
	local teachers seemed strongly critical. Additionally he was guided not to give more than 78% when marking work.	worked on improving interaction and communication with fellow teachers. STRATEGIC ACCOMMODATION	

10

The Curriculum and Cultural Identity Transformation

Candace SCHLEIN

—◌◠◌—

Abstract

Teachers undergo intercultural experiences when they develop themselves professionally in foreign educational settings. Through narrative inquiry and the storying of experience, I indicate the ways in which global education reforms influence the teaching of the curriculum in the foreign context and in the teachers' native countries. The findings of my inquiry show that the interweaving of educational landscapes leads to the transformation of teachers' cultural identities. This theme is considered within the context of my experiences as a Canadian English as a Second Language teacher with the Japan Exchange and Teaching (JET) programme, and a connection is made to education in Hong Kong.

The Curriculum and Cultural Identity Transformation

In recent years, curriculum reform efforts have focused on globalization as a prime goal. Throughout the world, globalization has increasingly impacted curricula, and thereby teaching and learning. Many of the reforms often include the addition or strengthening of programmes in English as a Second Language (ESL). Therefore, ESL educators play a crucial role in implementing curricular changes that aim for globalization.

Furthermore, many countries, such as Japan and China have recruited teachers from Western countries to teach native English in local classrooms via respective programmes, such as NET (Native-Speaking English Teacher) in Hong Kong and JET in Japan. These programmes invite foreign teachers to their countries in order to teach English, but they also serve to offer students lessons in foreign culture. In this way, measures have been taken within the curriculum to prepare students for participation in the global village.

Countries that promote ESL education, the use of British and American textbooks, and the hiring of teachers from Western countries need to consider the vision of globalization that they are propagating to their youth. It is also significant to examine the experiences of the foreign teachers, as they engage with students, teachers and curricula in foreign contexts. Much insight can be gained by investigating the intercultural experiences of these "ambassadors of globalization" as they move back and forth between schools and curricula in their native countries and those on a foreign landscape.

In this chapter, I consider my own narratives of experience as a Canadian ESL teacher who participated in the JET programme for a period of 2 years. I share stories of my intercultural experience of acculturation and reacculturation in order to indicate the ways in which foreign teachers, and the curriculum, are impacted when they allow themselves to develop professionally in foreign educational situations. As a means of setting up a contextual framework for my stories of experience on the Northeast Asian landscape, I begin with a discussion of narrative inquiry and the storying of experience as a prime methodology for investigating teachers and teaching. I continue with a brief outline of the JET programme and its commitment to global education. Then, I explore theories regarding cultural adaptation and re-entry in the context of teachers and teaching. Next, I indicate the relationship between teachers' experiences and the actualized curriculum. These issues are then considered in light of my teaching stories from Japan and Canada.

Narrative Inquiry and the Storying of Teaching Experiences

The stories of my own experiences as a teacher on the Northeast Asian and Canadian landscapes result from narrative investigations into my memories of experience. Narrative inquiry into teachers and teaching produces a richness of data that would not be accessible via other forms of study. This type of research involves a multi-layered investigation of experience according to the research framework of the "three-dimensional narrative inquiry space" (Clandinin & Connelly, 2000, p. 50). This inquiry space comprises the intertwining of the temporal dimension of the past, the present and the future, the interactive dimension of the personal and the social, and the dimension of place (Clandinin & Connelly, 2000, p. 50; Erickson, 1986, pp. 127–128).

Furthermore, narrative inquiry enables researchers to investigate experience through the use of stories of experience (Clandinin & Connelly, 1994). The strength of storying teaching experiences is manifold. Firstly, stories enable researchers to access past teaching experiences in a manner that includes the emotional and the intentional aspects of situations. Secondly, the storying of experience has a transformative effect. Stories provide teachers with the opportunity to reflect on and reconstruct meaning from their past experiences. Then, teachers are able to gain new insight into the way that they teach or react to teaching situations, which could lead to new ways of approaching future teaching experiences (Johnston, 1994, p. 538).

Over the past 3 years, I have actively researched my own experiences as both a Canadian teacher in Japanese schools and as a Canadian teacher-returnee from Japan. I have storied my experiences in written form, focusing mostly on stories that are related to the theme of my cultural identity transformation that derived from my intercultural teaching experiences. These stories were assessed to be valid and plausible by referring to the literature on foreign teachers who lived in Northeast Asia (Bauer, 1995; Benjamin, 1997; Hill, 1997; Holm, 2000; Howard, 2000; Thompson, 1998) and by telling and retelling these stories to other teacher-returnees from Northeast Asia.

The Japan Exchange and Teaching (JET) Programme

The JET programme and the context of Japan are considered here both as an example of curricular reforms that aim for globalization, as well as to bring contextual meaning to my own stories of teaching experiences. It can be claimed that the first attempt at globalizing education in Japan began after World War Two. In the late 1940s Japan's formal educational system was restructured, following the model for schooling in the United States (Ishizaka, 1993, p. 2). American ESL educators were hired to teach English in Japan on a small scale since the 1950s. In the 1960s programmes such as the Mombusho English Fellows Programme and the British English Teaching scheme were created (McConnell, 2000). These programmes aimed to globalize the curriculum via English language instruction by native speakers. In this way, these predecessors to the JET programme set the tone for future curriculum reform efforts that linked education and globalization concerns with English instruction and teachers from Western countries.

In 1987, the National Council on Educational Reform agreed that some of the most important objectives for education include "educating the Japanese individual to live in a global human society" (Kanaya, 1995, p. 482). In the same year, the Japan Exchange and Teaching programme was introduced. While the programme offers three different positions to foreigners: assistant language teachers (ALTs), coordinators for international relations (CIRs), and sports exchange advisors (SEAs), only the position of ALTs is discussed here. The following quote from the JET web site illustrates the stated mission for its programme.

The Japan Exchange and Teaching Program seeks to help enhance internationalization in Japan, by promoting mutual understanding between Japan and other nations. The program aims to enhance foreign language education in Japan, and to promote international exchange at the local level through fostering ties between Japanese youth and foreign youth (Japan Exchange and Teaching Program, 2000).

The term "globalization" has been replaced here by the word "internationalization." The objectives incorporate the notion of a two-way exchange of language and culture between Japanese junior and senior high school students and university graduates from Western countries.

Responses to the JET Programme

The JET programme has been in existence for a period of 15 years, and its efforts in internationalization have produced various responses. Janesick (1993) praises the Japanese educational system for its concept of internationalization. She cites the strong English curriculum in junior and senior high schools, as well as the study of the history of Western civilization and of the United States as its strong points. Janesick asserts that "in Japan, the term *internationalization of the curriculum* carries a certain amount of awareness that we are only beginning to address here in the United States" (1993, p. 361).

Howard (2000) studies the experiences of Japanese English teachers and former JET teachers. The Japanese English teachers in the inquiry criticize the use of the word internationalization for the JET programme, as only teachers from Western countries are hired, whose native language is usually English. They wonder why the languages and cultures of people from African or other Asian countries are not included (pp. 26–27). The participating former JET teachers do not question the use of the term "internationalization." However, they feel uncomfortable teaching Western culture, since cultures vary within each country, as well as among Western countries. The JETs also resent the primacy of American pronunciation and spelling in the English curriculum in Japan, as JETs also come from Canada, Australia, England, Scotland, Ireland and New Zealand (pp. 28–29).

The positive and negative responses to the JET programme and efforts at internationalizing the curriculum in Japanese schools all focus on the interpretation of the term "internationalization." It seems that Janesick (1993) accepts internationalization to be equivalent to the study of English throughout all levels of schooling, as well as instruction in the history of Western countries. The Japanese teachers that participated in Howard's (2000) study indicate the weakness of globalization reforms that have been implemented in their own country. They argue that to truly create global or internationalized education, curricula must include an international array of languages and foreign teachers from non-Western countries.

Hall and Ames (1999) approach the topic of globalization in Eastern countries. The authors determine that most efforts at globalization thus far have been comprised of covert agendas to Westernize the world, rather than to bring together different nations under a blanket of common values:

Until now, the principal elements of globalization involve those economic, political, and technological dynamics originating in, and sustained by, Anglo-European cultures. Thus, the West is colonizing the rest of the world in accordance with its decidedly parochial values, and the consequential "global" culture looks more and more like the provincial Western world. (p. 9)

Although Hall and Ames do not discuss the example of Japan and the JET programme, their statement rings true for a programme that aims to bring about internationalization via the study of English, the preference for American pronunciation and spelling, and the hiring of teachers solely from Western countries. Although the JET programme has fostered a generation of Japanese youth who have attained a basic proficiency in English and who have become knowledgeable about the culture of the Western world, it is uncertain as to whether the programme has realized its objective of internationalizing Japanese students through curricular reforms. The next section of this chapter will shift the focus to the situation of the foreign teachers who are given the opportunity to participate in a global teaching and learning exchange.

Cultural Identity Transformation

The JET programme, in its stated goals, aims to provide both foreign teachers and Japanese students with an opportunity for mutual exchange. However, there are few studies of the experiences of foreign teachers who take part in the programme. Additionally, studies dealing with cross-cultural or re-entry issues usually focus on the effects of the experiences of students who traverse borders in search of linguistic and cultural education (Brabant, Palmer, & Gramling, 1990; Kanno, 2000; Martin, 1984).

It is of prime significance to provide a voice for teachers who deliberately take measures to develop themselves professionally in a foreign country and who actively work towards realizing goals for globalizing curricula. It is clear that ESL teachers play a special role in globalization. In the foreign context, the foreign teachers are utilized as tools for teaching foreign language and culture, which serves to open the eyes of young students to a world of countries, cultures and languages. When these teachers return to their native countries, their experiences will influence the way that they teach ESL and how they approach students in multi-cultural classrooms.

Cross-cultural Experiences and Re-entry Issues

Adler (1975) asserts that intercultural experiences are marked by encounters of culture shock, as people are forced to "survive in, and grow through immersion in a second culture" (p. 14). The author further maintains that most people perceive the experience of encountering and acculturating to a foreign culture as a negative experience (p. 14). However, intercultural experience has the potential to lead to significant growth, since "the more one is capable of experiencing new and different dimensions of human diversity, the more one learns of oneself" (p. 22). Martin (1984) discusses intercultural experiences in terms of re-entry to the native country. She states that the process of reacculturation involves a form of culture shock, as individuals relearn how to live in their native countries through recognizing the ways that they have changed while they were abroad (p. 123). Brabant et al. (1990) investigates the re-entry experiences of foreign students who had studied in the United States. They conclude that reacculturation is largely unproblematic, although the participants who did not visit their native countries frequently, as well as females in general, were seen to have some problems adjusting during the period of re-entry (p. 399). On the other hand, Kanno (2000, 1996) in her inquiry into the cross-cultural and re-entry experiences of Japanese students, argues that her participants continue to face difficulties related to re-entry, as they deal with pressure to conform to Japanese ways.

Cross-cultural Experiences and Teachers

Much of the discussion on acculturation to foreign contexts and reacculturation to native countries has centred on the situation of students. It is certain that teachers who interweave between schools and curricula on different landscapes undergo similar problems, such as culture shock and reverse culture shock. However, there are some aspects of this experience that are unique to teachers who work in schools in foreign countries.

Teachers in foreign contexts must learn to adapt their teaching to reflect the educational values of their host country. In the context of the JET programme, Western teachers must learn how to become effective teachers on the Japanese landscape. Although the programme promotes internationalization through the inclusion of foreign teachers into their schools, the foreign teachers are expected to do so within the constraints of the Japanese educational system. The JET teachers are required to learn how to team teach with a Japanese teacher of English, they must deal with a strictly enforced standardized national curriculum, and they need to comprehend the influence that the system of entrance examinations has on teaching and learning in that country.

Other issues of acculturation to the foreign context are related to learning, understanding and accepting the foreign cultural values for teaching and learning. "There are different attitudes in different cultural groups about which characteristics make for a good teacher. Thus, it is impossible to create a model for the good teacher without taking issues of culture and community context into account" (Delpit, 1988, p. 291). Teachers from a minority culture, especially those who work in Japan, need to learn the foreign culture so they could teach in an effective and meaningful manner (Shimahara & Sakai, 1995, p. 184).

For this reason, JET teachers undergo acculturation to the Japanese context on two levels, the personal and the professional. From the first day of classes, JETs need to learn the Japanese way of schooling. This includes understanding a myriad of culturally-specific aspects of education in Northeast Asia, such as the proper attire and behaviour for teachers; the rhythm of the school day, teacher-student relations, teacher-teacher relations, the Japanese work ethic, testing, homeroom, morning meetings, group lesson planning, classroom management techniques and the notion of saving face, after school club activities, class leaders, and pre-assigned groups of four for seat work activities and lunch time. Furthermore, the JETs must learn how to teach English through the use of English textbooks that adopt American spelling, with a minimal use of audio-visual equipment. JET teachers are expected to conform to the Japanese system of education so that internationalization can occur in a way that makes sense to and reaches Japanese students and Japanese colleagues. Thus, JETs struggle with personal and professional culture shock as they find or create a path on the foreign landscape.

Teachers' Personal Practical Knowledge and the Curriculum

The experience of teachers engaging in their profession in foreign contexts is significant, as it impacts the way that teachers interpret and enact the curriculum on the foreign landscape and upon re-entry to their native countries. King (1986) labels teachers as developers of the curriculum, since the teacher ultimately designs and enacts the curriculum (pp. 36–38). Connelly and Clandinin (1988) argue that teachers make the curriculum according to their own past personal and professional experiences (pp. 4–25).

Ben-Peretz (1995) states that teachers' professional memories influence the decisions that they make in the classroom (p. 7). Clark and Peterson (1986) assert that teachers' thought processes guide curricular decisions and actions (p. 255). Elbaz (1981) claims that teachers employ personal, professional, interactive and practical knowledge in teaching (p. 47). Schulz (1997) further maintains that teaching practices are influenced by teachers' life experiences (p. 1).

Researchers have indicated that teachers interpret the curriculum and implement teaching methods and practices according to their own experiences, and the specific needs and interests of their students. Teachers' cultural identity, or the cultural affiliations and experiences that teachers hold, has also been examined as a component of their personal practical knowledge, and thereby, an influence on the making of the curriculum (He, 1998; Li, 1998; Phillion, 1996).

Cultural Identity Transformation

JET teachers undergo many personal and professional changes when they live and work in Japan. Even if the foreign teachers do not subscribe to the culturally prescribed ways of living, teaching and learning in Japan, compromises are necessitated as a means of adapting to life in a largely monocultural and monolingual country. The compromises and changes that are made by the foreign teachers often result in an acceptance of, as well as a partial assimilation to, Japanese culture. Foreign teachers desire to assimilate to the Japanese culture, as its rewards include friendships with Japanese people, good relationships with fellow teachers, and competence in teaching and interacting with Japanese students. In effect, foreign teachers must first learn, adapt to and adopt the Japanese culture before they are able to approach a curriculum that includes internationalization as one of its objectives.

Over time, JETs learn how to teach English in Japanese schools, according to the Japanese curriculum and Japanese methods of instruction. The foreign teachers suppress their own instincts in the classroom in favour of those that they have been conditioned to utilize. Eventually, the new cultural way of teaching becomes less foreign and more familiar. Conscious changes to teachers' cultural identity unconsciously become natural, as teachers' cultural identity becomes transformed (Schlein, 2001, pp. 19–20). The effects of such a cultural identity transformation on foreign teachers in the Japanese context are most apparent when the teachers return to their native countries and reenter the schooling system in that context.

Consequently, JETs face serious difficulties when they reenter their native countries that are not shared by students that have intercultural experiences. Teacher-returnees experience reverse culture shock in both the personal and the professional realms, as they come to realize the extent of the changes that they have undergone during their cross-cultural experience. Many of the teaching practices and norms for teaching and learning that have been acquired while teaching in Japanese schools do not translate to the context of schools and schooling in their native countries due to different cultural values and expectations for teaching and learning. An awareness of change does not necessarily lead to the resolution of their cultural identity transformation. Many JETs embraced their experience in Japanese schools as an opportunity to learn about novel teaching methods and practices. Upon re-entry, they desire to teach with respect to their intercultural experiences, with the intention of bringing globalization to schools in their own native countries. Due to the fact that teachers create the curriculum according to their past experiences, it is clear that teacher-returnees' cultural identity transformation has a substantial effect on their present and future professional endeavours.

A Search for My Cultural Identity Transformation

Culture Shock

My first impressions of Japan began as soon as I got off the plane in

Tokyo for a period of orientation to the JET programme. My initial period of adjustment to life in Japan was marked by culture shock:

> As I stepped off the plane, I immediately noticed a few things: the intense heat and humidity, huge crowds of hurrying people, and a complete absence of Caucasians and the English language. When I got settled into my apartment, I made a trip to the local supermarket to get some provisions. I made my way down the aisles, unable to recognize the foods by sight, nor by the Japanese labels. One little boy spied me in the rice aisle and quickly began crying, rushing toward his mother to hide behind her skirt.
>
> I soon learned the word 'gaijin', 'foreigner' or 'alien'. That was the role that I would play for the next two years. I was a white-skinned, brown-haired, green-eyed, English-speaking Canadian. All those qualities ensured that I could never integrate into Japan. I was a foreigner in a monocultural society. As such, I was always conspicuous, living in a fish bowl. (Schlein, 2000a, pp. 7–8)

It was clear that culture shock and the grave differences between Japan and Canada impressed me within moments of my arrival.

I also indicate some immediate responses to the JET programme and its attempts at internationalization.

> My first days in Japan consisted of an orientation period at a hotel in Tokyo. Looking around, I could see a few thousand other foreigners who had been hired for the same purpose. I had not been accepted into the Japanese educational system for my own individual skills as an English as a Second Language teacher. Instead, I had been part of a mass hiring of teachers from various English-speaking countries around the world. In the eyes of the Japanese Ministry of Education, we were all identical. As teachers, we were all expected to be equally qualified to perform our teaching tasks. (Schlein, 2000a, p. 32)

The first days that I spent in Japan were comprised of an orientation to the professional role that I would play in Japanese schools during my stay in Japan and settling in to my new environment. It was stressed that every JET teacher was expected to teach English, teach Western culture and take part in various activities within the school and the community in order to promote internationalization. I experienced a form of professional culture shock, as I became informed of the details of my job. I felt lost in a sea of foreign teachers, as we were all expected to march out of the orientation eager to fulfill our mission of internationalization.

Professional Culture Shock

My first day as a teacher in Japan commenced with a learning experience. I arrived at the appropriate train station and walked in circles, attempting to find my new school. After a while, I stopped several people, seeking directions to my destination. Finally, a kind stranger escorted me to the gates of a building that I had already passed several times. As a Canadian teacher, I was accustomed to the North American style of schools. In Japan, I was unable to recognize a school that consisted of several buildings amongst landscaped grounds, surrounded by a wall and a gate. My first teaching period also indicated cultural adjustments that I would have to make so that I could teach in that country. I had wanted to do cooperative learning and have groupwork, but instead, I was faced with practicing teacher-centred instruction.

Adaptation and Acculturation

In the ensuing days, I became a student of Japanese culture, determining how to teach within the Japanese educational system. I slowly learned how to teach according to Japanese methods and gained a sense of understanding as to how I was able to make changes to those methods and incorporate some of my own ideas, such as creative classroom activities that involved the students working in groups of varying sizes.

Furthermore, I had to learn how to team-teach with a Japanese teacher of English, and all lesson plans and teaching materials were created as a group with all of the other English teachers. The English teachers in the schools that I worked at provided me with much insight into what was deemed to be acceptable teaching methods and practices in Japan. In Canada, teaching was an isolating experience, where each teacher planned lessons on an individual basis, without an opportunity for guidance, feedback and the sharing of ideas. In some schools, I was able to play language learning games, as long as they covered areas of the standardized national curriculum. In other schools, I was urged to practise pronunciation and grammar without communicative goals.

Additionally, I learned through trial and error the significance of the cultural notion of saving face in classroom interactions. Many of my students appeared to be shy and hesitant to speak in English. I was informed that this was due to the fact that many students are afraid to make mistakes in a foreign language. This may make them appear to be foolish or unintelligent in front of their peers, or in front of myself, the native English speaker. As a result, I was unable to prepare activities that required individual competition, or to expect students to voluntarily offer answers to questions. Instead, I prepared curricular activities that made use of "han," the pre-assigned groups of four, or I conducted whole class activities. My team teachers often translated my words into Japanese for the students, and as I learned some Japanese, I was encouraged to make use of that language during class.

As a Canadian teacher in Japanese schools, I had a difficult time understanding the classroom management techniques that were employed, as they were based on foreign cultural notions. In many instances, I witnessed my Japanese team teachers react to student misbehaviour with class discussions. It is believed that it is the teacher's duty to point out the correct way to behave without blaming specific members of the class. The underlying assumption is that the misbehaving students will rectify their behaviour after they understand its inappropriateness. In this way, the teacher also does not have to single out specific students for embarrassment in front of their peers. Other methods of managing student behaviour include calling out a student's name, or asking students to stand up in front of their desk for the remainder of the period if they have not done their homework. It seems as though this punishment provides the embarrassment of being separated from the group, which prevents repetition of the misbehaviour. Students are also encouraged to regulate the behaviour of their peers and correct each other's mistakes on homework assignments. Corporal punishment is rare, but it is not forbidden.

> The Japanese Ministry of Education had warned me that corporal punishment was practiced in Japanese schools. Although this form of punishment did not occur frequently, the Ministry of Education wished to inform foreign teachers of this possibility, thereby reducing adverse reactions to instances of physical discipline. It seemed strange to me that an educational system that promotes self-discipline among the students would also provide teachers with the power to physically punish their students.

I had been working with a Japanese teacher of English for a month. She was a kind, soft-spoken woman who rarely raised her voice in class. Most of her classroom management techniques involved calling out the names of misbehaving students or glancing at the disruptive student with a glaring eye. One afternoon, my team-teacher and I were walking towards our classroom, several minutes before the next period. As we passed a young boy, my team-teacher quickly raised her hand and slapped the boy twice on the back of his neck. She then began to reprimand him in rapid Japanese.

The boy properly tucked in the shirt of his school uniform, looked down at the floor and walked away. It seemed that his terrible offense was the fact that he was walking around the school with the shirt of his uniform not tucked into his pants. My mind became numb and my ears rang as this episode took place. I had never experienced physical punishment as a student in school, and I would never consider hitting a student in order to discipline him or her.

A year later, I was teaching a class at a school with many students that were severe discipline problems. On the particular day in question, I was teaching the worst class. Two other teachers habitually accompanied me to the class as a method of aiding me in controlling the students.

During the class, one of the students stood up at his desk and began to sing loudly. The other two teachers quickly ran over to the boy and requested that he stop singing. The boy continued with his serenade, and the teachers grew louder in their desperate attempts to quiet the student. I soon felt as though I were teaching in a circus. The noise level from the boy and the two teachers in the front, right-hand corner of the room grew. Finally, I turned to the student and requested that he leave the classroom for some quiet time. It was my hope that he would reflect on his behavior and then soon reenter the class. The student began crying and left the room.

The next week, that student looked at me with hatred throughout the lesson. The other students in the class refused to participate in the class activities. After class, the other two teachers reprimanded me. By requesting the misbehaving student to exit the room, I had disrupted the harmony of the classroom unit. As a teacher from the Canadian landscape, I found it difficult to reconcile the matter of discipline in the Japanese context. I could not comprehend a system that enforces the hitting of students and disapproves of what I believe to be standard, harmless, North American methods of managing misbehaving students. (Schlein, 2000b, pp. 55–57)

Although I needed to become informed about these techniques for managing classroom behaviour, I was also not faced with many instances of severe misbehaviour. In fact, as a teacher, or ìsensei,î I enjoyed a certain degree of respect from my Japanese students that does not exist in Canadian schools.

The most problematic area of my teaching experiences in Japan was related to the rhythm of teaching in Japanese schools. In Japan, I had to learn to arrive at school early in order to set a good example for my students. I was also expected to stay after school to exhibit my dedication to my job. I witnessed many of my colleagues remaining at school until evening, pretending to look busy, in order to make a good impression as a hard worker. Teachers begin classes late, as they only leave the faculty room after the bell has rung to signal the next period. Free time is regularly allotted during each lesson, rather than making use of extra class time by teaching new items or playing English games. Additionally, spare periods and the lunch period are spent in the staff room, while homeroom teachers eat lunch in class with their students.

I particularly remember the fact that I never attempted to arrive at school before the morning meeting. My teachers placed negative value judgments against me because I did not match my rhythms of the Canadian teaching landscape to those of the Asian landscape. I would usually arrive at school around 8:15 in the morning, under the watchful eyes of the teachers at the gates of the school. I sometimes felt as though the teachers, my colleagues, wanted to reprimand me for not getting to school at 7 or 7:30 in the morning in order to provide the students with a good example.

How could I explain to them the difficulties that I had to face on a daily basis? The days when culture shock depleted my energy, and I would stare at my six o'clock alarm clock wake-up call, wondering how I could face the hour-long commute with the train pushers, cattle-car rush hour packed trains all filled with judgmental eyes focused on me. The days that began and ended with meetings I could not understand due to linguistic and cultural difficulties.... The days that saw me teaching in thirty degree, ninety-percent humidity weather, trying to appear energetic, as my students slept on their desks without attempting to feign an interest in my subject matter. The days in which my fellow English teachers corrected my English grammar, pronunciation and knowledge of Canada. (Schlein, 2000b, pp. 63–65)

The rhythm of teaching in Japanese schools was based on unfamiliar cultural precepts. My sense of the rhythm of teaching has been ingrained in me throughout a lifetime of experiences in Canada as a student and a teacher. Even though I understood what was expected of me as a teacher in Japanese schools, following the Japanese rhythm of teaching sometimes felt wrong. In turn, grappling with the embedded cultural ideals for teaching and learning that underlie the rhythm of teaching in the Japanese context often led me to instances of culture shock.

Re-entry to Canada and Canadian Schools

My re-entry to Canada proved to be as difficult as my period of acculturation to Japan and Japanese schools had been. Upon re-entry, I felt a great deal of frustration that I had to relearn how to be a "regular" Canadian. I returned to Canada with the intention of attending graduate school. From the first day of classes, I felt as though I did not belong. I attended classes that were populated with other Canadian teachers. However, when they spoke about curricular guidelines, student testing, teacher-student relations, and classroom management techniques, I realized that my cross-cultural experiences had alienated me from the quotidian experiences of "normal" Canadian teachers and that I had to relearn what it is to be a Canadian teacher. I felt as though the personal and professional changes that I had undergone during my stay in Japan had left me with a hybrid Canadian-Japanese pedagogical outlook. I had to come to terms with the experiences of Canadian teachers in Canadian schools as a means of reacculturating to Canada.

Re-entry to the teaching profession occurred gradually. The first year after my return, I felt hesitant to resume teaching. I continually questioned what I had to offer ESL students in Canada, since I also felt like a stranger in my own native country. I also had to resolve my Japanese teacher self with my Canadian teacher self. Last year I began to teach adult students who have been relocated to Canada by their companies for varying periods of time. At first, I compared my students to those that I had taught in Japan. I frequently caught myself anticipating certain reactions or errors in my students that I typically encountered in Japan.

My students have all complimented me on my slow and clear

pronunciation of English, my attention to pronunciation practice, and my explicit demonstration of English grammatical and spelling rules. These are all teaching traits that I had learned in the Japanese context. One student recently commented that I am unlike any other teacher that she has ever had. Immediately, feelings of inadequacy surfaced, as I thought about my cultural identity transformation as a Canadian teacher-returnee from Japan. She expanded on her statement, claiming that my way of teaching has finally given her the confidence to speak English during her daily activities without embarrassment. I exhaled a sigh of relief and pondered over the meaning of global education, when a Canadian teacher successfully and meaningfully instructs ESL students in Canada according to a combination of teaching methods and teaching experiences from the contexts of both Japan and Canada.

Educational Globalization in Hong Kong

The preceding sections of this chapter present the findings of a narrative inquiry into my experiences as a Canadian ESL teacher in Japanese schools, as well as upon my re-entry to the teaching situation in Canada. In this section, I draw attention to the curricular implications and effects of educational globalization in Hong Kong. Curriculum reform efforts in the Hong Kong educational system face challenges that are both similar to and unique from schooling in Japan. Many of the underlying cultural notions of teaching and learning in Hong Kong are shared with Japan. However, Hong Kong also faces a past under British colonial rule and a present reunification with the People's Republic of China. Therefore, it is certain that the goals and intentions for globalizing Hong Kong reflect the specific needs of its dynamic society.

Nevertheless, the findings of my experiential investigation into teaching within Japan's programme for curricular internationalization leads me to the same conclusions, which culminate in the following suggestions. Namely, it is of the utmost significance for educators in Hong Kong to define globalization in a way that is the most meaningful for that context. The use of English language instruction or foreign cultural lessons should be questioned for its value in globalizing Hong Kong. Programmes such as NET invite foreign teachers into local classrooms as a means of promoting globalization. I argue that students in Hong Kong may also benefit by being taught by local teachers who have had global experiences, or by participating in international activities such as periods of time studying abroad.

Furthermore, foreign teachers who provide language instruction in Hong Kong schools should be given explicit training in the local cultural and curricular expectations for teaching and learning in order to aid the teachers in adapting successfully to their foreign professional environment. Perhaps, the foreign teachers may also be able to include some methods of instruction from their native countries so that students in Hong Kong would be exposed to novel ways of teaching and learning alongside their foreign language instruction.

Lastly, it is crucial for foreign teachers in Hong Kong to be welcomed and included as full members of the faculty in their schools. In this way, the foreign teachers will become enthusiastic participants in educational globalization, and their teaching experiences will translate into global teaching methods and practices both in the foreign context and upon return to their native countries and schools.

Conclusion

This chapter considered the theme of globalization through the lens of curricular reform efforts that aim to globalize education via the strengthening of the ESL curriculum and the recruiting of foreign native English speakers to teach in local schools. The JET programme was discussed as an example of such a programme that has been in place for a period of 15 years. The JET programme lists the desire for internationalization as its major goal, and it attempts to reach that objective by hiring English teachers from English-speaking, Western countries. Critics of the JET programme and similar curricular reforms that strive for global education warn educators and administrators of the danger involved in subscribing to such a narrow view of globalization or internationalization. They advocate new curricular reforms that include the instruction of many cultures and languages, so that the resulting education is genuinely global.

Furthermore, global education reforms make an impact on the

entire educational system, from the students to teachers and curricula. Nevertheless, most research on intercultural experiences focus on the situation of students. Throughout this chapter, I argued that it is of prime significance to attend to the experiences of teachers who are involved in curriculum reforms for globalization. Specifically, there is a need to comprehend the impact of foreign ESL teachers' experiences, as they teach in foreign contexts and return to educational settings in their native countries. Teachers develop themselves professionally in accordance with the students, schools, colleagues, and cultural values for teaching and learning that they encounter while abroad. In order to become effective teachers on the foreign landscape, these teachers need to reconcile their cultural narratives regarding teaching and learning with those of their host countries. This leads to the formation of a new teacher identity, which culminates in a transformation of the teachers' cultural identity.

Cultural identity transformation in teacher-returnees influences the enacted curriculum in both the foreign and native educational contexts, as the decisions and actions that are made in curricular situations are based on teachers' past personal and professional experiences. In this way, teachers who work in foreign contexts within the framework of global education return to schools in their native countries with international experiences and global perspectives. I included stories of my own teaching experiences in Japanese schools and those of my re-entry to teaching in Canada as a means of exemplifying the fact that teachers who practice their profession on foreign landscapes undergo cultural identity transformation, which impacts the curriculum.

The findings of this study, that teachers involved in foreign global education reforms are influenced by their experiences abroad, even upon re-entry to schools in their own countries, displays the fact that globalization through education has significant, if unintentional, resonating consequences. There is a great need for future studies to investigate the experiences of teachers' intercultural professional experiences. The development of a body of literature in this area could serve to shed light on the effects of international global education reforms on local ESL instruction, and it could provide a voice to the experiences of teacher-returnees, as they endure professional reacculturation in isolation.

References

Adler, P. S. (1975). The transitional experience: An alternative view of culture shock. *The Journal of Humanistic Psychology, 15*(4), 13–23.

Bauer, G. (1995). *Tokyo, my Everest: A Canadian woman in Japan.* Toronto: Hounslow.

Ben-Peretz, M. (1995). *Learning from experience: Memory and the teacher's account of teaching.* New York: New York State University.

Benjamin, G. (1997). *Japanese lessons: A year in a Japanese school through the eyes of an American anthropologist and her children.* New York: New York University.

Brabant, S. C., Palmer, E., & Gramling, R. (1990). Returning home: An empirical investigation of cross-cultural re-entry. *International Journal of Intercultural Relations, 14*, 387–404.

Clandinin, D. J., & Connelly, F. M. (1994). Personal experience methods. In N. K. Denzin & Y. S. Lincoln (Eds.), *Handbook of qualitative research* (pp. 413–427). Thousand Oaks, CA: Sage.

Clandinin, D. J., & Connelly, F. M. (2000). *Narrative inquiry: Experience and story in qualitative research.* San Francisco: Jossey-Bass.

Clark, C. M., & Peterson, P. L. (1986). Teachers' thought processes. In M. C. Wittrock (Ed.), *Handbook of research on teaching* (3rd ed., pp. 255–296). New York: Macmillan.

Connelly, M. F., & Clandinin, D. J. (1988). *Teachers as curriculum planners: Narratives of experience.* Toronto: OISE Press.

Delpit, L. D. (1988). The silenced dialogue: Power and pedagogy in educating other people's children. *Harvard Educational Review, 58*(3), 280–298.

Elbaz, F. (1981). The teacher's "practical knowledge": Report of a case study. *Curriculum Inquiry, 11*(1), 43–71.

Erickson, F. (1986). Qualitative methods in research on teaching. In M. C. Wittrock (Ed.), *Handbook of research on teaching* (3rd ed., pp. 119–145). New York: Macmillan

Hall, D. L., & Ames, R. T. (1999). *The democracy of the dead: Dewey, Confucius, and the hope for democracy in China.* Chicago: Open Court.

He, M. F. (1998). *Professional knowledge landscapes: Three Chinese women teachers' enculturation and acculturation processes in China and Canada.* Unpublished doctoral dissertation, University of Toronto, Ontario, Canada.

Hill, J. (1997). *A bend in the Yellow River.* London: Phoenix.

Holm, B. (2000). *An alphabet of China essays: Coming home crazy.* Minneapolis, MN: Milkweed.

Howard, C. (2000). *An inquiry into the role of the Assistant Language Teacher within the Japan Exchange and Teaching Program.* Unpublished Qualifying Research Paper, University of Toronto, Ontario, Canada.

Ishizaka, K. (1993). *School education in Japan.* Tokyo: International Society for Educational Information.

Janesick, V. (1993). Of chrysanthemums and Confucius: Some impressions of recent Japanese educational reforms. *International Journal of Educational Reform, 2*(4), 358–362.

Japan Exchange and Teaching Program. (2000). *The JET Program.* Retrieved August 1, 2002, from http://www.mofa.go.jp/j_info/visit/jet/outline.html

Johnston, S. (1994). Resolving questions of "why" and "how" about the study of curriculum in teacher education programmes. *Journal of Curriculum Studies, 26*(6), 525–540.

Kanaya, T. (1995). Japan. In T. N. Postlethwaite (Ed.), *International encyclopedia of national systems of education* (2nd ed., pp. 482–489). Tarrytown, New York: Pergamon.

Kanno, Y. (1996). *There's no place like home: Japanese returnees' identities in transition.* Unpublished doctoral dissertation, University of Toronto, Ontario, Canada.

Kanno, Y. (2000). Kikokushijo as bicu-ltural. *International Journal of Intercultural Relations, 24,* 361–382.

King, N. R. (1986). Recontextualizing the curriculum. *Theory into Practice, 25*(1), 36–40.

Li, X. (1998). *Becoming an intersubjective self: Teacher knowing through Chinese women immigrants' knotting of language, poetry, and culture.* Unpublished doctoral dissertation, University of Toronto, Ontario, Canada.

Martin, J. N. (1984). The intercultural re-entry: Conceptualization and directions for future research. *International Journal of Intercultural Relations, 3,* 115–134.

McConnell, D. L. (2000). *Importing diversity: Inside Japan's JET program.* Berkeley, CA: University of California Press.

Phillion, J. (1996). *Narrative inquiry in a multicultural landscape: Multicultural teaching and learning.* Unpublished doctoral dissertation, University of Toronto, Ontario, Canada.

Schlein, C. (2000a). *Teaching a second language and a second culture in Japan: My house on fire.* Unpublished manuscript.

Schlein, C. (2000b). *The teaching landscapes of Asia and Canada: An inquiry into the personal practical knowledge of a Canadian teacher-returnee from Asia.* Unpublished Qualifying Research Paper, University of Toronto, Ontario, Canada.

Schlein, C. (2001). *Stumbling through China and Japan with a maple leaf: A Canadian teacher's quest to understand education in Japan and China.* Unpublished manuscript.

Schulz, R. (1997). *Interpreting teacher practice: Two continuing stories.* New York: Teachers College Press.

Shimahara, N. K., & Sakai, A. (1995). *Learning to teach in two cultures: Japan and the United States.* New York: Garland.

Thompson, P. L. (Ed.). (1998). *Dear Alice: Letters home from American teachers learning to live in China.* Berkeley, CA: Institute of East Asian Studies, University of California.

11

Contrasting the Profiles of Schools in Extreme Stages of Organizational Learning: Localization in Globalization

Jack Yee-lay LAM

—᙭—

Abstract

Under the decorous mode of dissecting change processes, globalization is depicted as some unifying, homogenizing force that transforms organizational, institutional and societal values and configurations. Localization, on the other hand, seems to epitomize idiosyncratic indigenous modification of the existing framework. This chapter takes exception to such a rudimentary dichotomy by referencing to Hong Kong and Taiwan schools in diverse stages of organizational evolution. Perceptual interpretations tinted by socio-cultural experiences and upbringings of individuals regulate collective organizational behaviours and administrative orientations, bearing strong testimony to the much neglected fact that globalization must be juxtaposed with localization to provide a comprehensive lens of scrutinizing change.

Backgrounds

Cast under the global spell of school reforms, recent educational changes in many developed regions and countries bear striking similarities in spirit and in forms. Shepherded by the pervasive neo-conservative ideology of "economic rationalism" (Harrold, 1998), the contemporary reform agenda are deeply engulfed in the corporate culture, punctuated with business terminology like efficiency, effectiveness, productivity, and accountability. For the first time as well, resource distribution is no longer based on input needs but on the demonstrated performance of individual schools. Restructuring of the school system resulted in realignment of power distribution, reshaping the entire working environment for all public educators. Devolution of decision making power to site base legitimizes laymen's intrusion into a domain once exclusively monopolized by the professional. Marketization of schooling in the form of parental choice has loosened the very solid foundation of a domestic enterprise (Carlson, 1975) so that the continued survival of the school as a public institution is no longer guaranteed.

Short of a crystal ball that can foresee what is to come, the bewildered public educators, at this critical juncture, are at a loss when rambling for alternative coping strategies. To scholars, researchers and practitioners alike, the only reliable counter-measure in this uncertain, turbulent external context is to enhance school's learning capacity so that on-going self-renewal will emancipate schools from a state of stagnation and transcend it into a vibrant one more resilient to impending challenges ahead. The subsequent proliferation of journals, articles and scholarly writings on learning organizations, in a large measure, reflect some urgency in unmasking the potentials of group learning in institutions.

Taking a historical perspective, one cannot overlook the seminal work of Senge (1990) who has exerted profound impacts on scholars interested in undertaking additional work in this domain. His five disciplines encompass private pursuit of new knowledge (i.e., acquisition of new models and personal mastery) and public endorsement and implementation (i.e., systems thinking, shared vision and team learning). Close examination of these five disciplines suggests that while they are systematically and sequentially ordered, they may belong to different levels of development. Key factors and motives fostering organizational progression from one stage to another are not explicitly stated. Housed in the entire process of theoretical development, Senge's work furnishes some tentative scaffold for further refinement and expansion.

Unfortunately but not uncommonly in the field of education, exultation in this rich but unexplored territory does not lead scholars to belabor the conceptual framework pioneered by Senge. Rather, they begin to wander off in diverse directions. Some, for instance, are interested in relating organizational learning with staff professional development (e.g., Sadler-Smith, Allinson, & Hayes, 2000). Some attempt to establish the linkage between organizational learning, efficiency, and effectiveness of organizations (Bastiaens, 2000; Simkins, 1994, Stoll, 1999). There are still others who attempt to chart the relationship between collective learning and the improvement of the basic characteristics of the organization (Salaman, 2001; Snell, 2001). By adopting a wide latitude in mapping the uncharted landscape, we see the field littered with diffused, piece-meal and totally uncoordinated pieces of works that distract rather than present a united front in fathoming this new phenomenon.

To bring some order to this chaotic scene, a revisitation of Senge's work is useful. We need to complete the missing gaps that may be implicitly alluded to but not explicitly stated. These include how new information is acquired (e.g., Garvin, 1993; Slocum, Megill, & Lei, 1994), how it is disseminated throughout the organization (Sahin & Simsek, 1996), and what motives provide the primary drives for organizational transition (Lam, 2001). By integrating these missing gaps with the original disciplines, Lam (2001) advances a model depicting three distinct stages of development towards attaining "learning organization" status.

While providing instant references to gauge schools' ability to engage in collective learning, Lam's initial model resembles all the static frameworks when attempting to bridge empirical findings with conceptual interpretation. For one thing, conceptual purity of stages may not adequately cover diverse "hybrid" types of school development that display features harbored in different stages. Subjective interpretation and categorization of data may deviate from schools' actual developmental conditions. Additionally, classification of schools' development by stages may only be temporarily useful as all developmental processes in schools are highly complex, dynamic and transitional as they can be easily altered by changing personnel and leadership style (Adamson, Kwan, & Chan, 2002).

Toward Some Synthesis Through Model Construction

The identified pitfalls of mismatch between data and interpretation, and possibly misclassification of developmental stages can be readily rectified when an alternative approach is employed. Lam (2003a) proposes making a direct reference to the amount of organizational learning processes that members of a school organization experience, and assessing the outcomes they have achieved. Within this parameter, we can ascertain the degree of a school's effort toward accomplishing the status of learning organization. In light of the significance of "processes" and "outcomes" as yardstick for measuring the amount of organizational learning that is actually taking place in schools, their conceptual origins, measurement, and empirical characteristics need to be critically reviewed.

Tracing the theoretical root of "process," we discover that the term was derived initially from the systems model (e.g., Campbell, 1977) which is concerned about individual actors and about the organic nature of organizations within which they function. "Outcome" measured, according to the goal model (Hoy & Miskel, 1991), the degree that incumbents of the organization achieve established goals. In the classical rational comprehensive model, "process" and "outcomes" represent "means" and "ends" stages of collective learning. An interesting twist in the context of organizational learning is the management of learning "outcomes." In contrast to individual learning where new knowledge and experience are internalized and stored in one's mind, organizations do not have equivalent cognitive capacity to accommodate it (e.g., Wegner, 1987). They must be registered in tangible forms, or as Lam and Punch (2001) argue, in demonstrable performance or written records of one kind or another.

Instrumentally, "processes" pertains to the cognitive, affective and perhaps the psychomotor dimensions of the organization's incumbents in executing a series of actions related to collective learning. In a small measure, the concept was borrowed from the qualitative work of Leithwood, Leonard, and Sharratt (1998) but modified for quite a few cross-cultural studies (e.g., Lam & Pang, 2003; Lam, Wei, Pan, & Chan, 2002). The subsequent items constructed for assessing "organizational learning processes" encompass "collective ability to adapt to change," "satisfaction with group learning," "pride in collective effort," "on-going search for ways to improve collegial coordination," "beneficial effect of team work on personal viewpoints and experience" and "effectiveness in achieving group goals."

For "outcomes," the measurement is inclined to reflect tangible achievement through collective learning, arriving at mutually gratifying results, success of breaking new grounds and documentation of group decisions. Accordingly, six items were constructed. These include "continuous revision of developmental objectives and direction," "establishment of partnership with parents in supporting student learning," "experiment with diverse methods of enhancing teaching and learning process," "large scale revision of curriculum," "success in bringing about innovative teaching strategies," and "development of various manuals to improve administrative procedures."

Empirically, these two sets of items registering organizational learning processes and outcomes have been subject to repeated factor analyses using data from diverse regions (Lam 2004b; Lam et al., 2002; Lam & Pang, 2003). The results consistently point to the fact that these two factors are pure and distinct from each other. Each has high inter-item homogeneity as Cronbach's reliability coefficient for each variable is over .80.

Armed with the evidence that organizational learning processes and outcomes are distinctive in concept, precise in measurement and valid in empirical evidence, we may proceed to construct a model of school's developmental stages based on these two critical criteria. Implicitly and explicitly, a school's engagement in processes and achievement in learning outcomes can be demarcated along "high" and "low" categories, creating a two-by-two typology, or four possible developmental stages or conditions (Lam, Chan, Pan, & Wei, 2003). To avoid unnecessary confusion in dealing with individual school's means and deviations, all values are converted into standard scores and deviations when plotting into a graph.

The detail of this typology is described elsewhere (Lam, 2003a). Suffice for the present reference is the fact that Condition 1 depicts a stage where both organizational learning processes and outcomes are "low." This clearly illuminates a situation where no collective learning is taking effect. Schools in this condition are stagnant due to factors that exert stronger pressure for inertia than change. In contrast, Condition 4 denotes a situation when a school organization attains "high" in both organizational learning processes and outcomes, showing quite evidently that it has successfully evolved into a "learning organization." Conditions 2 and 3 display "high" in one dimension and "low" in another, suggesting that school organizations in those stages are undergoing certain transitional phases. In their search for new directions for development, they are in a state of flux.

The purposes of this chapter are threefold: The first is select school systems from two regions, in this case, Hong Kong and Taiwan to analyze schools in their extreme developmental stages (i.e., Conditions 1 and 4) along the path toward "learning organizations. " The second is to locate global or universal as well as localized factors that influence the development of these schools in the two regions. The third is to propose some tentative thesis that offers a more in-depth explanation as to how schools in those extreme stages of development came about.

The selection of the above two regions is deliberate as similarities in many background factors permit an easier extraction of universal as well as unique factors from the sampled schools for comparison without fear of contamination by unaccounted for extraneous variables. In our present situation, reforms in Hong Kong and Taiwan are comparable, and the Chinese as the major ethnic group cherish similar cultural traditions in both places. These allow the historical heritages embedded in the socio-cultural characteristics of the two regions to be the sole major variations. In this respect, Hong Kong has inherited much from the British rules, with many of the reform agenda being passed on by the departing Colonial government. Taiwan, on the other hand, has been under strong American influence. As observed by many scholars (e.g., Huang, 1999), the Americanization of Taiwan's educational system and reforms is by no means accidental, given the close historical, political, military, cultural and migration ties between the two places.

By scrutinizing the external environmental factors, internal school factors and contextual variables, many of which are either universal or culturally specific factors, we should be able to pinpoint critical factors that explain the momentum for organizational developmental status for schools in both regions. Furthermore, through the rank ordering of these variables, we should be able to construct more systematically, a comprehensible lens in analyzing the complex phenomenon of school development.

To ensure that the schools' profiles were distinct and unambiguous, only those that were statistically significant (attaining .05 or better) from the standard mean scores were included. In the final count, out of the 67 sampled schools approached for data collection in Hong Kong, there were 3 schools that fell into Condition 1 (i.e., no fundamental change), but no Hong Kong schools belonged to Condition 4 (i.e., achieving mature learning organizations). On the other hand, of the 88 sampled schools selected from Taiwan, 2 fell into Condition 1 while 3 displayed characteristics of Condition 4. These school aggregate scores had been derived from the standard mean scores generated from 90% of the staffs in all sampled schools taking part in the investigation. In other words, of the 8 schools in both regions that exhibited extreme opposite stages of development, and were the subjects of the present scrutiny, over 660 teaching staffs constituted the basic data for compiling the present school scores. Figure 11.1 displayed the score distribution of these schools.

What accounted for the variations of these three subgroups of schools, as alluded to earlier, became the focal points of the present investigation. To focus our discussion on this topic, we need to undertake three tasks:

Figure 11.1. Distribution of Schools by Levels of Organizational Learning

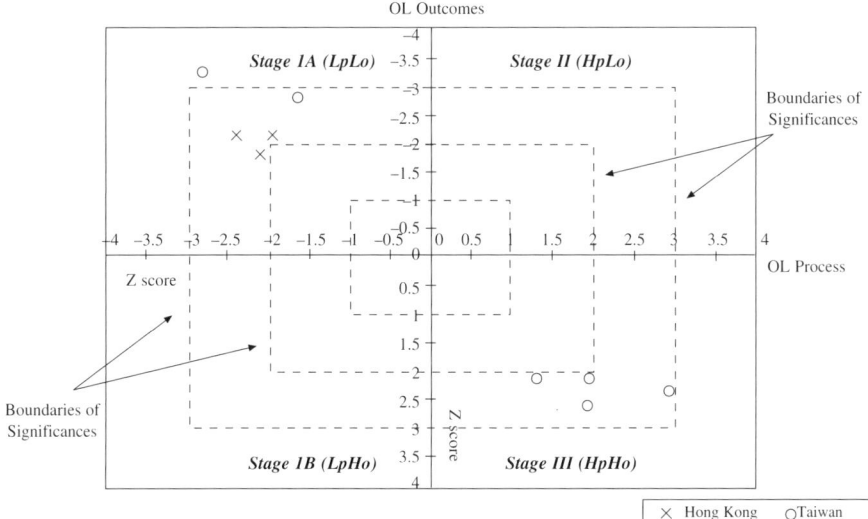

- To examine how the staffs of the chosen sampled schools perceive their external environment and internal school conditions.
- To detect divergent forces that assist school organizations progressing from one stage (condition) to another.
- To probe the inner feelings of school leadership so as to gauge their mentality and adopted strategies in preparing school organizations for stability or change.

Evidently, by taking task one, we will have a more holistic understanding of how the teaching staffs understand their external environment. When they begin to comprehend how the external contexts change the nature of their jobs and render them more accountable for their performance in schools, they will start making more preparation for role changes to accommodate externally imposed demands. Problem sensing (Kiesler & Sproull, 1982) and awareness at the psychological threshold has often been viewed as the first mechanism to trigger coping strategies.

Task two carries a clear objective of mapping relevant factors that motivate school organizations to break away from inertia. Divergent forces must be at work, which accounts for the fact some schools are progressing more smoothly than others are. Without dwelling on too much speculation, we might hypothesize that the propelling forces may come from three sources. First, they can come from external environmental changes, as most environmental deterministic proponents emphasize (e.g., Haveman, 1992), since external ìpunctuational changesî (Gould, 1980) leave no room for organizations to procrastinate. Or, they may come from favorable internal school conditions such as leaders who are willing to bring about change, culture that is supportive of individual or group initiatives in learning, and flexible structure, which allows groups opportunities to meet and work on regular basis (Leithwood et al., 1998). Or, the changes may be related to staffs' and schools' characteristics, the effects of which are broadly reported in literature (see Lam & Pang, 2003). By comparing and contrasting the forces of changes at work, we may identify both the global and local factors that schools in each setting seem to respond to.

Task three highlights the omnipotent role that school leadership plays in setting the stage for their schools either to remain stationary or to move forward. Literature seems overwhelmed with works that substantiate the claims that school principals exert a dominant influence in organizational learning (e.g., Kofman & Senge, 1993; Mohrman & Mohrman, 1995; Silins, Mulford, & Zarins, 1999). While recent empirical evidence points to the fact that transformational leadership may be linked to cultural conditions (e.g., Jung, Bass, & Sosik, 1995; Lam, 2002), its impact on organizations cannot be minimized or denied (e.g., Fiol, Harris, & House, 1999; Wren, 1995). Revelation of leadership inner feelings, perceptions, and mentality will furnish not just additional insight as to why some actions were adopted while others were not considered at all, but also some socio-cultural factors that may condition how leadership behaves as well.

Observed External Environmental Constraints

Of the six factors derived from Lam's School External Constraint Instrument (1985) that were conceived to have impacts on schools' operation, only enrolment fluctuation, incompatibility of social values (between school and students), and educational policy changes initiated by the government were found to be common between schools of Hong Kong and Taiwan.

On the other hand, localized decision making mode was no longer a constraining factor for teaching staff in Taiwan. Likely "teacher empowerment" and "school based management," the two main thrusts of Taiwanese reform have taken roots in the system. Funding and resources, having perceived to have some constraints by teaching staffs in Hong Kong, were viewed as "separate" entities by their counterparts in Taiwanese schools. The latter being the case is, as claimed by some participants of the study, primarily due to insufficient curriculum resources and in-service support that are supposedly available for schools in streamlining their syllabi from Grade 1 to Grade 9.

When looking at the perceived level of external constraints, it is surprising to note that the staffs of Hong Kong schools which remain relatively stagnant experienced a level of constraint higher than their Taiwanese counterparts, even though statistical analyses did not yield noticeable differences. In this parameter, enrolment fluctuation problems were less in Taiwan and so was difficulty of interpreting government educational policies. On the other hand, constraints arising from resources and funding were perceived to be "high" by staffs of Taiwan schools that progressed well to become learning organizations, but less so by their colleagues in schools that remained more or less unchanged when compared with their previous situations. Most probably, change needs resource and those that embarked upon transition would find funding and resources more acute than those which procrastinate.

The only area where constraints seemed comparable "high" was "the incompatibility of social values" between schools and students. Rising cases of students' misconduct and disruptive behaviours troubled teachers of both regions. Yet, surprisingly, there were no systematic deviations from the routine management. Neither could we find evidence of collective learning or action in dealing with the increasingly complex issues. Most likely, teaching staff of the concerned schools in both regions must be preoccupied with other important issues such as curriculum reorganization, performance appraisal, and greater involvement in the governance restructuring (e.g., the newly created school management committees, or parent councils). Alternatively, they may perceive "student problems" as routine problems and hope to resolve the emergent crises in a traditional way.

Observed Internal School Conditions

Of the three critical internal school conditions that foster schools' evolution towards organizational learning, that is, culture, structure and transformational leadership (Leithwood et al., 1998), it is interesting to note that teaching staffs from the four Taiwan schools that have evolved successfully into the status of learning organizations, perceive these internal school conditions of theirs far more favourably than those colleagues from Taiwan and Hong Kong schools which fail to make any substantial headway towards collective learning. Scheffe's multiple comparisons confirm these variations.

Indeed, for those stagnant schools, traditional self-centred norms, apathetic attitudes towards team learning, and highly compartmentalized structure have removed whatever incentive that the more risk taking individuals or groups might initiate. More importantly, if the school leaders are unwilling or unable to undertake the task of transforming their schools for one reason or another, the schools are destined to be immobile no matter what external or internal stimulus might be present. To those that have been actively engaged in organizational learning, the problems associated with the internal conditions should have been overcome. There is perhaps no clearer evidence to illustrate the contrast between schools in extreme stages of development than the mentality of these principals. The abstracts from the interviews with principals of Hong Kong and Taiwan schools below should illuminate the situation well:

Condition 1 (immobile schools)

(Hong Kong) "Decentralization as a government policy has complicated school administration far more than was expected...."

(Hong Kong) "I'll try to study the implications of the reform initiatives before I alert the school. Hopefully, I could come up with solutions myself without alarming the staffs."

(Hong Kong) "After I collected all the relevant information on this topic [curriculum changes), I'll approach some scholars or experts for advice."

(Taiwan) "I haven't restructured school to meet the current reform. I'm keeping a close contact with my fellow principals in other schools who're in the same boat to monitor the situation."

(Taiwan) "Devolution has greatly complicated school operation. What should be decentralized and what needs to be under central control remains unclear. I'll wait for a while...."

From these excerpts, one develops an impression that the school leaders in Condition 1 encountered considerable adjustment problems. Yet, consciously, these principals are unwilling to share their problems with their staffs, lest they fall into the "weak" leadership stereotype in the eyes of their subordinates. Alternatively, they may be ambivalent about sharing their newly won "authority" bestowed upon them through school-based management; for fear that they regress once again into "powerlessness" as they once were under centralized, bureaucratic control. In short, through their calculated assessment of the situation, these school leaders profess to justify their inaction through more studies, more networking with their counterparts in other schools or more consultation with experts in the field of their interest. Whatever the rationale, their reluctance to reshape their schools make their school organizations fall into the status quo.

In contrast, principals from Taiwan schools in Condition 4 (learning organizations) shared their inner feelings, reflective of a very different perspective:

> "We've regularly utilized our Wednesday (staff development days) to share new insights about teaching and to engage in self-reflection in order that we benefit our utmost from team learning."

> "To consolidate collective learning, I'll invite interested staff to plan and design new approaches and provide opportunities for them to share with their colleagues. I'll let them feel that public presentation is a great honour. I stress a lot on outcomes but leave the process for the staffs themselves to work out."

> "We've worked closely with neighbouring schools to solidify networking and team learning."

Here we find that principals have provided their staffs with opportunities to work together, have actively encouraged, promoted and rewarded staffs' efforts to experiment with new approaches, and shared with their colleagues both inside and outside schools. The intentional sharing of decision-making power seems to pose no psychological threats to the formal leaders. Instead, they grasp the opportunities to accelerate professional growth of their staffs. Such a demonstrated degree of trust and teacher empowerment in schools stand in great contrast to the paternalistic attitudes of the principals in Condition 1, who are unwilling to depart from their power monopoly.

Discriminant Factors Accounting for Developmental Variations Among Schools

In comparing factors that discriminate (and hopefully foster) school at different stages of development, we note that Taiwan schools that attained the status of learning organizations varied significantly from their stagnant counterparts in terms of funding, supporting culture, flexible structure and transformational leadership. The former further differed greatly from those stagnant Hong Kong schools in such factors as policy, culture, structure and transformational leadership. Between schools of Taiwan and Hong Kong that remained immobile, the only important discriminating variable was the "enrolment fluctuation."

Evidently, perceived favourable internal school conditions persistently permit progressive schools to outshine those which were less favourably inclined. These three internal factors can be seen as the prevailing common forces that distinguish quality schools from the average both between different and within the same socio-cultural conditions. Other empirical data collected from western countries (e.g., Lam, 2004b) lend additional weight to the claim that conditions within schools must be viewed as the "global" forces that accounts for organizational learning to take effect. External environmental factors, on the other hand, can be treated as the "local" factors since they are stained by contextualized situations when exerting their influences on school organizations.

Along this line of reasoning, we do find that within the same cultural setting, as in the case of Taiwan, either creative or unimaginable utilization of funding does make a substantial difference in school development. For those that actively seek collective learning to bring about change, creative or strategic application of resources frees them from stagnation. For those that seek refuge and security of the past, inability to reallocate existing funding offer them some convenient pretext for their lack of prompt action.

Between schools in the two regions, another localized factor seems to be operative. A major discriminating factor between the progressive Taiwanese schools and the stagnant Hong Kong schools was found to be government educational policies. Apparently, the rapidity of new guidelines directed at Hong Kong schools (600 messages from the Department of Education in 3 months—according to a principal's account) was so overwhelming that hardly had the principals digested one before another arrived. The urgency of the government's directives had the opposite effects on school leadership, as ambiguity and confusion might just encourage principals to display "avoidance behaviours," and adopted the "wait-and-see" mentality (Lam, 2003).

When we examine how stagnant schools in Hong Kong and Taiwan differed, only one localized factor emerged to be significant: enrolment fluctuation. Demographic data from both regions suggest that school-aged enrolment decline is more severe in Hong Kong than in Taiwan. However, such fluctuation, while affecting the stability of the school in terms of programme offerings and staffs need, fail to emancipate schools from organizational inertia. Quite a few Hong Kong schools appeal to the teacher organization to exert political pressure on the government for smaller class size to avoid job cut of teachers. Most, however, would just wait passively for enrolment attrition to take its natural toll. Indeed, the well-solidified complacency and lack of imagination on the part of some of the school leadership allow a slow but inevitable organizational disintegration to unfold without actively embarking upon a more rigorous intervention to reverse the trend.

Socio-cultural Influences

There is a generalized assumption that when school systems in different regions are under very similar global influences (in this case school reform agenda and ideological thrusts); the perceived external environment should have imposed comparable impacts on schools. This is not necessary the case as the present data show. Globalized trends and factors, when interacting with local socio-cultural conditions, may produce highly indigenous factors that have restrictive significance to the incumbents of the school systems concerned. In other words, the numerous attempts of conceptually segregating globalization and localization become futile academic exercises when we seriously apply these concepts separately to dissect the impacts of the contemporary school reforms.

To a common set of external factors that supposedly exert homogenous influence on school operation, funding constraints are more pronounced in Taiwan than in Hong Kong. Yet, on the other hand, policy interpretation should pose more difficulty for school heads in Hong Kong than their counterparts in Taiwan. Digging behind the scene, one would have no problem of understanding how these problems arise. Reforms were ushered into Taiwan at a time when the Island suffered severe economic downturns. Demands on school changes were not accompanied with the injection of additional financial resources. Consequently, schools were asked to do more with no corresponding increase of financial support from the central government.

This was not the case in Hong Kong. With the initiation of school reforms, substantial financial backing to the schools was assured. Individual schools were allocated with so much cash at one time that some principals privately admitted that they had difficulty of disposing with it. And yet, with the demonstrated impatience of the government, schools were flooded with directives and guidelines in terms of how to execute reforms. The rapid succession of these directives was overbearing that many principals experienced disorientation toward the whole process of school reforms. Based on the unique characteristics of their schools, principals had adopted different fashions of adjustment, many of which displayed what the current data showed—"inaction" to avoid too deep an involvement in something that they believe to be transitory (Lam, 2003).

The ironic mixing and meshing of globalization of major trends and localization of impact factors tend to recur in that of internal school conditions that foster organizational learning. While the generalized pattern of supportive culture, flexible structure and transformational leadership are shown to be persistently critical to the developmental stages of the schools in both regions, they differ immensely in nature and characteristics.

More specifically, in Taiwan schools, the presence of election system for principalship has transformed top echelons into politicians with the cultural emphasis largely reflective of "consideration" dimension of leadership. Behaviours, norms and values of the staffs centre on the notion of a "big family." Those, including leadership, who do not accept the established patterns of values experienced "cultural excommunication" (Lin, 2002). In structural terms, even though Taiwan schools are much larger and more complex, the professional power of teachers is remarkably more noticeable than those in Hong Kong. Principals have to look for special time before teachers can be brought for collective learning. Such conscientious efforts of arranging team learning occasions become highly treasured moments for brainstorming and collective decision-making. Leadership performance depends therefore on how they maneuver their staffs to capitalize on the situation to become more innovative or to fall prey to a comfortable but illusionary state of immobility.

In Hong Kong, principalship, in most occasions is appointed for good. They do not need to be answerable to their staffs as their counterparts do in Taiwan. Running schools is often compared to running business. School cultures are broadly ingrained by corporate culture, particularly when such models are accentuated in reforms. The structures of the schools are governed by specification of roles. So refined is the division of labour that sessions for collective decisions become far and few, rending coordination at time difficult. Leadership stands primarily aloof from grass-root staffs, making it at time difficult to mobilize the entire schools. These observations helps account for the fact as to why less schools in Hong Kong can overcome innate organizational problems to achieve the status of "learning organizations."

Taking a macro-level of cultural analysis along the framework developed by Hofstede (1991), we do find that the patterns of thinking, feeling and acting that underscore the collective programming of the mind vary substantially between public educators of the two regions even though they are of the same ethnic group. Principals of Hong Kong schools project a more masculine, assertive role when they lead their schools. Heads of Taiwan schools seem more feminine in dealing with their staffs in their attempt to rally their support. Cultivating amiable relationships and looking after the welfare of their staffs are some common administrative strategies among Taiwan school leaders.

Along another dimension of power distance (i.e., power distribution), Hong Kong principals tended to display a higher power distance when compared with those in Taiwan. As the appointment of Hong Kong principalship does not involve staffs input, leadership of the school does not feel any obligation to their staffs. On the other hand, the presence of electoral system of principalship in the current Taiwan school reforms dis-stabilize the tenure of principalship, making them extremely vulnerable and sensitive to staff assessment and comments. Attempts to avoid unfavorable perception of their staffs encourage Taiwan principals to draw socially closer to their subordinates. Given the present situation when major changes are taking place, we see much common concerns and fears of uncertainty among leaders of both regions, in contrast to what has been reported in earlier decade (Dimmock & Walker, 2000). Likewise, earlier conclusion that people of the oriental societies tend to have a long-term perspective is again invalid as the emphasis on outcome-based education rewards instant evidence of achievement to justify school success and leadership capability.

What might still ring truth, perhaps, is the choice of individualism versus collectivism. There is sufficient reluctance on the part of Hong Kong principals to challenge or modify existing culture and tradition of the schools, even though some of the characteristics do not synchronize with demands for change. The painstaking, colossal efforts of altering norms and values of the staffs without a priori assurance of success have paralyzed many principals in Hong Kong into inaction. For a different but equally convincing rationale, Taiwan school principals with no assurance of support of their staffs are unwilling to commit politically incorrect and professionally suicidal move of unconventional action which calls into question past practices. Seeking the safety of collectivism becomes a common haven for school leaders when they are in doubt.

There is perhaps no better way to demonstrate the subtle relationship between global trend and localized factors in shaping some institutions in a period of transition than to bring Hofstede's (1991) grand cultural framework to interpret school data from the two regions. While some of the generalized observations made by Hofstede remain correct while comparing and contrasting institutions from different regions, many show inadequacy or obsolescence when empirical evidence is brought under closer scrutiny. This does not necessary mean that any grand conceptual proposals or theories are futile efforts, it does show that localized elements or factors may at work which render ubiquitous statements less reliable or more debatable. More works perhaps need to be undertaken to ensure what presents here as a challenge can be pursued further to ensure that important grand theories can be further refined.

From the perspective of defining the relative roles assumed by global and localized factors, re-sorting the present findings may be a promising starting point. Clearly, globalized patterns of internal conditions that determine the development of schools are the unmistaken results of unique socio-cultural traditions that continue to interact and modify the concerned institutions locally. It would seem quite impossible to sort out the effects of localized factors in order to assess global influence. Neither is it beneficial to parcel out globalized effect to ascertain the role of local factors. I will subscribe that, given continued interactions as they are, intermingling globalized and local effects constitute a very rewarding and enlightening aspect of comparative education research.

References

Adamson, B., Kwan, T., & Chan, K. K., (2002). *Changing the curricular: The impact of reform on primary schooling in Hong Kong.* Hong Kong: Hong Kong University Press.

Bastiaens, T. (2000). Results: How to assess performance, learning, and perceptions in organizations. *Human Resource Development Quarterly, 11*(4), 414–417.

Campbell, J. P. (1977). On nature of organizational effectiveness. In P. S. Goodman & J. M. Pennings (Eds.), *New perspectives on organizational effectiveness* (pp. 13–55). San Francisco: Jossey-Bass.

Carlson, R. O. (1975). Environmental constraints and organizational consequences: The public school and its clients. In J. V. Baldridge & T. E. Deal (Eds.), *Managing change in educational environments* (pp. 187–200). Berkeley, CA: McCutchan.

Dimmock, C., & Walker, A. (2000). *Future school administration: Western and Asian perspectives.* Hong Kong: The Chinese University Press.

Fiol, C. M., Harris, D., & House, R. J. (1999). Charismatic leadership: Strategies for effecting social change. *Leadership Quarterly, 10*(3), 449–482.

Garvin, D. A. (1993). Building a learning organization. *Harvard Business Review, 71*(4), 78–91.

Gould, S. J. (1980). The episodic nature of evolutionary change. In S. J. Gould, *The panda's thumbs* (pp. 179–185). New York: Norton.

Harrold, R. (1998). *Resources in education.* Melbourne: The Australian Council for Educational Research.

Haveman, H. A. (1992). Between a rock and a hard place: Organizational change and performance under conditions of fundamental environmental transformation. *Administrative Science Quarterly, 37*, 48–75.

Hofstede, G. H. (1991). *Cultures and organizations: Software of the mind.* London: McGraw Hill.

Hoy, W. K., & Miskel, C. G. (1991). *Theory, research, and practice: Educational administration.* (4th ed.). New York: McGraw-Hill Inc.

Huang, H. M. S. (1999). Educational reform in Taiwan: A brighter American moon? *International Journal of Educational Reform, 8*(2), 145–153.

Jung, D. I., Bass, B. M., & Sosik, J. J. (1995). Bridging leadership and culture: A theoretical consideration of transformational leadership and collectivist cultures. *Journal of Leadership Studies, 2*, 3–18.

Kiesler, S., & Sproull, L. (1982). Managerial response to changing environments: Perspective on problem sensing from social cognition. *Administrative Science Quarterly, 27,* 548–570.

Kofman, F., & Senge, P. (1993). Communities of commitment: The heart of learning organizations. *Organizational Dynamics, 22*(2), 5–22.

Lam, Y. L. J. (1985). Toward the construction of a school environment instrument: A conceptual framework. *Candaian Journal of Education, 10,* 362–382.

Lam, Y. L. J. (2001). Toward reconceptualizing organizational learning: A multi-dimensional interpretation. *International Journal of Educational Management, 15*(5), 212–219.

Lam, Y. L. J. (2002). Defining the effects of transformational leadership on organizational learning: A cross-cultural comparison. *School Leadership & Management, 22*(4), 439–452.

Lam, Y. L. J. (2003). Implications for professional preparation and development of principals in Hong Kong. In P. Hallinger (Ed.), *Reshaping the landscape of school leadership development: A global perspective* (pp. 175–190). Lisse, Netherlands: Swets & Zeitlinger Publishers.

Lam, Y. L. J. (2004a). Reconceptualizing a dynamic model of organizational learning for schools. *Journal of Educational Administration, 42*(3), 297–311.

Lam, Y. L. J. (2004b). Exploring the sources and relationships that propel organizational learning: An investigation of some Western Australian schools. *Learning Environments and Research, 7*(1), 81–102.

Lam, Y. L. J., Chan, C. M. M., Pan, H. L. W., & Wei, H. C. P. (2003). Differential developments of Taiwanese schools in organizational learning exploration of critical factors. *International Journal of Educational Management, 17*(6), 262–271.

Lam, Y. L. J., & Pang, S. K. N. (2003). The relative effects of environmental, internal, and contextual factors on organizational learning: The case of Hong Kong schools under reforms. *The Learning Organization: An International Journal, 10*(2), 83–97.

Lam, Y. L. J., & Punch, K. F. (2001). External environment and school organizational learning: Conceptualizing the empirically neglected. *International Studies in Educational Administration, 29*(3), 28–38.

Lam, Y. L. J., Wei, H. C. P., Pan, H. L., & Chan, C. M. M. (2002). In search of basic sources that propel organizational learning under recent Taiwanese school reforms. *International Journal of Educational Management, 16*(5), 216–228.

Leithwood, K., Leonard, L., & Sharratt, L. (1998). Conditions fostering organizational learning in schools. *Educational Administrative Quarterly, 34,* 243–276.

Lin, M. D. (2002). *School leadership: Concepts and principals' professional careers.* Taiwan: Higher Education Press.

Mohrman, S. A., & Mohrman, A. M. (1995). *Designing team-based organizations: New forms for knowledge work.* San Francisco: Jossey-Bass.

Sadler-Smith, E., Allinson, C. W., & Hayes, J. (2000). Learning preferences and cognitive style: Some implications for continuing professional development. *Management Learning, 31*(2), 239–256.

Sahin, A. E., & Simsek, H. (1996, October). *A qualitative assessment of organizational learning processes in selected Turkish public and private high schools.* Paper presented at the Annual Meeting of the University Council for Educational Administration, Louisville, KY.

Salaman, G. (2001). A response to Snell: The learning organization: Fact or fiction? *Human Relations, 54*(3), 343–359.

Senge, P. M. (1990). *The fifth discipline: The art and practice of the learning organization.* New York: Doubleday.

Silins, H., Mulford, B., & Zarins, S. (1999, April). *Leadership for organizational learning and student outcomes.* Paper presented at the Annual Meeting of the American Educational Research Association Montreal, Quebec, Canada.

Simkins, T. (1994). Efficiency, effectiveness, and the local management of schools. *Journal of Education Policy, 9*(1), 15–33.

Slocum, J. W., Megill, M., & Lei, D. T. (1994). The learning strategy: Anytime, anything, and anywhere. *Organizational Dynamics, 23*(2), 33–47.

Snell, R. S. (2001). Moral foundations of the learning organization. *Human Relations, 54*(3), 319–342.

Stoll, L. (1999). Realizing our potential and developing capacity for lasting improvement. *School Effectiveness and School Improvement, 10*(4), 503–532.

Wegner, D. M. (1987). Transactive memory: A contemporary analysis of the group mind. In B. Mullen & G. Goethels (Eds.), *Theories of group behavior* (pp. 185–208). New York: Springer-Verlag.

Wren, D. J. (1995). School culture: Exploring the hidden curriculum. *Adolescence, 34*(135), 1–14.

12

Managing School Change Through Self-evaluation in the Era of Globalization

Nicholas Sun-keung PANG

—॥॥—

Abstract

Leading a school organization involves much more than managing. Principals need to have a vision and should possess good inter-personal and group skills, and should be able to be creative and innovative in leading school members towards the accomplishment of pre-determined goals. An effective leader plays a central role in placing school self-evaluation (SSE) on a development cycle of continuous improvement. The implementation of self-evaluation enables schools to: (1) identify priority in the areas of school improvement, (2) define important questions to be investigated and answered in self-evaluation, (3) collect appropriate data for consideration and reference, (4) analyse data for further interpretation and sharing, (5) report and communicate results of self-evaluation to stakeholders; and (6) formulate school development plan and action plan.

Through the procedures of self-evaluation a self-renewal strategy will be institutionalized in the schools' management structure. The central purpose of SSE is to improve the knowledge and skills of organizational members to diagnose and solve problems on an everyday basis. The main focus should be on developing skills for solving inter-personal and inter-departmental problems. It is a process of acquiring skills in dealing with on-the-job problems. The ultimate aim of SSE is to convert the school organization into a community of learners.

This study is part of the research in a school improvement project, which was sponsored by Quality Education Fund in Hong Kong and was launched in 20 schools in the year 2000–2002. This chapter investigated into the effectiveness of implementing self-evaluation in a sample of Hong Kong schools as well as the factors that hinder and facilitate self-evaluation in these schools. Based on interview data collected from the principals of the 20 participating schools and evidence from the schools' performance in various domains of evaluation, the study posits that principals are the crucial agents of change and the key players in changing the schools' organizational culture and climate.

In this chapter, different approaches to intervention strategies to cultivate a climate of educational change in schools are introduced. These intervention strategies include, for example, (1) rational-empirical strategies, (2) power-coercive strategies, and (3) normative-re-educative strategies. If a principal is to lead and manage a school towards continuous improvement, an integrated approach to change, which includes developing a shared vision, building value and culture, and focusing on evaluation of progress should also be adopted.

Introduction

Globalization and educational change are inextricably intertwined. Economically and politically, globalization has been affecting the identity and independence of nation states, and the ways in which public education is undergoing change within these states. Agenda in educational reforms in response to globalization in this respect include marketization, privatization and decentralization on the one hand, and standardization of curriculum and assessment and a growing emphasis on nationhood on the other. Socially and culturally, globalization has been simultaneously influencing: teaching and learning; the curriculum and the ability to deal with difference and reshaping student lives through market influences; and symbolic concerns with identity and nationhood. As both China (the PRC) and Taiwan have been admitted to the World Trade Organization quite recently, the boundaries between East and West will, inevitably, be further blurred and parts of the world will merge more rapidly than ever before. The impacts of globalization on education will continue to increase.

The Inevitability of Change in Schools

Globalization and changes in information processing during the last 2 decades have had a great impact on education systems and organizations. The modern values of contract, market, competition, efficiency, accountability, planning, continuous evaluation, quality assurance, and so forth, have been emphasized in the education system and even exaggerated under the impact of globalization. There have been some noticeable changes in schools, and numerous scholars have warned educators that public schools should keep pace with societal changes and expectations in order to survive in the changing environment (Gamage & Pang, 2003). Now, almost daily, educators are confronted with demands from society to reform organizational structures and educational processes.

According to Beer and Nohria (2000), two dramatically different approaches to organizational change are being employed in the world today, namely: Theory E and Theory O. These two theories are guided by very different assumptions on the part of corporate leaders about the purpose and means for change. Theory E aims at the creation of economic value and maximizing shareholder values. It emphasizes the changes in structures and systems, motivates through financial incentives, and involves the processes of planning and establishing programmes. Thus, Theory E changes are managed from the top down, planned and programmatic. Theory O, on the other hand, aims to develop the human capability of organizations to implement strategy and to learn, from actions taken, about the effectiveness of changes made. It encourages participation from the bottom up, focuses on the building up of a corporate culture, motivate through commitment, and make use of the processes of experimentation and involvement. Thus, Theory O changes are emergent, less planned and programmatic. Both Beer and Nohria thought that these theories were only archetypes. An examination of many organizations will show that a mixture of these strategies often coexists. They suggest that a hybrid of these theories is likely to produce better results in organizations (Gamage & Pang, 2003).

Hong Kong schools are confronted with more or less the same challenges brought about by the huge information flow and vigorous innovative moves owing to globalization. They necessitate schools transforming into learning communities in order to meet the expectations of their stakeholders (Pang & Cheung, 2004). If a school has to become a learning community, it needs enhance its own learning capacity in such a way that the whole school seeks organizational improvement by a continuous process. School leaders have to submit to a paradigm shift from hierarchical, supervisory and controlling roles to facilitative and supportive roles needing careful planning.

The Quality Assurance Movement in Hong Kong

There have been rapid changes in both the education system and Hong Kong schools due to the recommendations made by Education Commission Report No. 7 (ECR7) in 1997. ECR7 recommended a two-pronged approach to assure the quality of education in Hong Kong: an external assurance mechanism and an internal quality assurance framework. While the external quality assurance mechanism was achieved through the establishment of the Quality Assurance Inspectorate (QAI) in 1997, for accountability purposes, the internal quality assurance framework has been relying on schools' own capability to self-evaluate its process of school improvement. The external quality assurance mechanism is done through adoption of a whole-school approach to inspection by the QAI, which assesses a school's effectiveness, identifies its strengths and weaknesses, makes suggestions for ways of improvement and development and releases inspection reports for public reference (Cuttance, 1993). In order to continuously improve the quality of school education, all schools are also expected to engage in the cyclical processes of evaluation, planning, implementation and on-going self-evaluation (Moelands & Ouborg, 1998). Every school must work towards meeting the educational needs of its students as effectively as it can and self-evaluation provides information on which to base plans for improvement. Through self-evaluation, all schools should produce documents which outline the long-term goals, prioritize development areas, set out specific targets for implementation, evaluate progress of work during the school year, and set improvement or development targets for the coming year (Ministry of Education, 1984; Scottish Office, 1996, 2002).

However, the two strategies in the two-pronged approach to assure the quality of education in Hong Kong as recommended by the ECR7 may not have been as effective as expected. First, the external assurance mechanism is a quite limited tool for enhancing the quality of school education through since a whole-school inspection will only last for 2 to 3 weeks each time and the QAI will not re-visit the same school for at least 4 to 5 years, given the present manpower in the QAI teams (Harris, 1999). Since the inception of Whole School Inspections in the 1997/98 school year, the number of schools inspected (up to the 2001/02 school year) is only 12.1% (see Table 12.1). Secondly, after conducting whole-school inspections in over 200 schools in the last 5 years, the QAI found that most of these schools had not established a self-evaluation framework in the daily management and no appropriate school-based indicators developed for use in school self-evaluation (SSE). Schools can only improve when they have a good understanding about their present environment and situations and when they have a clear vision of the future. There is concern that it is impractical and unrealistic to expect a school to be able to establish a self-evaluation framework and to develop a comprehensive set of school-based indicators on their own within a short time. Most schools lack the resources and expertise in setting up such indicators for measuring their performance in significant aspects.

Schools can only improve continuously when they have institutionalized a self-evaluation framework in daily practices and when there is a set of valid, reliable and school-based performance indicators for use in self-evaluation. Practicing self-evaluation enables schools to (1) develop formal procedures for setting school goals; (2) gain the participation of teachers, parents and alumni in school management, development, planning, evaluation and decision-

Table 12.1. No. of Whole-school Inspections Conducted by QAI Since 1997

	Secondary schools	Primary schools	Kinder- garten	All schools
Whole-school inspection	77	141	50	283
Total no. of schools in Hong Kong*	486	816	1,040	2,342
% of schools inspected	15.8%	17.3%	4.8%	12.1%

Sources of data:
1. Minutes of the 15th meeting of the Advisory Committee on Quality Assurance Inspectorate, November 25, 2002.
2. Education and Manpower Bureau (2002).

making; (3) assess their progress towards their goals as well as their own performance over time; and (4) take appropriate steps for improvement. When school-based indicators are translated from the aims of the schools, they are useful tools for measuring and monitoring school performance in areas of interest. Self-evaluation with appropriate school-based indicators provides information to schools, teachers, parents, students and the community with the general profiles of schools for reference and for comparison with schools of similar background or within the same quality circle. SSE and school-based performance indicators are the crucial elements for continuous improvement in schools (Cuttance, 1994; Scottish Office, 1996, 2002). A summary of the pros and cons of the two-pronged approaches to quality assurance in education is given in Table 12.2.

Managing Change Through Self-evaluation

Evidence-based organizational change is a very recent trend in the school reform and improvement movement. It is important that school organizational change should be based on objective and reliable evidence of school performance. Schools should have a self-renewal mechanism (with the implementation of SSE) for managing change. This can be built upon (1) a clear and appropriate diagnosis

Table 12.2. **The Pros and Cons of the Two-pronged Strategies to Quality Assurance**

Quality assurance	External mechanism	Internal mechanism
1. Approach	An innovative approach	A Kaizen approach
2. Changing agent	Quality Assurance Unit	School Self-evaluation
3. Changes	A "crash-through" approach with radical surgery.	An evolutionary development.
4. Drives	Top-down and from external	Bottom-up and from within
5.Pace of Change	Fast, on schedule and intermittent	Slow, continuously, and long lasting

of the school as an organization, and (2) the role of administration in the school. Experience in research and practice has shown that if school reforms are to succeed, organizational changes need active support from the principal. The principal needs to be an active advocate of self-evaluation and be prepared to articulate a vision of self-renewal for the school. School development cannot be copied and imposed from outside. The leader needs to understand the current situation, including strengths and weaknesses, opportunities and threats (SWOT) to the organization, determine the goals to be attained within the next 1–3 years, and develop the strategies necessary to achieve them. Institutionalization of self-evaluation in the organizational framework and daily managerial practices allows the principal managing the school towards effective educational change (Macbeath et al., 2000; Pang, 2005).

To successfully institutionalize a self-renewal framework in daily managerial practices as well as to lead and manage change effectively, the leader first of all needs to: (1) acquire appropriate knowledge and understanding of the theoretical framework and concept of SSE, (2) develop and acquire the necessary skills and attitudes in self-evaluation and manipulation of performance indicators, (3) think through the leadership role as a guide to action, and (4) clarify for himself/herself the strategic elements that are essential to effectively implement the school development plan. Then, the principal should examine the types of knowledge, kinds of skills and attitudes that need to be developed for successful implementation of organizational change (Pang, 2003a).

What is School Self-evaluation?

What is school self-evaluation? School self-evaluation (SSE) is a mechanism through which schools can help themselves review the quality of education, improve continuously and develop themselves into effective schools. The three major questions usually asked in SSE are: (1) What is our school's present performance? (2) How do we know about the school's performance? (3) What will we do after knowing the performance? These seem to be simple questions, but it may be a very difficult task to produce a full picture or thorough understanding of the school through systematic and objective evaluation of the school's performance (Pang, 2003b, 2005).

The Basic Steps in School Self-evaluation

There are several identifiable stages in SSE, such as problem recognition, prioritizing, defining important questions, data collection, data analysis, reporting and communicating, school developing planning, team building, and feedback and evaluation. All these need to be fully implemented in sequence. Thus, this schema is useful to a leader for initiating change in the organization. It needs to be emphasized that the leader should have a good understanding of the concept of SSE or self-renewal process. Its major steps and the sequence of events should be:

- *Problem identification.* Organization becomes aware of the existence of a problem that needs to be fixed. The leader either recognizes and confronts it, or ignores it.
- *Identifying priority.* There may be many problems in a school in different domains, for example, organization and management, teaching and learning, ethos and support, as well as academic and affective performance. However, a school cannot solve all problems within a single year. Administrators should ascribe a priority to tackling these problems according to the teachers' will and the students' needs.
- *Defining important questions.* Within an identified problem, the school should specify the key questions. These will be answered following a systematic procedure of data collection and analysis.
- *Data collection.* Data can be collected through questionnaires, observations and/or interviews, to ascertain whether the problem still exists. Consideration should be given to the source of data since this may be significant to a genuine assessment of the school's performance.
- *Data analysis.* On the basis of data collected, attempts should be made to clarify, verify or re-define the problem as required.
- *Reporting and communicating.* Staff should be briefed on diagnostic data and involved in developing strategies to solve the problem by providing opportunities for staff training on group dynamics, communication techniques, and goal setting.

- *School development planning.* An attempt should be made to fix the gap between the current situation and what should have happened. A consultant or similar expert may help in determining what steps should be taken? By whom? When? And how? Implementation should be monitored to fix any difficulties as they arise.
- *Team building.* Efforts should be made to build a culture of trust and confidence, improve communications, team building, skills in problem solving, and develop cooperation between and amongst different subsystems of the organization.
- *Feedback and evaluation.* Feedback should be provided to staff at the completion of a school self-evaluation cycle. The cyclical process needs to be continued to institutionalize school development as an ongoing process of innovation and change (Rudd & Davies, 2000).

Schools should acquire information and qualify perceptions of administrators, teachers, parents, students and the community for reference and comparison with schools of similar background or within the same quality circle, for continuous improvement and development (Pang, 2004).

The QEF Project on School Self-evaluation in Hong Kong

After conducting the first few cycles of whole-school inspections, starting in 1998, the QAI found that a self-evaluation framework was not commonly established in most of the schools inspected and no appropriate school-based indicators had been developed for use in SSE. In response to these weaknesses, the author with the support of the Hong Kong Centre for the Development of Educational Leadership (HKCDEL) and Quality Education Fund (QEF) launched a school improvement project entitled SSE and School-based Performance Indicators to help 20 schools institutionalize a self-evaluation framework useable in daily practices, acquire the required skills and techniques and develop a set of valid, reliable and school-based indicators for use in self-evaluation. The project aimed to help schools (1) develop their own models of school-based management in the spirit of the recommendations of the Education Commission Report No. 7, (2) institutionalize a self-evaluation framework in daily practice for continuous improvement, and (3) develop their own sets of school-based performance indicators for use in SSE.

A sample of 10 primary schools and 10 secondary schools took part in this project in the year 2000–2002. The project aimed to benefit the participating schools in the following ways: (1) A self-renewal strategy was institutionalized in the schools for continuous improvement through establishing a self-evaluation framework and using school-based indicators. (2) Administrators' and teachers' professional competence, confidence and performance in these schools was promoted through a series of training courses well designed for them. (3) Students' school life and learning was improved since school effectiveness was enhanced and a quality culture was fostered. (4) The schools were more accountable to parents and the wider community as the self-evaluation process had led to annual reports that contained fair, reliable and objective information about the schools.

A normative-re-educative strategy was used to initiate changes in the schools, that is, a user-centred, bottom-up approach to school reform in order to establish a climate of change and to cultivate a quality culture in the participating schools. In the improvement project all teachers in the schools were allowed to participate in shaping the reform by identifying their own needs, assessing the school's present conditions and performance and formulating the school development plans. Hence activities organized in each school included (1) setting-up of a Self-Evaluation Committee (SEC) in the management structure, (2) providing staff development programmes for members of SEC, and (3) conducting workshops for all teachers in the school to facilitate the practice of SSE and formulation of school development plans.

The project lasted for 2 years. Since changes and transformations are slow, progressive and incremental processes, it is unrealistic to expect to see sudden, radical changes in the schools. Nevertheless, noted effects of the project were as follows: (1) The schools fostered a culture of self-evaluation and a culture of organizational learning for continuous improvement. (2) A few training packages on SSE and the use of school-based performance indicators were developed, which were useful for other schools with a similar endeavour. (3) There were texts produced to disseminate good practice in SSE.

A Qualitative Research Into the Effectiveness of Implementing School Self-evaluation

After conducting the school improvement project in 20 schools as mentioned in the previous section, the author conducted a qualitative research which gathered the views of principals on the effectiveness and usefulness of the project and exploring the factors that hinder and facilitate the implementation of SSE. Out of the 20 principals, 18 were interviewed. Teachers' views of the project and their opinions about the factors that facilitate or hinder the implementation of SSE were also collected, this during whole-school workshops conducted in the schools. About 900 teachers from the 20 schools participated in group discussions through the activities organized in the workshops. Views and opinions of both principals and teachers were summarized and transcribed. Afterwards, the data collected were analysed and categorized into themes. The conclusions are given below.

Factors That Hinder the Implementation of SSE

Generally, most principals and teachers opined that SSE was not a normal practice in schools and it was a new and innovative concept to them. They thought that since the implementation of SSE involved a paradigm shift in school management and change of practices in normal school lives for all teachers, external support including financial resources, staff development programmes and sharing of personal resources, and consultancy services should be provided. In addition, most principals and teachers would like SSE be implemented in phases, since they needed more time and space to acquire the new knowledge and skills necessary. There were many existing factors which could hinder the implementation of SSE in Hong Kong schools. Based on their views and opinions gathered, these factors are summarized as below and classified as those at the system level and those at the school organizational level.

Hindrances at the System Level

1. *A loosely coupled system.* The Hong Kong education system clings to a loosely coupled system, because aided schools form the major sector. About 85% of schools in Hong Kong are

aided schools, 5%, government schools and 10%, private schools. Although aided schools receive financial support from the government, they have their own school sponsoring bodies and management committees. Aided schools, when compared to government schools, have greater autonomy and discretion in response to requests for change and the implementation of education policies. That is, resistance to change in the Hong Kong education system is much greater than that in other education systems in other countries, where the state or government schools commonly form the major sector.

2. *A too ambitious plan.* There were around 1,300 primary and secondary schools in the Hong Kong education system. Conducting whole-school inspections throughout the territory within just a few years was an unrealistic goal. Asking most schools to rely on their own resources to conduct self-evaluation and to raise their capacity for change within a year or so was again impractical and unattainable, especially at a time when the government was under great financial constraints. School reforms and improvement should be a continuous and incremental process which takes time.

3. *Too many existing reforms.* There have been many reforms proposed for the education system in Hong Kong for the 21st century, in addition to those left over from the last decade. Most of these reforms and policies were implemented without good planning and coordination. Schools have been suffering from the great burdens and confusion arising from them. Any introduction of further reforms and programmes in schools would meet with indifference or even resistance because of this.

4. *SSE is a complex process.* The implementation of SSE involves changes to school culture and general practices. Such changes cannot be achieved by directives promulgated by the education authority alone but require in addition, a well-planned, bottom-up strategy of initiation and introduction which needs extra resources and support from outside.

5. *Lack of resources.* Effective implementation of new reforms or initiatives needs extra resources and support. At a time of economic recession such as that which presently exists in

Hong Kong, the shortage of financial and human resources creates more difficulty for the implementation of SSE throughout the territory.

Hindrances at the School Organizational Level

Implementation of SSE at the school level is not an easy task, given the present conservative cultures found in most schools. The major factors that hindered the effective implementation of SSE are summarized as follows and they are worthy of the special attention of school leaders and administrators.

1. The plurality of categories of stakeholders and the diversity of views and opinions in schools might lead to many ideal sets of reforms being opposed.
2. Past experience of failure in the implementation of educational policy encouraged schools to take passive and conservative roles in educational reforms.
3. Schools are inevitably political arenas and power struggles are common. These created resistance to educational change in the schools.
4. The school leaders and the teachers in some schools might have become embroiled in conflicts, which caused tensions, fears, and low morale among teachers.
5. The communication breakdown between teachers and administrators found in some schools resulted in a very weak basis for professional collaboration and commitment.
6. Most teachers and principals had no knowledge and skills in SSE and a misconception of SSE was common.
7. There were no performance indicators developed for use in SSE and there were no guidelines or criteria for success that were commonly agreed in evaluation.
8. There were no formal, systematic, and in-depth professional training programmes well designed and developed for the implementation of SSE.
9. Most schools were passive to change and there was a lack of culture of organizational learning in the schools.
10. Most schools lacked a long-term vision and planning for school development and improvement.

Factors That Facilitate the Implementation of SSE

Though there were many factors that hindered the effective implementation of SSE, a few schools out of the 20 participating schools in the research had been successful in creating a culture of self-evaluation and organizational change. Such organizational characteristics existed in these schools before they took part in the project. Guidance and consultancy on school development provided in the school improvement project facilitated the implementation of self-evaluation in these schools and enhanced their transformation into learning organizations (Lam & Pang, 2003). Factors that facilitated the implementation of SSE in these schools are summarized below.

1. *An enhanced leadership.* There was an enhanced leadership in the schools that succeeded in implementing SSE and initiating organizational change. The management of organizational changes calls for "stronger" leadership. The success of organizational change in these schools was due to the strong leadership that unified people in accepting the organization's goals and clarified the technology in achieving goals.

2. *Shared values.* To a great extent, there were shared values among the staff members in those schools which had successfully implemented SSE in the management and organizational structure. Shared values are the binding forces that hold the organizational members together and unified the school's long-term and short-term goals and visions.

3. *Focused attention.* There was special attention paid to specific relationships in the management system in the schools that had successfully implemented SSE. Small step strategies within a confused, turbulent and ever-changing environment may produce more effective and efficient organizational changes. Effective leaders in these schools, when facing multiple and conflicting goals, they selected targets carefully, controlled resources cost-effectively, and acted forcefully.

4. *Good team spirit, high staff morale and a strong sense of professionalism.* The schools which were very successful in the implementation of SSE possessed a very strong teaching force with good team spirit and high staff morale as well as a strong

sense of professionalism. The formation of the strong and professional teaching force was not an accident but the result of deliberate and careful selection and recruitment in personnel management. High teacher morale and strong team spirit were resulted from the enhanced leadership and effective management systems in the schools.

The above findings from the qualitative research into the effectiveness of implementing self-evaluation in schools and the factors that hinder and facilitate organizational change shed light on how to lead and manage organizational change in school development and improvement. The details of this are delineated in the following sections.

The Basic Strategies of Organizational Change

In organizational change the three traditional types of strategy for introducing changes are: (1) rational-empirical strategies, (2) power-coercive strategies, and (3) normative-re-educative strategies (Chin & Benne, 1985; Pang, 1998a).

Rational-empirical strategies emphasize that people consider rational self-interest to determine needed changes in behaviour. Research evidence of improvement is the impetus and guidance to changes. Facing the external changed environment or expectations, schools and teachers seek ways to define their own problems, to identify alternative solutions and to choose the best alternative for actions. The logical sequence of activities in these strategies involves (1) a central team conducting basic research, (2) trailing of the innovative ideas, (3) planning dissemination to the masses, and (4) implementation of the strategies by users. Usually, these strategies are top-down and packaged solutions, produced by a team of more talented and experienced and introduced to users at the school level.

Power-coercive strategies are usually used by bureaucrats in a highly centralized system and are top-down. These strategies are associated with rewards and sanctions. If improvements are achieved, schools are rewarded with increased funding, autonomy and/or recognition. If orders are not followed, schools are penalized by removal of grants, dismissal of chief executives in schools and/or reforming the school management structure. These strategies are effective when there are time constraints and easiest and cheapest to apply in the short run. However, the effects of these strategies may be short-lived and less effective if resistance and hostility is met during implementation.

Normative-re-educative strategies are a user-centered and bottom-up approach. The self-renewal process of innovation is carried out within the school by (1) identifying its needs, (2) assessing the organization's present conditions and performance, (3) searching for probable solutions, (4) selecting the best alternative, (5) trying out and evaluating the innovation, and (6) implementing the innovation. In the process of change, the role of the outsider is essentially consultative, providing ideas guidance and temporary inputs of aid. A strong belief in the strategies stems from a philosophy that people should be allowed to participate in the shaping of reforms, because people are more likely to commit to the implementation of the reform when they are involved. The basic changes brought about by these strategies are the shifting of the members' attitudes, beliefs, values and norms towards a more productive culture (Owens, 1995).

Although the implementation strategies of planned change can be traditionally classified into three categories as mentioned, these theoretical distinctions between the various strategies of change are not clear cut and absolute in practical cases. None of them are usually used in their pure form and several different strategies are often used effectively at the same time. In managing organizational change effectively, school administrators must be capable of implementing appropriate strategies and tactics of organizational change (Chin & Benne, 1985; Pang, 1998a).

Different researchers may categorize different strategies of change differently (Havelock & Havelock, 1973; Katz & Kahn, 1966). In general, the two very basic strategies for introducing changes at the organizational level are evidence-based strategy and professional development strategy.

Evidence-based organizational change is a very recent trend in the school continuous improvement and reform movement, in which self-evaluation and the use of performance indicators (PIs) in monitoring change are the crucial components. Schools should have information on, and the perceptions of administrators, teachers, parents, students and the community from schools of similar background or within the same quality circle, for reference and comparison. Continuous school improvement is difficult to be show if appropriate performance indicators have not been developed for use in self-evaluation.

The evidence-based strategy emphasizes that people in organizations are rational and act in their own self interest when determining changes in behaviour needed when they are fully informed. Research evidence of improvement is the impetus and guidance to changes. The logical sequence of activities in these strategies involves (1) implementing SSE at the whole-school level, (2) collecting views of concerned stakeholders about the school's performance, (3) interpreting the results of self-evaluation with a full involvement of the staff, (4) brainstorming on the subject of school improvement and development, (5) devising the school development plan by consensus, and (6) implementing the innovative measures with teachers' commitment. Usually, this strategy is bottom-up and holistic and packaged solutions are produced by the involvement of all staff in the school.

The professional development strategy is the integration of work-group training, in such skills as communication, problem solving and managing change, the normal functioning of the school. Tailor-made training programmes, courses, seminars and workshops are provided for school administrators and teachers, which not only promote their professional skills and commitment in the process of continuous school improvement, but also enhance their professional competence and confidence in the quest for excellence in school education. The main outcome of professional development should be a self-renewing system that intrinsically motivates people to monitor their own functioning within a changing environment and that the system should be flexible enough to modify the school's own organizational form and functioning to meet its needs effectively.

Overcoming Resistance to Change

In the previous section, the strategies to organizational change have been explored. The approaches discussed, based on work with a few schools which succeeded in initiating organizational change, may form either the "pulls" or the "pushes" which are the important driving forces of organizational change. Even with these strong driving forces, it is common to meet resistance to change. The findings in the qualitative research into the factors that hinder the implementation of SSE are evidence of the existence of resistance.

With respect to overcome resistance to change, Pang (1998a) suggests a two-pronged approach to organizational change in pursuit of a quality culture in schools: a Kaizen (improvement) approach and an innovative approach. Both quality and culture are subtle, intangible (adjectives are highly contestable for "quality") concepts, which take time to develop in schools. The pursuit of quality school education and self-renewal may require a change in the school practitioners' beliefs, values and norms. Schools should be given more autonomy, time and resources to develop on their own. A Kaizen approach (Imai, 1986; Japan Human Relations Association, 1992) is recommended when organizational change is at the school or classroom level. The Kaizen approach adopts mainly rational-empirical and normative-re-educative strategies in driving change. However, those factors, which hinder the development of a quality culture in schools, should be eliminated as quickly as possible. For example, those schools with unclear goals and missions, with inaccurate appraisal systems, with poor quality school management committees should be mandated to change as soon as possible. In such cases, an innovative approach with the use of power-coercive strategies used for effecting changes is suggested.

Since schools are unique social organizations which have different organizational structures and cultures. Resistance to change varies from school to school. There is no a single panacea for overcoming all sorts resistance to change within a school. Educational leaders and managers should adopt a contingence approach and be flexible in adopting different approaches to overcome the resistance to change in their own situations and contexts (Zhang & Pang, 2005).

Conclusion

Globalization has inevitably led to educational change. Publicly funded schools should keep pace with societal changes and expectations, in order to survive in such a changing environment. Agenda in educational reforms in response to globalization include marketization, privatization and decentralization. Hong Kong schools, like those in other countries, are also confronted with the challenges arising from globalization. The two-pronged approach adopted in the recent quality assurance movement in Hong Kong—that is, employing whole-school inspections as the external force and SSE as the internal force—will produce better results in managing organizational change. The school principal is an important agent for change, and in response to the ever-increasing expectations of school education, should make use of these two forces in managing organizational change (Pang, 1998b).

Evidence-based organizational change is a very recent trend in the quality assurance movement, in which SSE plays an important role. SSE allows school leaders to successfully institutionalize a self-renewal framework in daily managerial practices as well as to lead and manage change effectively and efficiently. Due to various hindrances at both the system level and the school organizational level, most Hong Kong schools have not established a self-evaluation framework and the culture of self-renewal is weak in many schools. Nevertheless, the experience in a few successful schools in Hong Kong can shed light on ways other schools can transform themselves into learning organizations through the implementation of SSE.

The fundamental purpose of SSE is to convert the school into a learning organization. It aims to improve the knowledge and skills of organizational members in diagnosis and solution of problems on an everyday basis. SSE is a process of acquiring skills necessary for dealing with on-the-job problems. The experience gained in SSE should be utilized to track down other problems and, when they arise in the organizational context, should follow a similar process in solving them (Pang, MacBeath, & McGlynn, 2004). Because individuals are linked to other groups, the SSE concept tends to spread to the whole organization and encourages them to get involved in a cycle of continuous improvement or self-renewal. Institutionalization of self-evaluation in the organizational framework and daily managerial practices allows the principal to manage organizational change effectively and efficiently.

In order to facilitate change in school, administrators should have enhanced leadership that clarifies the school's goals and identifies the technology for achieving them. They should promote the sharing of values among all members, reach agreement about preferences; and be focus attention by careful selection of targets, control of resources, and forceful action. Not only do good team spirit, high staff morale and a strong sense of professionalism form the crucial basis of the change, but they also help reduce the resistance to change.

References

Beer, M., & Nohria, N. (2000). Resolving the tension between Theories E and O of change. In M. Beer & N. Nohria (Eds.), *Breaking the code of change* (pp. 1–34). Boston: Harvard Business School Press.

Chin, R., & Benne, K. (1985). General strategies for effecting changes in human systems. In W. G. Bennis, K. D. Benne, & R. Chin (Eds.), *The planning of change* (4th ed., pp. 22–45). New York: Holt Rinehart and Winston.

Cuttance, D. (1993). The development of quality assurance reviews in the NSW public school system: What works? Sydney: NSW Department of School Education. (ERIC Document Reproduction Service No. 384 141)

Cuttance, P. F. (1994). Monitoring educational quality through performance indicators for school practice. *School Effectiveness and School Improvement, 5*(2), 101–126.

Education and Manpower Bureau. (2002). *Education statistics.* Hong Kong: The Printing Department.

Gamage, D. T., & Pang, N. S. K. (2003). *Leadership and management in education: Developing essential skills and competencies.* Hong Kong: The Chinese University Press.

Harris, P. B. (1999, September). *The battle for raising standards: Can improvement be mandated?* Paper presented at the European Conference on Educational Research, Lahti, Finland.

Havelock, R. G., & Havelock, M. C. (1973). *Training for change agents: A guide to the design of training programs in education and other fields.* Ann Arbor, MI: Center for Research on Utilization of Scientific Knowledge, University of Michigan.

Imai, M. (1986). *Kaizen: The key to Japan's competitive success.* New York: Random House.

Japan Human Relations Association, The. (1992). *Kaizen Teian 1: Developing systems for continuous improvement through employee suggestions.* Portland, OR: Productivity Press.

Katz, D., & Kahn, R. (1966). *The social psychology of organizations.* New York: John Wiley and Sons.

Lam, Y. L. J., & Pang, S. K. N. (2003). The relative effects of environmental, internal and contextual factors on organizational learning: the case of Hong Kong schools under reforms. *The Learning Organization: An International Journal, 10*(2), 83–97.

Macbeath, J., Schratz, M., Meuret, D., & Jakobsen, L. (2000). *Self-evaluation in European schools: A story of change.* London: Routledge/Falmer.

Ministry of Education (1984). *School self-evaluation.* Victoria, Australia: Ministry of Education.

Moelands, H. A., & Ouborg, M. J. (1998, September). *School self-evaluation in primary education in the Netherlands.* Paper presented at the European Conference on Educational Research (ECER98), Ljubljana, Slovenia.

Owens, R. G. (1995). *Organizational behavior in education* (5th ed.). Boston: Allyn and Bacon.

Pang, N. S. K. (1998a). Should quality school education be a kaizen (improvement) or an innovation? *International Journal of Educational Reform, 7*(1), 2–12.

Pang, N. S. K. (1998b). The binding forces that hold school organizations together. *Journal of Educational Administration, 36*(4), 314–333.

Pang, N. S. K. (2003a). Binding forces and teachers' school life: A recursive model. *School Effectiveness and School Improvement, 14*(3), 293–320.

Pang, N. S. K. (2003b). Initiating organizational change through school self-evaluation. *International Journal of Knowledge, Culture and Change Management, 3,* 245–256.

Pang, N. S. K. (2004). Teachers' feelings about school life: A multilevel analysis. *Hong Kong Teachers' Centre Journal, 2,* 64–84.

Pang, N. S. K. (2005). *School self-evaluation and organizational change* (in Chinese) (School Education Reform Series, No. 21). Hong Kong: The Faculty of Education of the Chinese University of Hong Kong and Hong Kong Institute of Educational Research.

Pang, N. S. K., & Cheung, M. (2004). Learning capacity of primary schools in Hong Kong. In J. C. K. Lee, L. N. K. Lo, & A. Walker (Eds.), *Partnership and change: Towards school development* (pp. 269–294). Hong Kong: The Hong Kong Institute of Educational Research and The Chinese University Press.

Pang, N. S. K., MacBeath, J., & McGlynn, A. (2004). *Self-evaluation and school development* (School Education Reform Series No. 19). Hong Kong: The Faculty of Education of the Chinese University of Hong Kong and Hong Kong Institute of Educational Research.

Rudd, P., & Davies, D. (2000, September). *Evaluating school self-evaluation.* Paper presented at the British Educational Research Association Conference, Cardiff University, Cardiff, United Kingdom.

Scottish Office. (1996). *How good is our school? Self-evaluation using performance indicators.* Edinburgh, United Kingdom: The Scottish Office of Education and Industry Department.

Scottish Office. (2002). *How good is our school? Self-evaluation using performance indicators* (2nd ed.) Edinburgh, United Kingdom: The Scottish Office of Education and Industry Department.

Zhang, S. Z. Q., & Pang, N. S. K. (2005). *An analysis of the elements and strategies of school development* (in Chinese) (School Education Reform Series No. 22). Hong Kong: The Faculty of Education of the Chinese University of Hong Kong and Hong Kong Institute of Educational Research.